CONTENTS

Part 1

BACKGROUND

CONSIDERATION OF TERMINOLOGY

I have no great opinion of a definition, the celebrated remedy for the cure of this disorder (uncertainty and confusion). – *Edmund Burke*[1]

Uncertainty and confusion both become apparent in any discussion of the terminology of non-book materials. The subject is invested with an excess of jargon and technical language; general and specific terms abound. It is further complicated by three worlds – television, computers and publishing – merging. Interactive multimedia are giving us new processes for education, leisure and information.

A consideration of the literature on the subject is an obvious starting place for establishing a consensus view. What terminology is used in the general literature of non-book materials? Have these terms been standardized at a national or international level? Are there approved glossaries? If the specialists within the subject agree on standardized terms, do the non-specialists use them?

On checking the titles of books in this area, it becomes apparent that there is as yet no general agreement on a single term to describe the subject. *Non-book media: collection management and user services* (1987),[2] *Bibliographic control of audiovisual materials* (1986),[3] *The media lab* (1987),[4] *Legal deposit of non-book materials* (1986),[5] and *Non-print production* (1988)[6] are all relatively recent publications . Attempts to combine terms include *Audiovisual and microcomputer handbook* (1984)[7] and a particularly ingenious title, *Non-print cataloguing for multimedia collections: a guide based on AACR2* (1987).[8] In 1976 the British Standards Institution identified a similar picture of the range of general terms,[9] which included:

> medium,
> non-book material and its synonyms audiovisual materials and meta-book,
> non-book media and its synonym non-print media,
> multimedia and its synonym non-print materials.

Thus in the last decade, despite many efforts and much individual endeavour, no consensus about one general term to describe this subject has emerged. Consequently, the terms used in this book need to be defined.

Media
These are the channels used for the transmission of a message, as shown by the difference between print, sound and vision. The channels are: printed message, usually on paper or on a screen, which can be writing, graphics or photographs; still pictures, which are transparent for projection or viewing; sounds, as in a live radio broadcast, or recorded as on a sound disc; moving pictures, as in a live television broadcast or recorded on a cinefilm.

Materials
This term is used to describe the complete range of physical forms for the recording of information carried by the media; for example, books, wallcharts, pamphlets, videorecordings, sound recordings and computer discs.

Non-book materials (NBM)
Strictly speaking, this should cover all those materials which are not bound into a book. However, it is used here to exclude any printed message presented in the form of a pamphlet, leaflet, manuscript, map, serial or music score. The range is therefore wide, and also includes those materials which have been excluded above when they are re-presented in a different form, such as a map on a slide or serials on microfiche.

Four materials may be used:

(a) Paper, which can be arranged in a variety of ways; cards, charts, art reproductions, portfolios, photographic prints.
(b) Film, which includes:
    filmstrip
    slide
    cinefilm: 35mm, 16mm
    microform: 35mm roll, 16mm roll, aperture cards, microfiche, microfiche jackets.
(c) Magnetic tape, which includes:
    sound tape: open reel, cassette
    videotape: open reel, cassette
    magnetic discs.
(d) Plastic, either flat and transparent or opaque and grooved:
    transparent plastic: overhead projector transparencies
    vinyl discs: gramophone records
    optical storage systems: laservision, CD audio, CD-ROM.

Other materials are, of course, used in models and artefacts. Specimens, which are actual objects themselves, are also referred to as NBM. There are also mixtures of these materials, commonly called kits.

Finally, there are collections of NBM materials which can be electronically accessed at a distance; for example, teletext and viewdata systems.

Document
A unit of material containing information. The emphasis is on the information content rather than on the physical form of the material.

Form
A general designator for a particular material; for example, cinefilm, sound recording, microform, videorecording, CD-ROM.

Format
A specific designator for a form of material; for example, sound cassette, microfiche, videodisc.

Each form and format will be described in Part 3, together with technical terms concerning the components of equipment. Other than there and in the foregoing list, this book contains no glossary of terms, and the reader is advised to turn to other works for such information.[10] The *Anglo-American cataloguing rules* (second edition, revised 1988) includes a glossary of terms which has some international credence. The area of computer terminology requires further work on a standard approach, for example computer laser optical disc or CD-ROM.

However, these are the works of specialists trying to establish a common language, and it remains to be seen how far non-specialists will use their terms and definitions. A term such as 'computer file' may have a clear meaning to the specialist who knows it is a generic term for computer software, but it is unlikely to find much favour with the library client who is searching for a computer cassette or floppy disc. The librarian needs to be aware of this 'natural language' if he or she is to succeed in remedying the disorder.

HISTORICAL DEVELOPMENT

It is generally agreed that the function of a library is the collection, preservation, organization and use of documents. However, it is the documents concerning one medium, print, that have dominated the operations of most libraries to date. This is hardly surprising considering the long tradition of writing, beginning with the earliest cuneiform system in Mesopotamia circa 3000 BC. Similarly, the development of the codex with pages like those of a modern book by the first century AD points the way towards the long tradition in which one physical form predominated in the preservation and dissemination of knowledge in every literate society. The development of printing in the second half of the fifteenth century made possible a revolution in thought and scholarship through the spread of multiple copies. With its mechanization in the nineteenth century the increased demands of an increasingly literate society could be met. It is hardly surprising that the mainstay of most library collections is the printed word, particularly in book form.

The physical materials used for the other forms have been the result of inventions of the late nineteenth and twentieth centuries. The more important dates for the various forms are presented below:

Still pictures
(a) Film
- 1841 William Henry Fox Talbot. Paper negative using the Callotype process. The true beginning of photography.
- 1884 George Eastman. Roll film system patented and the development of the film slide. Prior to this date only lantern slides used, which were glass with an image printed on them.
- 1888 First Kodak mass-produced camera.
- 1912 Rudolph Fischer patented basic principles of the Kodachrome process for colour photography.
- 1924 First crude picture containing all colours on a three-layer type of film.
- 1935 Kodachrome first marketed. Development of 35mm (2 in. × 2 in.) colour slide.
- 1951 Polaroid camera.
- 1952 Theory of holography patented by Dennis Gabor.

1960s Development of lasers made production of holographic pictures possible.
1976   Microprocessor controls exposure in a camera.
1988   Sony and Canon introduce electronic still cameras.
1989   Canon introduce Xapshot which records pictures on floppy disc for display on TV set.

(b) Microforms
1839   John Benjamin Dancer. First microphotography.
1870   Microforms sent by pigeon during Franco-Prussian War.
1901   Victorian age − commercial microphotographic views sold mounted on pen-holders, manicure sets etc.
1906   Idea of microfiche proposed.
1928   Eastman Kodak Co. Use of microfilming to prevent bank frauds.
1970   *Books in English* produced on microfiche.
1978   Whitaker's *British books in print* available on microfiche.

Moving pictures
(a) Cinefilm
1870   Eadweard Muybridge. Experimented with photographs and
−93   eventually made films of animal and human locomotion. Simple cameras and projectors used.
1889   First cine camera in which the successive pictures were taken on a strip of film with a single camera.
1893   Thomas Alva Edison invented the nickel-in-the-slot cinematograph machine.
1895   First cinefilm made by L. Lumiere.
1914   First animated cartoon, *The dachshund*.
1922   Technicolour process used for *Toll of the sea*.
1922   First sound recording on film.
1923   First practical 16mm camera projector and compatible non-flammable film. Prior to this date all films were made on 35mm.
1927   Sound on film with Fox-Movietone News.
1932   First practical sound on 16mm film.
1932   Introduction of standard 8mm film cartridges.
1950   Magnetic striping of 16mm film enabled amateur makers to add a sound track.
1952   Cinerama.
1965   Kodak introduced the 'super 8' film.

(b) Videotape and television
   1908   First successful electronic transmission of a picture between London and Paris.
   1926   John Logie Baird demonstrated first mechanical television transmission.
   1932   Radio Corporation of America demonstrated all-electronic television.
   1936   British Broadcasting Corporation launched the first 405-line public television service.
   1940   Colour television system developed.
   1958   Videotape marketed.
   1965   PAL scanning system patented.
   1965   Demonstration of MVR videodisc recorder.
   1967   Colour television broadcasting introduced in the United Kingdom.
   1971   Some 20 different 'videocassette' systems under development.
   1972   BBC introduced digital TV.
   1977   Philips 1700 videocassette recorder.
   1980s   Development of domestic camcorders.

Sound recordings
(a) Discs
   1877   Thomas Alva Edison. Patented the phonograph using a sheet of tinfoil wrapped around a cylinder.
   1889   Emile Berliner. First recording on a flat disc.
   1889   First use of sound recording in academic research.
   1920s   Use of electrical recordings.
   1933   Stereophonic gramophone patented.
   1948   Columbia Company introduced long-playing record using vinylite.
   1980   Philips and Sony introduced compact digital discs.
(b) Sound tape
   1899   Valdemar Poulsen. First practical system using a wire magnetic recorder.
   1927–8 Introduction of steel tape and coated paper tape.
   1930   Cellulose acetate tape used.
   1940   PVC tape used.
   1960s   Philips compact cassette developed.
   1968   Dolby 'A' system for reducing tape hiss.

1980 Sony Walkman miniature cassette recorder.
1985 Sony and Philips introduced digital audio tape (DAT).

Microcomputers and viewdata
1945 ENIAC (Electronic Numerical Integrator and Calculator).
      First fully electronic computer.
1956 Burroughs E-101. First desk-sized computer.
1969 Silicon chip designed as the central processing unit of a
      computer.
1971 Intel introduced microprocessor.
1973 Computer-coded labels introduced into supermarkets.
1974 Hewlett-Packard programmable pocket calculator.
1974 BBC Ceefax service.
1975 Altair home computer in kit form.
1975 Videogames.
1976 Apple microcomputer.
1979 Prestel service launched.
1981 Sinclair ZX81 microcomputer.
1983 Telesoftware service via Prestel and BBC Ceefax.
1984 American Library Association established library electronic
      mail system.
1989 Library Association established an electronic mail system.

Optical storage systems
1972 MCA and IBM Disco Vision.
1978 Philips Laservision digital videodisc system.
1981 'Kiddidisc' videodisc which allowed viewer participation.
1983 Audio CD released in Japan.
1984 CD-ROM drives introduced.
1986 Whitaker published pilot CD-ROM.
1986 BBC released the Domesday interactive videodisc.
1988 Philips CD video.
1989 CD interactive released.

How were these inventions and developments reflected in library
collections? There is a parallel with the early history of libraries in that
there is a general progression from service to select groups to service
to the general public. Such a picture may be seen with collections of
NBM, particularly those of sound recordings.

Private collectors went early into the field, recording folk songs and making anthropological recordings. The first instance of sound recording being used in academic research was by J. Walter Fewkes, who recorded the prayers, tales and songs of the Pasamquoddy Indians in 1889. The firstly officially recognized collection of sound recordings[11] was established in Vienna in 1899 for the language and dialects of Europe. Later collections such as the British Institute of Recorded Sound (1948) relied heavily on the donations of individual collectors. Other national institutions were also keen to establish an interest. The Library of Congress had copyright concerning paper prints or contact prints of motion pictures by 1894, but sound recordings were not covered by federal copyright law until 1972. The BBC established its sound library in 1935 to satisfy its own growing demands. But there is little other evidence concerning the beginnings of many NBM collections. However, there is some indication of involvement by public libraries from an early date, particularly in the United States.

Illustrations collections
These included prints, photographs, materials cut from periodicals and lantern slides. The first known picture collection was begun in 1889 at Denver Public Library, Colorado. In the UK the emphasis seems to have been on the collection of local illustrations, in particular photographs. Local photographic societies sponsored surveys, and in 1908 some 20 systematic collections had been preserved in local libraries or museums. Lantern slides were in use in a number of libraries and in 1923 Kent County Library had a collection of 6,000. Hereford County Library in 1926 had sets of lantern slides for 44 lectures on subjects agreed with the rural community council. Illustrations collections were available in half the municipal libraries in London and the Home Counties by 1939. However, Campbell,[12] writing in 1964, suggests that these were still peripheral in most UK public libraries and that there was nothing to compare with the developments in the USA, where at least three public libraries held over one million illustrations. The closest British comparison was Birmingham Public Library, with some 200,000.

Sound recordings
In the USA public libraries were early in the field. That at St Paul, Minnesota, established a collection in 1913 and by 1919 had a stock of 600 records and an annual issue of 3,500. In the UK the first gramophone record service to schools was organized by Middlesex County Library

in 1936, although it was soon transferred to the education department. Hereford County Library was the first public library to make discs available on loan to the general public, in 1945; and Walthamstow was the first municipal library to do that, in 1947. By 1950, there were 50 public library authorities lending gramophone records. In contrast, sound cassettes and CD audio were quickly introduced into libraries, perhaps because they were more robust and therefore less susceptible to damage by borrowers.

Cinefilm and video
Collections were slow to emerge in the USA, but by 1922 11 school systems had established them and by 1945 approximately a dozen large urban public libraries had organized film services. As early as 1929, the Cleveland Public Library had cooperated with a local movie house to publicize the film *Scaramouche*. Little has been discovered to indicate any services to the public in the UK, but the children's librarian of Rochdale in 1930[13] has been reported as using film, primarily to encourage reading!

Yet it should not be thought that librarians were slow to realize the potential of film. A writer in 1912 stated that 'a few years ago there were people who prophetically said that the cinematograph would not live long: it was just a craze, the popularity of which would soon diminish, but we are compelled to acknowledge that the moving picture is a force to be reckoned with'. He cited its use to train medical students and reported that in this way 'a large number of unnecessary operations are obviated'.[14]

Librarians quickly saw the potential of videorecordings for their collections. The resource centre growth of the 1970s saw a steady increase in educational establishments of collectors of videorecordings. Similarly, the domestic videorecording boom in the UK in the early 1980s was matched by services in many public libraries.[15]

It is ironic that cinefilm itself as a form is in decline in libraries. The growth of videorecording titles and the ease of use of the form has helped to accelerate this decline. In the UK a number of film hire companies have completely switched to videorecording only. In 1982 a survey in the USA indicated a reduction in the 16mm film service and by 1988 libraries in the USA were putting their film collections up for sale.[16]

Viewdata and computers
Librarians have readily accepted computers as valuable tools for the

'house-keeping' duties of a library. However, they have also been keen
to develop client services based on this technology. Public access micro
services are available in a number of libraries; for example, the Have-
a-go-Micro provision at the Central Lending Library in Stockport,[17]
aimed at increasing public awareness of the computer.

Similarly, viewdata facilities have been offered to the general public
and developed by librarians who have seized the initiative to create new
bulletin boards. Particularly interesting because of its enterprise is the
viewdata guide prepared by Robert Gordon's Institute of Technology
for the Glasgow Garden Festival in 1988.[18] The Library Associations
of the UK and the USA have also reacted speedily to the new growth
of electronic newsletters.[19]

This short history of the development of collections of NBM in libraries
is slanted towards developments in the public libraries of the USA and
Britain. There were some developments in other types of libraries, but
there is still a lack of research into the early history of NBM collections.
One writer has suggested that the lack of written evidence concerning
the early collections of sound recordings may have been because they
were 'considered ephemera and as such were likely to be disposed of;
therefore, the librarian was reluctant to make their presence official by
accessioning or cataloguing them'.[20]

The interest of librarians
Why were these early librarians so slow and in some cases so reluctant
to include NBM in their collections? Four reasons may be considered:

(a) The long history of the book and the printed word as the main
    medium for recorded information.
(b) The librarian was a collector and preserver of books and not of
    all forms of information.
(c) There was a strong belief that the book was an educational force
    and the other forms were mere novelties.
(d) The cost and fragility of NBM.

In spite of the absence of detailed research, some general points may
be made. Media other than books have been readily accepted by the
general public. The spread of cinemas, the large sales of sound discs
and the number of home movie makers and photographers indicate a
favourable use of all these forms. Yet librarians have often been in
opposition to these other forms and have linked this closely to a defence
of books. In 1917 Doubleday questioned 'what may be the educational

value of the picture palaces after sixty years or more of existence, is and must be a matter of speculation. In the writer's opinion they can only hope to serve as auxiliaries to libraries much as libraries are now an auxiliary to education; and they may never even attain to that utility.'[21] An anonymous writer some 20 years later believed that 'films are substitutes for reading. At the present time they are, at their very best, poor substitutes; at their very worst, they are pernicious.'[22]

Film was considered necessary in order to encourage reading rather than appreciated or valued in its own right. McColvin (1927), commenting on extension activities, said 'the chief objections are that suitable films are difficult and expensive to obtain, and that they are not sufficiently related to books. Without a doubt they would attract a different public.'[23]

The librarian has also worried about the expense, safety and fragility of NBM. The cost would be prohibitive:

> for a rate-supported institution to bear the expense of such a scheme . . . It is surely carrying our ideal of public service to such an extreme as to make it sentimental and American . . . To keep on adding to our extraneous undertakings will mean that we shall have soon departed so far from the fundamental idea of the public library that we shall regard the issue of a good book as a mere side-track.[24]

Savage was particularly concerned about the damage to discs by borrowers 'scraping the life out of them with steel needles or . . . blasting them with a blunt needle'.[25] Cinefilm was not being used in 1931, Sayers suggested, because the 'obstacles of inflammable films and local regulations have made its use difficult'.[26]

During the early period of libraries, their champions defended books on the grounds that they were of educational value to the general public. Paradoxically, after 1945 NBM were excluded from libraries on the grounds that they were of value only to educational institutions and not to the public. The only form that did develop outside the educational setting was the sound disc, and even this was seen as an adjunct to music. One writer in 1946 commented: 'Since librarians first began to discuss gramophone records, those in favour of them have on various occasions stressed the value of non-musical recordings — such as sound effects, local council proceedings, play readings, and, in particular, language-teaching records . . . It seems doubtful whether they will ever be of great significance in public libraries.'[27] Thus the major impetus for the development of collections of NBM after 1945 came from the educational system. Even when the public library was supplying a service to schools, the librarians were chiefly interested in books and ignored other materials. It has been a long road away from this position.

The value of film in education was stressed in 1948 by the National Committee for Visual Aids in Education, which sought to establish 'what types of material should be purchased, and how best to establish local visual aids libraries'.[28] As a result, local education committees were advised to set up lending libraries for 16mm film and to support the establishment of a national film library by the Educational Foundation for Visual Aids. These recommendations were eventually implemented.

Attention during the 1950s and 1960s was also focused on resource-based learning, and in 1970 both the National Council for Educational Technology and the Schools Council established projects on resource centres,[29] the former for higher education and the latter for schools. These considered that the key area was the organization of recorded knowledge to meet the individual learner's needs. Both stressed the importance of libraries collecting all forms of materials. The Library Association recognized this in a number of policy statements, culminating in 1973 with *Library resource centres in schools, colleges and institutions of higher education: a general policy statement*. This document stressed that 'books, duplicated and audiovisual materials complement each other in their contribution to teaching and research, and should be regarded as part of a unified collection'. It is heartening that in the 1988 national debate concerning the need to charge for public libraries the library profession was united in defending access to information in whatever form it was published — forms other than the book were part of the core service.

It is interesting to compare the hesitancy shown by librarians to the earlier NBM and the attitude shown to the more recent formats. The great interest in videorecordings was perhaps fuelled by the belief that this was a service that could be financially profitable.

In the 1980s the easier acceptance of microcomputer, viewdata, and CD-ROM perhaps stems from the strong push given by the UK government to establish computer literacy in schools and throughout commerce and industry. This created a climate which enabled local government councillors to sanction the purchase of computers, ironically at a time when book funds were cut.

VARIETY OF APPLICATIONS

Communication is conducted through the senses, the most powerful of which is sight. In competition with the other senses, sight dominates in the reception of information, a factor which producers of NBM need to take into account. However, any of the senses can be used to receive information – taste, smell, touch, hearing and sight. In practice, stored NBM make little use of taste for every examination will see a little of it disappear. Sugar manufacturers once marketed a teaching pack which included samples of different types of their products, but these naturally survived for a very short time only.

Smell too is a sense that is not commonly used in NBM. In the broadest interpretation of this word, chemicals and cooking materials would be included; but even in the most comprehensive library of the present and future these are unlikely to be a significant feature. Smells in information collections are usually signs of decay or potential mechanical breakdown, although there are a few books produced for young children scratching the pages of which elicits an odour which children can identify or associate with a picture. Attempts to produce films in the commercial cinema in which appropriate aromas were released into the auditorium during suitable scenes failed because the smells could not be removed from the atmosphere quickly enough. The scenes changed, but the aroma was the same.

On the other hand, touch is an underused but significant sense. The importance of it to the blind is well known, and their whole world can be described and manipulated through touch. From birth, exploration of objects by hand contact has formed a significant element of information gathering. Caressing and feeling stimulate strong sensual perceptions which are an important adjunct to artistic, cultural and emotional experiences in learning and leisure. It is therefore an important part of the appreciation of art to be able to touch sculpture and cloth materials in order to explore the surface and texture, just as it is helpful in the study of geology to be able to feel the relative roughness of rocks. Excessive physical handling may cause deterioration, but the opportunity to touch and explore introduces insight, understanding and emotional empathy.

Museums are much less restrictive on the use of touch to explore exhibits than they were. Some items, particularly those of especial fragility or in advanced stages of deterioration, remain behind barriers, but increasingly visitors are encouraged to participate in the experiences provided by the items on display. In many modern museums there are experiments in which visitors are actively encouraged to pull levers, insert limbs or subject their senses to different experiences in order to understand the exhibit and learn from it. Interactivity is increasingly important in encouraging those who enter museums to achieve deeper understanding and insight into that which is being displayed. In some, such as the Heritage Museum at Wigan and the Museum of the Moving Image on the South Bank in London, actors are employed to play roles from the past and they include the visitors in dialogues to encourage empathy and gain a greater sense of appreciation.

The value of sound and sight needs no elaboration. It is often overlooked that sight dominates sound: many people therefore find it valuable to listen to dialogue and music with their eyes shut in order to eliminate visual distraction. The more visually realistic the message, however, the less it encourages imaginative participation. Someone reading a novel has imaginatively to construct both the appearance and the sound of the characters involved. Hearing a dramatization of the same work leaves only the visual experience of the characters and the setting to be imagined. The film of the book provides the user with all the information except the touch, taste and smell of the atmosphere. Perhaps because of this, it can be argued that books are reread more often than dramatic recordings are replayed, and reviewing is generally less frequent again. A natural identification with characters varies little in each situation, although the physical appearance of a particular actor may inhibit such participation in a visually realized recreation.

These responses are important factors in the borrowing rates of materials, and create difficulties for those deciding on the selection of items for mass distribution. Naturally there are exceptions, and there are constantly changing records for the reseeing of films. However, the principle is sufficiently strong to be of concern to producers and distributors of the different media.

On the other hand, audio and visual experiences are close to the way in which people learn about their environments and interpersonal relationships. They are the sensory channels through which information is expected for efficient mental processing and the development of understanding. For many people, now brought up in an audiovisual environment, the printed word is less easily interpreted than the information provided by sound and images. Indeed, they may need to turn words into audiovisual images before they can be understood.

Frequently, these media can carry information more concisely and directly than the printed words in a book. Because there are generally fewer imaginative requirements in mental translation, the nuances, inflections and relative emphases are less ambiguous; the comprehension is quicker and more complete. However, good presentation of information demands simplicity and careful explanation, because paradoxically the user finds it more difficult to consider the meaning of a single word or phrase in an audiovisual programme than in the pages of a printed book. Information can be more complex and more completely cross-referenced in a book than in an audiovisual presentation.

The effectiveness of NBM is not dependent merely on the senses which are used in addressing those materials. The environment in which they are used also affects their value. For example, a film may be viewed in a commercial cinema in which the surrounding darkness isolates the senses and induces complete concentration on the audiovisual experience being transmitted. The group response of the anonymous audience enhances any personal reactions to situations in the film; for instance, to shock in a horror movie and to laughter in a farce. The same film may be shown in a classroom in only partial blackout, when the senses are alerted and distracted by the other activities within the room and by the interpersonal relationships with the other students and the teacher. Emotional responses are different because the people are known and the relative positions in the group dynamic have to be maintained. Viewing the same film on television from a videorecording in the home environment introduces a different perspective again. The distractions of the room and its vicinity as well as the ability to halt the film at any time introduce a different set of responses. Shock is dissipated by the proximity of familiar objects and the facility of the kitchen and refreshment, while the impact of humour is reduced by the absence of group enhancement. Add to this, for example, the cropping of pictures from the cinema to fit the television frame, and the experience in each environment is considerably altered.

Thus the appreciation of NBM through the relevant senses can be much affected by the environment in which the material is used. Progressively, the trend is towards increasing interaction with the materials, as was described earlier in the modern museums and even as in the use of smell-generating books. With computer-controlled items becoming more prevalent, the ability to encourage such an approach is easier. Computer programs are more interesting and memorable when they require participation and responses from their users. In its most dramatic form, this is vividly illustrated by the computer games that are now available, ranging from the 'shoot-'em-up' variety, when the level of participation is merely one of rapid reaction, to the adventure games involving the solution of a variety of complex puzzles presented both in text and graphic forms. The appearance of CD-ROMs and optical formats of video storage have introduced further possibilities of interaction with databases and images. Different texts can be compared and contrasted on the same screen, and images can be rearranged at the whim of the user. At this level, the users of NBM are no longer passive observers, but have developed into participants in the environment, being able to alter and amend the sequence and activity which is being presented and to turn it into a shape that is more relevant to their needs. The level of interaction introduces the possibility of changing the conditions to investigate what happens − the so-called 'what-if' approach − to forecast financial changes to see the effect on profits, to promote the growth of more reeds to find out the impact on the ecology of a pond, to send a space ship towards a particular star to discover whether any aliens attack it, and so on.

As explained earlier, NBM consist of a wide variety of different materials, some used independently, others collected together as kits. The simplest forms are combinations of two items, sound tape and slides, computer program and booklet, but some kits are considerable collections of different formats. Thus the Microprimer pack produced by the Microelectronics Education Programme[30] to introduce teachers to the use of microcomputers in primary schools contained 70 items. It included an overview, guidelines for the teacher, a study text and reader, 30 computer programs and a database system, two audiocassettes of case studies, a video, 30 overhead projector transparencies and an easel-like guide to using the machine.

While the majority of these kits have been prepared for educational purposes, the definition of learning must not be confined to the school environment. For example, several years ago, the *Observer* newspaper produced kits in support of a series of articles on the history of Britain in its colour supplement. *The making of the British*[31] kit included information cards, supplementary articles, slides and a sound disc or tape. It was available to and purchased by the general public, not just by teachers, and while some were undoubtedly used in schools, others were purchased for their general interest value. Certainly not every purchaser was an academic historian. For many, the materials offered added interest to the information in the articles, giving a different perspective and providing an extension of general knowledge. Certainly kits tend to be instructive rather than purely entertaining, but it would be wrong to conclude that they are not frequently of value to the general user.

Kits flourish because they bring together a diversity of formats of NBM and books. As computer-based systems develop, so there is a trend towards integrating many of these different formats. The optical storage systems are good carriers of text, sound and visual elements, all individually selectable as well as capable of being linked together into integrated presentations. Audio and visual materials, once separately purchased as slides and cassette tapes, can be held together on a CD-ROM or videodisc and used as an integrated item. There is no difference in their impact on the senses and, as projection television improves, little difference in the size of the audience that can receive them at the same time. Text can be viewed on a screen separately or overlaid on top of video images projected from a videodisc. Through mechanisms like this, the variety of formats for the user will gradually be reduced, although producers will continue to originate a great deal of the information to be distributed using the same range of materials. Still images that a user obtains from a videodisc will continue to be originated as photographic transparencies in order to achieve the highest quality.

The uses of NBM are wide ranging, penetrating most of the areas where communications and the storage and passage of information are involved. The principal applications are for entertainment, learning and enrichment, but there are a variety of uses. The arrival of information technology and computer-based systems has created major changes in administrative and management activities, which are now dominated by them. Exchange and movement of information is increasingly being undertaken by cable, phone line and satellite, the outputs being either entirely electronic for viewing and manipulation on screens or facsimile printouts on paper. Both are capable of carrying graphics and pictures, usually monochrome, as well as text. Commerce also makes widespread use of NBM for advertising, promotion and sales. Slides, audiocassettes and videotapes all find a place in the travelling bag of the contemporary sales staff, providing opportunities for expressing more directly and explicitly the applications and values of products. Electronic communications between the sales staff and company head office can be established in order to obtain instant quotations as well as to finalize orders. Through facsimile transmissions, signatures can even be exchanged before the sales staff leave a client's office.

While there is still some sponsorship of entertainment films by the larger companies, this is gradually being replaced by the production of videocassettes, the quality and performance of which have now reached a sufficient standard to make an attractive impact. Such is the simplicity of the packaging and its relatively inexpensive duplication cost that videocassettes have tended totally to replace cinefilm as the mechanism for distribution. International companies also use NBM for communication between their various subsidiaries. For decision-making meetings, videoconferencing is becoming more commonplace, superseding the audioconference as it is so much easier to introduce graphics and models into the discussion. Videorecordings of major pronouncements by senior management can be distributed to the staff on videotape or transmitted directly by satellite. Providing a clearer presentation of procedures and announcements of future developments, the video message carries with it an impression of personal interest and concern from an apparently remote headquarters.

NBM are also frequently used as a means of recording information and events, both for immediate analysis and as historical archives. While sound recordings, still photography and video are still widely used, computer-based systems are beginning to have an important role, particularly with the associated optical storage systems. A photographic record may be needed to differentiate the places at the finish of a race or the climber may use a camera to freeze that unique moment at the summit of a mountain. The decision at a football match is recorded on video from many angles and can be analysed frame by frame to determine the truth; sources of unrest in the crowd can be similarly recorded, enhanced and used for identification and judgement in court. In conjunction with overlaid computer calculations, a speeding car can be identified and its driver prosecuted from similar evidence. Birth, marriage and death records are now held in electronic form, and CD-ROMs containing lists of all the names and addresses of the population are available, complete with postcode, for indicating environment and social type analysis.

News and events of all kinds are captured through NBM, sometimes for personal satisfaction, sometimes in order to prove an achievement has been made or to keep as a record. The film and video record of contemporary society and its activities is now considerable. The addition of computerized control and enhancement techniques for increasing the clarity of pictures makes it possible to undertake a detailed analysis of each frame and even part of the frame. By using optical stores, particularly in digital form, it is possible to locate and review items from the mass of information at considerable speed. Whereas books and other traditional means of keeping records often present interpretations of happenings and people, NBM tend to provide a more open representation of reality, although inevitably the producer has selected angles and viewpoints as well as editing out imperfections. A verbal description of the Zeebrugge car ferry tragedy requires imaginative interpretation from the reader, probably from a base of total inexperience; whereas the videorecordings of the searches and rescues bring closer the sense of enclosure and tension and of the heroism of many of those involved. Hearing and seeing the oratory of President Kennedy and Martin Luther King adds perspective and understanding through the force of their personalities and expressions, facets that are not apparent from merely reading the text of their speeches.

Valuable records should not be restricted to so-called important events and notable people. The continuing development of oral history on sound tape makes a permanent record of the feelings of the general populace as they react to their environment and the daily intercourse of their activities. Through the popularity and use of film and video cameras, immense libraries of visual records of the behaviour and mores of contemporary society are available, and they are readily convertible to optical stores for perpetual archiving. In the same way that Phiz's drawings for the novels of Dickens give a sense of the nineteenth century, so these video and sound recordings are essential elements in making clear the attitudes and behaviour patterns of our present society for future generations. Now that computer-based systems are available to help to organize and locate the different items, it is beginning to be possible to absorb these extensive collections of information in the knowledge that particular parts can be located relatively quickly. NBM are providing facilities for recording, storing, finding, examining and exploring these materials in ways that have not been possible before.

NBM are also a source of study in their own right. Knowledge, understanding and theory are developing rapidly. In the 1950s, the theory of film was discussed in a very few books, by Rotha, Grierson, Manvell, Seton, Montagu, Jacobs and − of course − Eisenstein. Most writing about the cinema was about its stars and their love lives, not its history and theory. Now, 40 years later, there are lecturers in film and video studies at universities, and there are degrees in media and communication studies which are dominated by NBM. At school level, too, courses in media studies continue to flourish, even within the national curriculum.

Music on disc and cassette and still photographs already have their own theoretical structure and methods of analysis. For computer-based systems, the studies in schools and higher education tend to be more technical than aesthetic and analytical, although there is a growing interest in this field as the variety of uses stretches further into art, music and design.

In summary, the argument developed here is that NBM extend the range of senses that are used in exploring documents for information, and that this activity demands greater participation and interaction on the part of the user. In doing this, methods are being employed that have been important from the earliest days of human development, involving the exploration of the environment through aural, visual and tactile stimuli. The range of formats available to the user remains extensive, but the trend is to move towards increased integration for the delivery system, making it more closely aligned to computer-based systems. As far as applications are concerned, the range is constantly expanding. Once principally seen as a means for carrying messages for the purposes of entertainment, learning and enrichment, NBM have come to dominate administration, storage and communication in business and commerce, and to play a large part in sales and marketing. Over the next few years they will provide the major mechanism for recording events and archiving the activities of society. The importance of studying these media in their own right assumes a greater significance as they become ever more essential to the infrastructure of society.

REFERENCES

1 Burke, E., *A philosophical enquiry into the origin of our ideas of the sublime and beautiful*, 1st ed., 1757, 1.

2 Ellison, J. W. and Coty, P. A., *Non-book media: collection management and user services*, Chicago, American Library Association, 1987.

3 Library Association Audiovisual Group, *Bibliographic control of audiovisual materials*, London, LAAVG, 1986.

4 Brand, S., *The media lab: inventing the future at MIT*, New York, Viking, 1987.

5 Pinion, C. F., *Legal deposit of non-book materials*, London, British Library, 1986.

6 Thomas, J. L., *Non-print production*, 2nd rev. ed., Littleton, Libraries Unlimited, 1988.

7 Henderson, J. and Humphreys, F., *Audiovisual and microcomputer handbook*, 4th ed., London, Kogan Page, 1984.

8 Rogers, J. V. and Saye, J. D., *Non-print cataloguing for multi-media collections: a guide based on AACR2*, 2nd ed., Littleton, Libraries Unlimited, 1987.

9 British Standard Specification 5408, *Glossary of documentation terms*, 1976.

10 Very few listings are available, and they are either highly technical or only of American terminology. A further problem is that the physical form of a given document may be described in more than one way. The following offer a history of the development of the terminology: *Anglo-American cataloguing rules*, 2nd rev. ed., Chicago, American Library Association; Ottawa, Canadian Library Association; London, Library Association, 1988. (Note the glossary and terms in Rule 1.1C1, general material designation and in the specialist chapters); Library Association, Media Cataloguing Rules Committee, *Non-book materials cataloguing rules*, London, LA/NCET, 1973, 9. (Lists the forms; some definitions given in the text); Gilbert, L., *Non-book materials: their bibliographic control*, London, National Council for Educational Technology, 1971, 12 – 15. (Defines some of the terms in LA/NCET); Groves, P. S., *Non-print media in academic libraries*, Chicago, American Library Association, 1975, 48 – 50. (A useful structured listing); IFLA

ISBD(NBM), *International standard bibliographic description for non-book materials*, London, British Library, 1977, 54–8; *Computer library*, New York, Ziff Communications, 1989; published on CD-ROM, contains an invaluable glossary of computing terms; Weihs, J. R., *Non-book materials: the organisation of integrated collections*, 3rd ed., Ottawa, Canadian Library Association, 1988. (Extremely useful source, highly recommended); Also note: British Standard Specification, op. cit.

11 The phonogramm-Archiv of the Akademie der Wissenschaften was set up on 27 April 1899 with three major aims: (a) to survey the languages and dialects of Europe, and then the rest of the world; (b) to record performances of music, particularly of primitive races; (c) to record voices of famous people.

12 Campbell, A. K. D., *Non-book materials and non-bibliographic services in public libraries: a study of their development and of the controversies which have surrounded them from 1850 to 1964*, FLA thesis, London, University Microfilms, 1965, 116.

13 Ibid., 131.

14 Lever, A., 'The cinematograph and chronophone as educators in public libraries', *The librarian*, **3** (5), 1912, 195–200.

15 Pinion, C., 'Video home lending service in public libraries', *Audiovisual librarian*, **9** (1), 1983, 18–23.

16 Rolstad, G. O. and Orlyk, D. J., 'Adult services: a myriad of messages and media opportunities', *RQ*, **27** (3), 1988, 318–20.

17 Skinner, H., 'Microcomputer software in public libraries', *Audiovisual librarian*, **13** (4), 1987, 200–8.

18   Wood, N., '(RG) IT at the Glasgow Garden Festival', *Library Association record*, **90** (9), 1988, 504–5.

19 Templeton, R., 'LA-net: a major new service from the Library Association', *Library Association record*, **90** (10), 1988, 569.

20 Gibson, G., 'Sound recordings', in Groves, op. cit., 82.

21 Doubleday, W. E., 'Current view', *Library Association record*, 15 February 1917, 41–2.

22 Campbell, op. cit., 134.

23 Ibid., 130, quoting L. McColvin.

24 Smith, F. S., 'Music and gramophones in public libraries', *The library assistant*, **316**, March 1925, 64.

25 Campbell, op. cit., 171, quoting E. A. Savage.

26 Ibid., 130, quoting W. B. Sayers.

27 Ibid., 165.

28   National Committee for Visual Aids in Education, *Planning a visual education department*, London, NCVAE, 1948, 1.
29   As reported in: Fothergill, R., *Resource centres in colleges of education*, London, National Council for Educational Technology (NCET working paper no. 10), 1973; Beswick, N., *School resource centres*, London, Evans/Methuen, 1972 (Schools Council working paper no. 43).
30   Microelectronics Education Programme, *Microprimer*, Loughborough, Tecmedia for MEP, 1983.
31   Cross, C., 'The making of the British: five invasions (600BC – 1066AD)', London, *Observer* CI Audio Visual, 1972.

Part 2

THE USER

INTRODUCTION

The term 'user' has been defined in a number of different ways in connection with libraries. Here it is being used to indicate a person using NBM, whether or not in a library context. The term 'non-user' therefore indicates somebody who does not use NBM rather than somebody who does not make use of libraries. In contrast, the term 'client' relates to somebody who actually makes some use of NBM within a library context; whereas a 'non-client' is anybody who uses NBM but has no knowledge of or desire to use them in a library context. An example may make this clearer. A safety officer who collects a videorecording from his office and shows it in a factory is a user of NBM, while one who lectures on safety in the factory may be described as a non-user of NBM. If, however, he were to go to the company library and borrow a videorecording on safety, he would be a client; whereas if he did not know that the company library had any NBM or refused to use the library, he would be called a non-client. The relationship is shown in the following diagram:

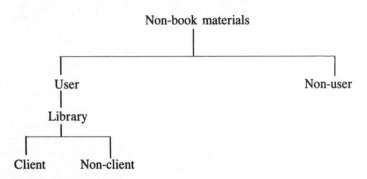

This is not merely playing with words; it is important to consider the user of NBM outside the library context in order to reveal the potential market for the services of the library. If librarians believe that the purpose of the library is to assist the economic, educational and social progress of the community, then their first duty is to analyse the use made of NBM by that community and to determine if, how and — perhaps most important — to what extent the library can help.

This use cannot be defined too narrowly; the full range of possible demands must be considered even if at the end the librarian concludes that help cannot be offered. The view which sees NBM within the public library context as being limited to sound recordings of music or entertainment confronts the belief that NBM are not just 'vehicles for artistic experience' but also a means of conveying ideas, information, learning and instruction. As Unesco (1968) has stated for one subject: 'The emergence of exciting and creative new forms for the presentation of scientific knowledge contributes to the progress of education and enriches the cultural heritage of mankind.'[1]

It is not the aim of this book to describe and analyse the impact that NBM have had on society. However, it is important to realize that the individual user has an immense range of information sources available. Within individual homes there are radios, televisions, midi sound systems, art reproductions, models, kits, photographs and viewdata services. Indeed, some would claim that the information sources not found within the home are books, newspapers and periodicals. In our day it is difficult to be a non-user of NBM.

A wide range of subjects and experiences is available: scientific exploration on television; rock music concerts in stereo on the radio; posters offered as free gifts in magazines, on subjects as diverse as child safety in the home and uses of glue; sound cassette guides around a stately home; and videogames. Within a factory, school or office an individual is similarly exposed to numerous NBM: the training video on safety; listening to the sound of recorded heartbeats in medical school; preparing a GCSE project on the mass media; desk diaries on microcomputers; and computer software on the genetics of the fruit fly.

THE VARIETY AND RANGE OF USERS

Users of NBM may be divided into two groups which, although not completely distinct, point to differing needs.

The producer

This type of user is one who, in creating a document in book or non-book format, has to extract previously recorded information from one or more forms of NBM. For example, for a television programme on Salvador Dali, the production team would incorporate material from his paintings, newsfilm, radio interviews and still photographs.

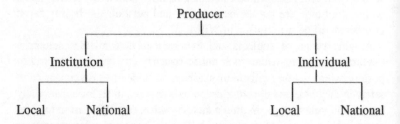

The diagram demonstrates that there are both individual and institutional producers. These may be differentiated into national and local, 'national' in this context meaning that the document produced will be sold or distributed beyond the reaches of the institution or individual producer. This is analogous to the process of books being published. In contrast, a local production is one that is primarily designed for use within the institution or by the individual. For example, an individual producing at a local level could be a student creating a tape-slide presentation for a seminar about Beatrix Potter, drawing upon her writings, contemporary still photographs and slides of her cottage. An example of an institution producing at a local level would be a media services unit creating an interactive videotape for a law lecturer incorporating maps, pages from law books, photographs and drawings.

In summary, the producer is a user who finds information in a variety of formats (be it book or NBM) and uses it to create something new.

The private user

This type of user takes a finished product in order to extract information from it. He may accept or reject that information but he makes no attempt to create his own document. Thus a student who plays a sound cassette of birds of the sea shore as a result gains knowledge of that subject but does not take parts of that recording and create his or her own document. Similarly, the parent who buys a copy of a sound cassette telling the story of Black Beauty in order to keep the children quiet on a long car journey is not intending to reorganize that recording. The private user may well be choosing the item not for himself or herself but for a known audience. For example, the training officer in a library may select a videotape presentation on enquiry techniques to show to a group of reference librarians.

The producer and private user described above appear in all aspects of society, and the following sections may help to show how wide ranging the demand is that these users can make on NBM.

In education

The librarian must be aware of trends within education which may alter the pattern of demands made on the library for information. There can be little argument about the attitude of the future clientele: their work within school is showing young people that non-books are powerful tools. It cannot be stressed too highly that NBM has permeated into all aspects of education, although it may not have reached as far as some claim. Major stimulants to this spread have been the growth of the ideal of the student as an individual learner, the concept of resource-based learning and the project method, all of which suggest that if the student is searching for information then he or she must have adequate resources in all formats. For example, the introduction of the GCSE has resulted in increased demands on the public library by the student interested in local history, who may well study via books, interactive video, still photographs, specimens and maps.

This should not be thought of as a recent development, although the use of electronic aids has developed during the latter part of this century. At the Beamish Open Air Museum, County Durham, there is an example of a late Victorian classroom which includes maps, wallcharts, a magic lantern, specimens and even a teaching kit. What may be new is the belief that these are more than teaching aids; they are the very basis of individual student learning.

The rapid introduction of microcomputers at all levels of the educational system is producing a computer-literate generation who see computing software as a natural part of their information requirements. In recording an essay they may use the BBC Domesday interactive videosystem for information, use computer software to manipulate the statistics on that system and finally use a wordprocessor for the final essay.

Even if one is not sure how far these developments may affect libraries outside education, it is salutary to see the figures concerning the number of students and teachers. In the United Kingdom in 1987, out of a total population of 56.9 million, some 9.4 million children attended school (nursery, primary, secondary and special). Some 25% of 18–24 year-olds were participating in further or higher education; 2.2 million students were undertaking full- or part-time further and higher education; about 1,600,000 people were attending adult education centres; and there was a total of 700,000 teachers in schools, further and higher education.

In the United States in 1985, out of an estimated total population of 238.8 million, there was a total of 57.4 million enrolments in all forms of education from elementary to higher. The US Center for Educational Statistics estimates that on 1 September 1987 approximately 23.8% of the population was enrolled in educational institutions. The total number of teachers in elementary and secondary schools was 2,645,000 and in higher education it was 700,000.

It can be seen that these represent sizeable percentages of the population of each country. If all these people are being involved with NBM in the educational sector, it is likely that many of them will be making similar demands outside it in the future.

There has been particular growth in education and training aimed at potential learners unlikely to attend traditional courses. Shift workers, workers whose responsibilities involve travel, geographically isolated workers, the housebound and those working via telecommuting etc. have begun to use open-learning systems, and they have become increasingly dependent upon new methods of audiovisual communication and computer-assisted learning.

Private users within education
Within primary education there are experiences which illustrate how far NBM and their equipment have become a normal part of the lives of some children.

> Examining historical evidence for clues, interpreting findings and collating results not only gives children tremendous enjoyment, but also makes them aware at an early age that history is a process of enquiry and that they are working as historians do ... Many forms

of historical evidence — artefacts and documents in particular — have immediacy.

Pictures in history books and the traditional type of school display poster was only a starting point . . . Original paintings of characters in historical costume and scenes from the past . . . Collections of old photographs . . . a series of old postcards showing the village about 50 years ago . . . a set of Ordnance Survey maps from 1904 to date . . . building plans . . . boxed sets of genuine artefacts provided by Bristol Museum . . . by using tape recorders to collect reminiscences from living witnesses, the children were able to gain valuable practice in developing communication skills.[2]

In secondary education the government's determination to counteract the growth of AIDS resulted in specially commissioned videorecordings with teaching notes which were designed to give detailed information within a supportive environment. The particular medium was chosen because it was one appreciated by the users, involved well-known television presenters and could be quickly and easily duplicated for school use. Similarly, the training package to help teachers prepare for the national curriculum consists of a 37-minute video showing classroom activity sequences, backed up by two folders containing information, practical examples and discussion points.

Pat Noble, in her work *Resource-based learning in post compulsory education*, notes:

Picture the learner in a resource-based system: busy with set tasks from a course workbook; submerged in a world of sound with headset and cassette player; trying to solve the decision-making problems with other students before rejoining a patient computer terminal; tuning into radio or television transmission; scanning a set of slides to find essential information; seeking out a teacher for help or guidance to other sources. All these activities belong to a resource-based learning system whether within institutions or at a distance from them. Learning in all such systems invites transaction with stored knowledge.[3]

Examples of the above may be drawn from all aspects of higher education.

The Granada Centre for Visual Anthropology at Manchester University is concerned with a field in which the practical use of film and video are of central importance. The directorate suggests that the surge of interest in this field is due to the fact that 'the ability to use visual media for communicating messages has become an essential precondition to both political power and commercial success, just as a command of verbal and literacy skills was essential in earlier times'.[4]

Distance learning is an avid consumer of NBM. The National Extension College has used videorecordings and computer software and, of course, the Open University was the first example in the UK of a full-scale multimedia system of higher education. Here the student is involved with television programmes, computer programs, videorecording and sound cassettes. All of this is supported by the library, which also provides the clearance of copyright for publications.

Outside the educational sector, there are a number of academic associations and professional institutions producing NBM. These include the Historical Association, the Royal Institute of British Architects, the Law Society and the Institute of Chartered Accountants.

Producers within education

In the previous section, the use of NBM has been considered in relation to the teacher and student as private users − in other words to their individual use of the documents available for study and teaching. However, teachers and students in all sectors of education must alo be considered as potential creators.

The primary school child involved in a project on the local park may take still photographs of the trees, interview the park-keeper (making use of the school cassette tape recorder), obtain photocopies of early maps of the area and borrow from the school library a slide set on the animals that may be found in a park. He or she will write up his or her experiences in compiling the project and package the complete work in a portfolio. At secondary school level, there are numerous examples of children and staff creating NBM, ranging from film making to writing computer software, in the process of teaching and learning.

Lecturers in higher education are also producers. A glance through the Higher Education Learning Programmes Database reveals many examples. The University of London Audiovisual Unit has published a resource videodisc, *The knee*,[5] which includes photographs of specimens and dissections radiographs, histological slides and film sequences of the movement of a freshly dissected knee.

At work

There are two key areas for the use of NBM within firms: training, aimed at middle management and salesmen; and marketing, aimed at advertising, public relations and sales.

From the point of view of the employer, the main purpose of training must be to achieve maximum efficiency. Employers have therefore focused on NBM which could meet this objective − for example, distance learning courses where the workers are able to study without attending college and therefore disrupting work needs. Some companies offer a 50/50 arrangement whereby they pay for the course materials provided the worker studies in his own time or they offer 50% of study time at work. Thus in the USA the Association for Media-based Continuing Education for Engineers provide 'video textbooks' which 'are cost effective − the flat-rate rental fee for videos makes unit costs for the employer far less than those involved in local university extension courses'. The flexibility of NBM is a key feature and the ability to question attitudes makes interactive video particularly important. The Training Agency has funded a one-hour interactive video business training course, *Start your own successful small business*; it asks entrepreneurs if they have what it takes to start up on their own and provides an overview of what is involved in doing so.

The Training Agency offers guidance for managers and trainees on training technology, through, for example, *The electronic brochure*, which is available on IBM-compatible computer discs and gives information on computer-based training, artificial intelligence, computer simulation, video, viewdata, satellite broadcasting and cable television. It also goes into the advantages and disadvantages of the various media, when they should and should not be used and current costings.

The armed services, industrial employers such as ICI, firms in the commercial sector such as Marks and Spencer, Boots and Barclays − all these have been keen users of NBM. The Post Office has installed videoplayers in its main post offices to provide information and advertise goods. Vast numbers of training films and specialist videos are made for firms such as Damart, Cuprinol and the Ford Motor Company in order to motivate their own workforce, increase profits and introduce new legislation. These firms also use them to encourage pupils to consider industry for a career. Government agencies are also keen to influence people; e.g. the Commission of the European Communities has its video *Agricultural Europe*, which highlights the common agricultural policy.

The need to update executives in new techniques has long been recognized, and a recent development stems from the North East Biotechnology Centre's finding that busy managers' time for updating knowledge is very limited. Sound cassettes that are short descriptions of the new biotechnology process and its likely impact on their future work have been produced for in-car use.

It is the growth of information technology that has perhaps most influenced current business practice. Packages for wordprocessing, spread sheets or databases have rapidly spread even into small firms as the unit cost has dramatically reduced. Microforms have similarly proliferated, principally because microfiche are still used for information storage in the administration of commercial enterprises. However, the development of CD-ROM with its speed of response may well see their demise.

In leisure activities

All libraries, consciously or not, cater for leisure activities. However, within this context the public library plays perhaps the leading role in relation to activities which occur outside the workplace or educational establishment. Its areas of concern include hobbies, club membership, sports, classical music and slide shows. The merit of these activities, intellectual or otherwise, need not concern the librarian. What is important is the fact that they involve a large number of individuals. Individuals in their homes listen to Beethoven on the radio, learn French from a sound cassette or watch soap operas on the television.

Probably the major leisure source is television, with over 51% of households having two or more sets. The average number of radios in each home is 3.76, although more than 72% of those who listen do so in their cars. In February 1987 the average time spent watching television was 25.5 hours a week, those over 65 years old watching the most.[6] The desire for home entertainment resulted in some 46% of households having a viderecorder by 1987.[7] The number doubled between 1983 and 1986. There was also a boom in home microcomputers, 17% of households having one in 1986 compared with 9% in 1984. Compact disc sales grew from 0.3 million units in 1983 to 18.2 million in 1987. In the USA in the same period there was a 130-fold increase. These growths were matched by expanding provision of videorecording and computer software through high street shops, and also by a surge in the number of magazines reviewing and evaluating the output and equipment.

Many public libraries and local education authorities offer a videorecording loan service, ranging from feature films to DIY guides for car maintenance, flower arranging and fitness. There are some ingenious new devices available; for example, the Bosch Travelpilot which promises in-car navigation on a TV screen on the dashboard coupled to a compact disc player with Ordnance Survey maps digitized on CD-ROM.[8]

A church society considering a visit to the Holy Land may want to borrow a film or slides on the subject. The local council that is twinning its town with one in Germany may have a need to learn a few German phrases by using a language sound cassette. Librarians are aware of many of the leisure demands and have certainly attempted to satisfy some of them. This is particularly true in the case of sound recordings. Westminster Public Libraries have loaned records since the 1930s and there are few public libraries which do not offer sound cassette and CD audio services, often for a fee. As early as 1983, public libraries in Scotland and England were loaning microcomputer software, and by 1986 some 97 authorities were considering it; the major concern was that they 'could not afford initial stock', not that it was not considered part of a public libraries function.[9] Of particular note is the provision of public viewdata services carrying local information supplied by the public library, for example Hillingdon, Hertfordshire and Birmingham.

NEEDS AND REQUIREMENTS OF USERS OF NBM

To what extent does the demand from users involve the functions of the library? Ely (1971) has defined a library as follows:

> A *function* (not a place) *whose responsibility is systematically* (there must be a plan for acquisition related to the needs of the institution to which it is attached) *to collect information* (information is used to include realia and non-book materials), *classify it* (the system must recognise the requirements of the retrieval system), *store it* (storage for retrieval purposes may require conversion to appropriate form) *and upon demand* (the art of identifying the existence of a unit of information must be efficient and systematic) *retrieve it and assist in adapting it to the use to be made of the information.*[10]

It is difficult to offer evidence for the view that users think of libraries in this way with regard to their requirements for NBM. They may well not see themselves as wanting NBM at all. However, there have been welcome signs that libraries are being increasingly viewed as the natural homes of NBM collections. Users have welcomed videorecording and computer software collections even where they have had to pay subscriptions. The speed with which librarians have introduced newer forms into such collections has reflected their growing confidence in the value of such services. However there may also be a pragmatic reason for this: such forms as videorecordings and microcomputer software have been a valuable source of income generation. They have often been introduced by public libraries through library committees on a self-financing basis. Ironically, such acceptance by users, librarians and local politicians has not been completely reflected at a national level. The government in its Green Paper on the funding of public libraries identified core services to be paid for out of the public purse; NBM and access to remote databases were not seen as part of these free core services. That this was vigorously attacked by the Library Association, and to some extent retracted by the government, is a heartening indication that NBM are now accepted by the users and the librarian. The resurgence of the public library as the natural focus for public information from government agencies through computer databases such as TAPS and ECCTIS is perhaps a more significant indicator of this change.

As has been stated, one of the library's main functions is to collect documents, whatever their form. Throughout this book it will be argued that lessons already learnt about the user needs and requirements for books may be used, suitably modified, for NBM.

The needs of the private user and those of the producer are similar in many ways, and there is one fundamental principle that is common to both, although its interpretation is perhaps different according to the community served. This is the paramount requirement to satisfy the user's need, which is coupled with the user's right of access to all information sources in all forms. Unfortunately, at the present time NBM are not as readily available as books. The user has only limited access to those items which are being offered. There is little opportunity to select retrospectively from the mass of recorded information. On the other hand, readers know that within the library system any particular book, no matter what its origin or level, can usually be obtained through the library network. The user of NBM does not have this choice. He or she has to buy a particular record, for if it does not have mass appeal it will be deleted. A television episode can be enjoyed only once, although a number of television archives have developed, for example the North East Television and Film Archive at Teesside Polytechnic for the regional output of Tyne Tees Television and BBC North East.

Private collections of off-air television recordings are not allowed under the 1988 Copyright Act. However, the freedom of access to commercial film through the purchase or hire of videorecordings is a welcome development. Major film companies such as United Artists and Twentieth Century Fox have seen the hire and sale sectors of their business become major income sources, in some cases larger than the first run income. Librarians have been able to make many videorecordings available that would have limited hire value through commercial outlets. Some companies have been unwilling to allow libraries to loan their products. Their argument has been that such provision limits their sales, but there is perhaps a need for them to consider wider issues.

The freedom of access so precious in the world of books has been achieved because libraries have collected and stored information presented in books, and have provided the facilities for its dissemination for both purposive and recreational needs. The words that spring to mind are those of R. C. Swank, that libraries enable clients 'privately and voluntarily to choose their own readings'.[11] Without this facility, the information recorded, whether in books or NBM, becomes the property of the institutions that own the copyright or those who can afford it. The practice of charging for the newer services runs the risk of restricting their use to those who are already 'information rich'. Private access to equipment such as interactive video is beyond the purses of the majority of the population. Children can gain access only if their parents or the institutions they attend can meet the costs and believe the services have a higher priority than other information services. One computer advertisement reads, 'so the money you would normally have spent on a good set of encyclopaedias for your children would now be more effectively spent on one of the new breed of personal computers'.

The library further offers the client the opportunity to use information sources privately, without a mediator. Perhaps an inherent danger in some student-centred learning schemes is that the teacher predigests the information for the learner, directing him or her along certain routes. The student uses learning packages and has no opportunity to compare and contrast the information in them; an analogy would be having the Bible available in a filmed version with no access to the original. Through the library other viewpoints and other routes are on offer.

Librarians must respond to the challenge of organizing NBM, for they should be:

> concerned with the products for the life of the imagination, the intellect, and the spirit of man; all formalized communication formats are of interest to librarians; audiovisual materials and services should have equal concern, equal familiarity, and equal support of library administrations and staff to those of printed materials. Integration of planning and programmes regardless of subject, format, or age level served is required for the library to continue as a relevant agency.[12]

In order to achieve this the library must act for its clients, by providing information about what exists and how access can be gained. This implies the provision of bibliographical tools which are current and retrospective, offer evaluation and state where the materials may be obtained. Individuals and institutions will require further information services geared to their specific enquiries. Furthermore, access to the materials in many cases will require collections organized in the way that books have been. The private user and the producer will require all of these services although their approaches may well differ in purpose and degree. Equipment will be necessary for the full implementation of much of this material and will require similar services.

Thus the needs of NBM users may be focused on three questions which have direct relevance to libraries: (a) What documents and equipment exist? (b) How does the user gain access to documents and equipment?

(c) How does he or she use the documents and equipment provided? The national producer does not have to face these problems to the same extent as the local producer and the private user do. There will often exist an institutional collection administered to meet specific demands, such as the BBC's film library. Where pressure of time is less, the national producer is likely to use external sources such as commercial picture libraries.

However, Hancock's comments (1973) should be noted:

for the producers of the media, the principal requirements are convenience and speed. A television company needs rapid access to film and tape footage; the ease with which a sequence can be located, retrieved and displayed is often the crucial factor behind whether it is used at all. The same is partly true of less professional users. Even for the private individual, a main interest is the ease with which he can find and secure what he wants.[13]

DOCUMENTS AND EQUIPMENT

What documents and equipment exist?
A client may request a set of slides on blacksmiths suitable for showing to a group of 10-year-olds. A similar request could be made for equipment; an organization may require, say, a videorecorder that can record from a microcomputer, costing no more than £1,000. Both these enquiries may well lead to a need for clients to see the items themselves, but at this stage a collection is not necessary. Requests can also be retrospective (for example, 'What archival videotapes exist to show students the changing nature of intellectual thought?') or current ('Have any sound cassettes been produced on the changes in the tax system as a result of the recent budget?').

Such demands must be answered with the same range of information regarding subject, authorship, format and full bibliographical details as would be given for printed material in the *British national bibliography* (BNB). The demand may be for access by purchase, borrowing or by reference, but the important fact is that the existence anywhere of the document or equipment has been recorded. If librarians searching for an index or catalogue reference to printed material cannot establish the existence of the work, it is assumed that either they have failed to use the tools correctly or that the enquiry was incorrect or misleading. It is very rare indeed for a book not to have been recorded in any bibliographical source. Yet this can well prove to be the case with NBM, because of the imperfections of the bibliographical organization involved.

Many clients' demands in this area could be satisfied by the creation of a British national media record with many of the attributes of BNB. However, there also seem to be needs and requirements that may be better met through information services for NBM. These will use the tools described above, but they will also need to create their own tools to satisfy requests.

Information services may be divided into two types:

1 *Those supplying information only for a particular type of client*
The British Universities Film Council Information Service is concerned with the production, availability and use of audiovisual materials in higher education. The needs of its clients may be seen in a sample of typical queries received by the information service:

- 'Please send me a list of British organizations, governmental and non-governmental, which make films on engineering, medical and scientific subjects.'
- 'Do you know of any audiovisual materials on the history of industrial relations?'
- 'I am preparing a series of lectures on Greek drama. Can you suggest any films or videotapes I might use?'
- 'Could you send me a list of slide suppliers in the field of physics?'[14]

These enquiries are answered without direct access to a collection of NBM through books, pamphlets, appraisals, bibliographies, catalogues and an information database.

2 *Those supplying information on both print and NBM for a subject*
The purpose of the Local Government Training Board is to provide an advisory service on training and development for local authorities in England and Wales. Its information services satisfy an ever-increasing demand for information covering NBM that can be used to meet the broad and specialist training needs of local government. A wide range of training publications including course materials, manuals, open-learning materials, overhead projector transparencies, illustrations, wallcharts, slides, videorecordings and computer software is available.

How to gain access to documents and equipment
Demand for NBM may be satisfied by a reference collection, or the client may require a loan service. The user may be happy to travel a considerable distance to a national collection, or may require a local service for immediate use.

At the national level, there may be the equivalent of the British Library Reference Division; that is, a central collection containing a wide range of NBM, linked to a programme designed to acquire all items as they are published and to make them available for reference. Some users may feel the need for a similar national reference collection for equipment. The Central London Polytechnic Information Technology Centre displays leading makes of microcomputers. Also at a national level, the example of the British Library Document Supply Centre could be followed, so that clients are supplied with NBM in the same way as they are supplied with books and periodicals.

There are no institutions which fully satisfy these demands for national reference and loan facilities. There are, however, a number of collections which partially satisfy the reference demand. For example, for particular formats there are the British Library National Sound Archive and the British Film Institute/National Film Archive. Unfortunately other formats are not so well covered at a national level. The picture is further complicated at a national level by the number of organizations that keep subject reference collections of NBM. For example, the Victoria and Albert Museum has a slide collection, and the Imperial War Museum has a sound records archive.

Clients require quick access to loan and reference facilities, and these may be met at an area or a local level. At the area level there has been the development of reference collections such as teachers' centres which have a reference collection of various types of commercially available materials which can be used to complement books in schools. A client can visit this service or contact the telephone information centre. It is likely that at national and area levels provision will be for reference and copying facilities only and this by itself is unlikely to satisfy clients' demands for a fast service. There are exceptions, of course, in that many videorecording users rely on external hiring agencies and they are prepared to accept this delay.

However, the local service would assume importance for most clients as a loan service, helping, for example, the student teacher wishing to use NBM on a teaching practice the next day, the works manager who wants a videorecording on safety for showing in a week's time, or the. child requiring a slide set about the area he or she is visiting on holiday. At a local level there is also the need for access to equipment. The public library has not to date supplied equipment, but this practice is fairly common in educational and industrial institutions. (Gateshead Public Library has enabled its local community to access viewdata equipment in its branch libraries.) Even here, however, it tends to be for use within the library area and the librarian will have to consider whether or not the client requires to take it elsewhere. Linked to this, and an aspect often neglected, the question is whether or not the client has access to the correct environment for using NBM. This may be as straightforward as a room with blackout facilities and sufficient power and telephone points, or rather more fundamental such as the provision of the relevant microcomputer for the software.

How to use documents and equipment
Many librarians take a neutral position with regard to information. They certainly regard it as their duty to help clients find the information they

require but there has been only limited attention paid to the question of helping clients use information documents and tools. Use is partly dependent on adequate guiding but, unlike the case of printed material (librarians do not find it necessary to teach their clients to read), they may find it vital to teach clients the correct method of, for example, handling slides and operating the microcomputer.

There is also the question of information concerning use of NBM and its equipment. Should the industrial trainer be tutored by the library in the correct way of using the slide with a small group, or when not to use the videotape recorder? This may not take the form of straightforward teaching but may involve the library in providing instruction sheets with each machine, pointing out not just how to operate it but also the best way to use it to achieve a particular learning goal. It will also be important for the library staff to understand the possible uses of the material and equipment. Does the librarian know how to use the videorecorder projector in story-telling sessions in the children's library? Or how to introduce a tape – slide sequence into a presentation on aspects of the library for clients?

It is at the local level and in particular with the individual producer that the library can assist in adapting information to new uses. This assistance may involve the library in two ways:

1 *The establishment of a production unit as part of the library* A client who lectures on local history may choose some early Ordnance Survey maps from the map collection in the library and ask the librarian to reproduce them as slides. The library will clear copyright, arrange with the library photographer to have them shot and mounted, and then deliver them to the lecturer. Indeed this is the equivalent of a lecturer asking the subject specialist in a library to prepare a bibliography on local history.

2 *Staff involvement* The librarian may work with the client to adapt the information as part of a course (as at the Open University) or work together with a lecturer to create a teaching package (for example, on children's literature). Packages made in this way include sound tapes of poetry reading, slides illustrating picture books and extracts from books of the winners of the Carnegie Medal. Students have consulted this package in the library and then found further information relevant to their own needs using retrieval techniques taught by the librarian; the student's final work being marked by the lecturer and the librarian together.

ANALYSIS OF CONSTRAINTS

It is important to consider the constraints which can prevent the development of an effective NBM library. Skinner (1987) lists a number of reasons public libraries gave for rejecting the possibility of lending software:

- Could not afford initial stock.
- Worries about possible restrictions applied by publishers and suppliers.
- Too many formats.
- Low priority against other demands (e.g. videocassettes).
- No staff available.
- Not considered part of a public library's function.
- Committee against the idea.
- No demand from the public.
- No space in the library.
- Consumer demand will fall.
- Possible corruption of programs by borrowers.[15]

From some of these difficulties librarians have little chance of escape, but others have been created by librarians and could be overcome by them with some thought, careful planning and perhaps some luck, to the benefit of the library's whole clientele.

The traditional view of the library

Throughout their education and in their professional life librarians have used the printed word and are well aware of its value. Their contacts with NBM may have been limited and they may see no reason why libraries should consider supplying these materials. Such a belief often carries a moral undertone implying that in some ways books are superior and richer in spiritual and intellectual values; it is considered acceptable to sit outside on a glorious summer's day and read a book, but a sign of moral turpitude to sit on the same lawn under the same sun and to watch a programme on a portable TV set.

There is no doubt that books have some technical advantages — for example, a page can be referred to over and over again, and the index can quickly help to pinpoint information. In contrast, anyone who has tried to trace a particular piece of information on a sound cassette will know how difficult this can be. Correct use of odometers, particularly with digital readings, makes it easier. On the other hand ... the song of a thrush can be described in print but a sound recording describes it much better. Photographs of the foetus increase our understanding of the miracle of birth in a way that mere words cannot.

Unesco (1968) states:

> that film ranks as intellectual work, in the same way as books, newspapers and periodicals, and that all such intellectual works should benefit from all measures conducive to the development of culture, to technical progress and to the intellectual and moral advancement of mankind, without any discrimination based on the material form on which works, or on the vehicle through which they, are transmitted.[16]

This first constraint against the use of NBM must be seen, then, as a simple misunderstanding of the role of the library — which is to supply information in whatever form it is required.

Clients' demands

A library necessarily reflects the demands of its clients, and it would be pointless to offer a service that is not required. However, this alleged constraint may hide a value judgement, suggesting that there is no demand because users do not think of the library as a supplier of NBM. Indeed they may like to see NBM in the library but have not been asked whether they would.

Users are often not aware of the value of having NBM available. In a school where there are individual departmental collections of teaching aids, the teaching staff can often see no necessity to have this material centralized in one place. This may well lead to a waste of resources. For instance, the geography department may have a model of Hadrian's Wall to show its underlying geographical features; the history department may hold the same model for its historical value. Such a model could also offer a stimulus to other departments which may not have considered it as a teaching aid: the English department reading Auden's poem on Hadrian's Wall could use it, for instance, and so could a school group organizing a climbing trip to the area. The librarian can have a role in the development of users' awareness of the potential of all forms of recorded information.

Even when NBM are available in the library, users may not be aware of it. Two-thirds of the population do not make use of the public library service anyway. However, there has been an increased emphasis on marketing of services as the political climate since 1979 has emphasized the consumer and payment at the point of use. The need to generate income was reflected by Pinion's research into public library video lending services. That concluded by stating: 'Public libraries have, generally speaking, been slow to publicize their services, having had little outside competition where books and sound recordings are concerned. Video libraries demand a much more aggressive approach, particularly by those authorities establishing a service on a self-financing basis.'[17] This need to publicize NBM services further is also true in academic libraries; ' surprisingly many academics had little idea of what the library could offer in computerized information, despite advertising our service, as we thought, widely'.[18]

The 'book fund first' syndrome

Library budgets are often under pressure, and cannot be stretched to cope with the demand for books and periodicals. However, libraries have increasingly recognized the duty set out in the UK Public Libraries and Museums Act (1964) 'to provide a comprehensive and efficient service'.[19] The Act states that:

> in fulfilling its duty ... a library authority shall in particular have regard to the possibility of ... securing that facilities are available for the borrowing of, or reference to books and other printed matter, and pictures, gramophone records, films and other materials sufficient in number, range and quality to meet the general requirements both of adults and children.[20]

It is interesting that the emphasis here is on form, rather than on why public libraries exist. Contrast that statement with one which states that public libraries today 'are fundamentally involved in the transfer of ideas, the stimulation of imagination and the development of adult learning through the use of all forms of communication media'.[21] Such a belief yields little to the finance argument, which it places in the same category as the belief that education is all about learning to read so that you can fill in your income tax forms.

However, it cannot be denied that the constraint of finance is an important one, nor that printed material is the major source of transfer of information at the present moment: 'Very large amounts of information are now created and distributed in electronic form ... It may be fugitive like Prestel or Ceefax newspages, which cease to exist when they are no longer current, or it may be actively or passively stored, on magnetic tape, floppy disc, hard disc, video disc, CD-ROM or even microchip.'[22] It is therefore dangerous to consider NBM as things which can be dropped at a time of financial restraint; at a future stage when money does become available the library may find that the material is completely unobtainable. As has been pointed out,[23] 'these ''new'' services must be seen as an integral part of the library's role, and adequate and continuing finance must be provided. Otherwise if the futurologists are right the world in general will bypass the library.'

Equipment

There are two concerns about equipment. The first is the suggestion that clients may not be able to use sophisticated equipment, the second is the suggestion that it is too expensive for most domestic budgets. It is probably true that many adults are unable to handle equipment competently, but it seems likely that the educational system will produce more and more people well able to use such equipment, that manufacturers will make their products 'idiot proof' and that people will expect to find forms of entertainment, education and training other than books. The relative cost of equipment is steadily reducing, and more people will soon be able to afford it; the real danger is that they will be disappointed with the library provision and will seek advice and help elsewhere. This is a plea not for the sanctity of libraries, but rather for recorded information to be kept together for the benefit of clients. Adequate guidance in using equipment and perhaps supplying it for reference use are the first steps, as in the Have-a-go-Micro scheme at the Central Lending Library in Stockport.

Subject v. form

The message transmitted by a film of an athlete running is not the same as a slide set of the same subject. The librarian must consider not only the subject his or her clients are interested in, but also the appropriate forms for it. Yet in some libraries the subject is subjugated to the form. The public library's disc collection has always been concerned with music, so the music librarian was often made responsible for all record purchases. However, a large number of fields are covered by recorded sound — including drama, poetry, social interviews, political debates and commentaries on important issues — and these could be of interest to all subject librarians.

Forms of communication can also change the way we look at our own experiences. Seymour Papert has clearly stated how he believes computers will affect our society:

> Computers can be carriers of powerful ideas and of the seeds of cultural change, and they can help people form new relationships with knowledge that cut across the traditional lines separating humanities from sciences and knowledge of the self from both of these. It is about using computers to challenge current beliefs about who can understand what and at what age.[24]

Traditional client divisions

It has been observed in public libraries where the adult and children's sections have been merged that the move often benefits the adult who is looking for a simple introduction to a subject. No longer constrained by the librarian's artificial decision that a book will be of use to one particular group of clients only, he or she is now able to find a simple introduction in a children's book.

Yet the readability of a book is still a constraint. A child with a reading age of 10 who is interested in ships might be induced to take out a book more suitable for a marine engineer. NBM to some extent overcome this barrier of client division, as they are more comprehensible across the age range. A slide of an oil tanker can be used by both the child and the engineer. The information received may differ, but there is not the same initial barrier to overcome in understanding the language of the message. Nevertheless, there is still a 'learning to read' process with all NBM.

Traditional subject divisions

Melvil Dewey described how during a long sermon, 'while my mind was absorbed in the vital problem, the solution flasht over me so that I jumpt in my seat and came very near shouting "Eureka!"'. He had conceived, in 1873, 'a solution to the problem of orderly and efficient arrangement of books in a library'.[25] In his resultant scheme, the whole of human knowledge was divided into 10 main classes, and many libraries since then have been arranged according to the Dewey Decimal Classification. But the artificial subject divisions pose problems, particularly in the case of NBM. For example, a slide of a diamond may be of use to the chemist studying crystallography, the student learning to cut glass, the mathematician concerned with volume, the art lecturer concerned with shape and the economist interested in forms of wealth.

The librarian must consider each of these needs and decide to what extent the library retrieval system can meet them. This problem will be discussed in more detail in Part 4 under the heading of cataloguing and classification.

Browsing

Librarians have usually been aware of their clients' need to browse, but worry about the fragility, durability, security and cost of NBM has introduced the notion that these must be stored separately or even locked away. Some may feel that closed-access policies are still necessary for some forms of NBM, but most forms can be safely integrated with the book stock. If this latter policy is adopted, someone looking for the novel *The hobbit* will, through the 'serendipity of browsing', find also the sound cassette of the work.

Future shock

Librarians may be unable to assist clients properly because of their own lack of knowledge or even fears concerning NBM and their equipment. Alvin Toffler (1970) has aptly summed up this inherent conservatism and lack of self-confidence as 'future shock', a 'concrete force that reaches deep into our personal lives, compels us to act out new roles, and confronts us with the danger of a new and powerfully upsetting psychological disease'.[26] However, he cannot hide from the truth of the statement that 'the use of the ubiquitous TV set as an information display and interactive personal electronic communication device will bring dramatic changes to the way in which we conduct our day to day affairs'.[27] Yet any change should build to some extent on the past. The library acquires, organizes, retrieves and issues units of information in book form, and these processes have been established after long practical experience. This book will demonstrate that NBM do not destroy these processes and that what is changing is the nature of the demand — clients now require that the library should acquire, organize, retrieve and issue units of information, whatever their form.

NBM AS ARCHIVE MATERIAL

Archives are not established to serve any particular group. Their sole aim is preservation, and they are the fundamental information sources upon which all other bibliographic organizations depend. Library services would be the poorer without them.

Some of the reasons for the necessity of our concern with the preservation of NBM are illustrated by the remarks of Mary Pickford, the silent screen actress of the 1920s:

> I never thought my films were important. I never did anything to save them. I just put them into storage and forgot them. I intended to destroy them because, frankly, I didn't want to be compared to the modern trend. If you look at the magazines of forty years ago, their writing is ridiculous. I mean it's so sentimental. I was afraid my films would be the same. When the Hollywood Museum started I tried to help, but found the tins of film were just full of red dust. Then we had two fires, one in our office building, another in the stores, and films were lost in both. Private collectors won't give up the pictures of mine — and they know they're bootlegged. But it's just as well — otherwise they'd be gone.[28]

She mentions the establishment of an archival organization, the Hollywood Museum, to preserve material. The organization and preservation of Britain's heritage of books is firmly established in the work of the British Library, in particular its Reference Division. One of the objectives of the British Library is the:

> preserving and making available for reference at least one copy of every book and periodical of domestic origin and of as many overseas publications as possible. The aim will be to provide as comprehensive a reference service of last resort as possible. If the reader cannot get what he wants nearer at hand he will know he can find it in the British Library.[29]

This is mainly possible because of the Copyright Act of 1911, which legally requires publishers to deposit one copy of each of their publications with the library. But the position with regard to the national heritage of visual and sound materials is not as well established. There is no national archive of NBM but the British Library and the Library

Association have recognized the need and in 1986 assisted a number of institutions with significant national collections of audiovisual materials to form the National Archive Collections of Audio Visual Materials Forum (NAVF).

The National Film Archive is the only truly national and general collection of film, while for sound there is the National Sound Archive. Neither of these collections has the benefit of legal deposit. They rely on donations and legacies for much of their material. The National Film Archive does receive gratis some material from the BBC, and the independent television companies pay the archive to record a representative sample of independent television programmes. A National Museum of Photography, Film and Television was founded in 1982 in Bradford.

A number of regional television and film archives have also been formed following the requirement by the IBA that: 'The Authority may require the company to make suitable arrangements for the accumulation and preservation of an archive of its programmes and for access to such an archive by the public.'[30] Thus archives such as the Thames Television Archive, and the North East Television and Film Archive at Teesside Polytechnic, have been established.

The National Sound Archive was founded in 1947 and has the largest collection of sound recordings in the UK, from wax cylinders to compact discs. The British Library is now responsible for this archive and has facilitated the development of an automated catalogue and free listening service.

There are other collections which have an archival function but this is secondary to their other roles. The BBC sound archive is more concerned with its in-house responsibilities; 'it is stressed that the most important object is to provide existing material for inclusion in new programmes'.[31] The BBC Hulton Picture Library, which has a collection of six million pictures, many of them unpublished and unique, 'is a commercial picture-lending library; it is neither a national archive nor a research institute, so it cannot help students or research workers unless it is a paying proposition'.[32]

Yet NBM are valuable archive materials and there is an obvious need for the nation to:

(a) Collect published NBM (such as the picture postcard, television programme, top 20 long-playing records) and to preserve them.
(b) Collect NBM of local interest: photographs of personalities and

buildings, records of singers, sound recordings of noises (such as the peal of cathedral bells or the sound of the last tram). The local studies collections of public libraries have perhaps exploited most effectively this function of NBM.

(c) Use NBM to preserve transient evidence, the growth of oral history being one manifestation of this. The historian who records on tape people's memories of the past offers the opportunity of access to the lives and outlooks of classes and groups who have left very little in the way of formal or written evidence. The North West Sound Archive, located in Clitheroe Castle, Lancaster, has established an extensive oral history collection.

(d) Use NBM to exploit more fully the material in the archives and give the public access to rare or fragile documents. The BBC Domesday disc has facilitated access to original materials from museums and public record offices.

The major problem lies in deciding what should be preserved and what destroyed, and this decision should not be left to private collectors. Mary Pickford pointed out, they 'won't give up the pictures of mine'. Because there is no national archive attempting to preserve all NBM, other collections have to worry about whether they are discarding the last copy of a document, and this function will probably not be central to their aims. As Hodges says (1989), 'We all have our priorities and these rarely include archives'.[33] There is no place of 'last resort'. Preservation is further hampered by a lack of coordination between the existing archival collections, clients being unaware of the location of documents. For certain formats it is necessary to rely on the collections of individuals, and librarians may have to create location records for these collections. Sample surveys by the British Library and the National Council for Educational Technology have shown that there is little archiving of computer software. The British Library and the Department of Trade and Industry funded a pilot study, which is called the Knowledge Warehouse, to collect from publishers the electronic versions of published works (generally, the tapes and discs used in computer typesetting), store and index them and make them available for reuse.

While the priority must be to preserve this material, there is still a need to consider clients' demands. The editor of the *Directory of recorded sound resources* writes in justification, 'we hope that the recordings held in over 480 different collections will become readily accessible to everyone from exhibition organisers, teachers, academic researchers and the general public, to broadcasters, film makers and even commercial users such as advertising agencies'.[34] The National Film Archive has available duplicate distribution copies of some of its films and will make stock available to the bona fide student on a reference basis. It also enables wider public access through its network of regional film theatres. The NAVF in particular strongly encourages local initiatives as 'They provide an invaluable way of ensuring that as complete a picture as possible is built up and allow greater public access than centralised national archives are capable of doing.'[35] The Sound Records Department of the Imperial War Museum has collected many hours of recordings on all aspects of war. Listening equipment is available and small groups of 8 – 10 students can be accommodated. A further service is that teachers can record archival material such as the BBC recording of the Battle of Alamein, or an interview with a soldier who fought in the First World War trenches, and bring this experience into the classroom. It has also released a videorecording, *The Battle of the Somme*, produced by the British Topical Committee for War Films in 1916.

Finally, there must be concern for the physical preservation of NBM. Mary Pickford's 'red dust' clearly illustrates the problem with early films. The cellulose nitrate stock used was highly inflammable and moreover decomposes within 50 years. Unless the film is reprinted, the material can be entirely lost. It should be noted that film archives rarely project the preservation copy – a viewing copy is always printed. Glass plates of the early photographers are also easily damaged. Thames Television found that its archival collection of 2in. videotapes had been affected by mould and by degeneration of the spools and associated packaging materials. A master copy of such material is invaluable if it is to be preserved. The advent of the laser videodisc may be a major advance in the preservation of material; however, caution is needed with the newer forms, for their stability is still open to debate. Nevertheless, a number of institutions have transferred to these new forms. For example, the International Museum of Photography has transferred some of its historic photographic negatives on to videodisc. Write only (WORM) optical systems are designed for archiving purposes in companies etc.

The nation's heritage of films, sound recordings and still photographs is in danger. Because often only a few copies are published, the chances of survival are reduced. Imagine how our knowledge and understanding of Dickens would be restricted if copies of *Oliver Twist* had not survived. Yet NBM produced more recently have already disappeared. Brownlow,[36] commenting on the silent film era, suggests that later generations' views of that period have been distorted by the relatively small amount of material that has survived. Ballantyne has asked: 'Who is going to file electronic journals? Is anybody making an archive record of a selection of pages from Prestel? Where will computer assisted learning packages be archived? Think about it. Knowledge does not exist until it has been recorded, and that knowledge is lost if no copy of the document is preserved.'[37]

It is salutary to compare the national archival situation in the USA. The US National Archive had set up a division of motion pictures and sound recordings as early as 1935. The Library of Congress has the largest archival collection of NBM in existence. It has an overall collection of 83 million items, which includes nine million photographs, 300,000 reels of movie films, 250,000 prints and drawings, 80,000 posters and a recorded sound collection of over a million items. Such a list conceals the multifaceted nature of the collections; for example, the playing card collection includes tarot, commemorative and standard decks from 25 countries. The collections are created through a mixture of donation, deposit for copyright and purchase. Perhaps an indication of the size of the Library of Congress collection is a report of the donation from *Look* magazine, consisting of '17½ million black and white photograph negatives, 1½ million colour transparencies, 450 thousand contact shots and 25 thousand movie stills'.[38]

The determination of the USA to preserve its national heritage of NBM is hardly surprising, bearing in mind that it invented the majority of these new forms and formats. However, it may also point to a particular awareness of the value of NBM as information carriers. This is not reflected worldwide, and IFLA in 1988 urged the need to address 'the problems emanating from restrictions imposed by the various copyright and other related laws and practices which, in many countries, affect the collection, preservation and access of AV materials for educational, research and private information purposes'.[39] Much remains to be done in the vital area of archives.

REFERENCES

1 Unesco, 'Text of the resolution adopted unanimously by the fifteenth session of the General Conference of Unesco at its forty-second plenary meeting on Wednesday, 20th November 1968, at Unesco House, Paris', International Film and Television Council, *International conference on the cataloguing of audiovisual materials, London, 1973*, London, IFTC, 1975, 30.

2 Davis, J., 'Evaluating evidence', *Junior education*, 11 (6), 1987, 26–7.

3 Noble, P., *Resource-based learning in post compulsory education*, London, Kogan Page, 1980, 15.

4 Henley, P., 'Granada Centre for Visual Anthropology', *Viewfinder*, 2, 1988, 13–14.

5 Reviewed in *Viewfinder*, 2, 1988, 10–11.

6 *Social trends*, no. 19, London, HMSO, 1989.

7 Reiss, P., 'TV audience: VCR's as the fifth dimension', *ADMAP*, November 1987, 44–9.

8 Hutton, R., 'Jam today, jam tomorrow', *Punch*, 23–30 December 1988, 40.

9 Skinner, H., 'Microcomputer software in public libraries', *Audiovisual librarian*, 13 (4), 1987, 200–8.

10 Ely, D. P., 'The contemporary college library: change by evolution or revolution', *Educational technology*, 11 (May), 1971, 17–19.

11 Enright, B. J., *New media and the library in education*, London, Bingley; Hamden, Ct, Linnet, 1972, 36, quoting R. C. Swank.

12 American Library Association Public Library Association, Audio-Visual Committee, *Guidelines for audio-visual materials and services for large public libraries*, Chicago, American Library Association, 1975, 12.

13 Hancock, A., 'Cataloguing and information handling for integrated audiovisual media utilisation at the national level', International Film and Television Council, *International conference on the cataloguing of audiovisual materials, London, 1973*, London, IFTC, 1975, 106–7.

14 British Universities Film Council Information Service, *Publicity leaflet*.

15 Skinner, op. cit.

16 Unesco, op. cit.
17 Pinion, C., 'Video home lending services in public libraries', *Audiovisual librarian*, **9** (1), 1983, 18.
18 Such anecdotal comments could, of course, be reported for all aspects of library work.
19 GB *Public Libraries and Museums Act 1964*, chap. 75, 6.
20 Ibid., 7.
21 Library Advisory Council (England), Report of the New Media in the Libraries Working Party, London, LAC 1976, p.6, quoting the chief librarian of Toronto Public Libraries.
22 Martyn, J., 'The knowledge warehouse and library users', *Journal of documentation*, **45** (1), 1989, 49.
23 Baggs, C. and Thompson, A. H., 'Video in libraries', *Audiovisual librarian*, **8** (1), 1982, 26.
24 Papert, S., *Mindstorms: children, computers and powerful ideas*, Brighton, Harvester Press, 1980, 4.
25 Dewey, M., *Dewey decimal classification and relative index*, 18th ed., Albany, Forest Press, 1971, 3.
26 Toffler, A., *Future shock*, London, Bodley Head, 1970; London, Pan, 1971.
27 *Videotex, viewdata and teletext*, Northwood Hills, Online Publications, 1980.
28 Brownlow, K., *The parade's gone by*, London, Abacus, 1973, 149.
29 *The British Library*, White paper, Cmnd 4572, London, HMSO. Note also the trenchant comment on the role of the British Library by the editor in *Audiovisual librarian*, **9** (2), 1983, 62−3.
30 Needham, E. and Emmett, J., 'Cinemac: an archive concept for Thames Television', *Image technology*, January 1988, 15−16.
31 Trebble, A., 'BBC Sound Archives: a general account, including a description of classification and cataloguing practice', *Audiovisual librarian*, **2** (2), 1975, 68; Davanagh, J., 'The BBC's written archive centre', *Audiovisual librarian*, **9** (2), 1983, 83−5.
32 Moss, D., 'Pictures: Radio Times Hulton Picture Library', in Aslib Audiovisual Group, *Audio-visual workshop May 7th−8th 1970*, London, Aslib, 1971, 13. This invaluable resource has had a chequered history in the last ten years and is an excellent example of the tensions that can arise between archival and commercial aims.
33 Hodges, A., '78's − preservation or disposal?', *Audiovisual librarian*, **14** (1), 1988, 29.
34 Weerasinghe, L., *Directory of recorded sound resources in the*

United Kingdom, London, British Library, 1989, v.

35 Cornish, G. P., 'Audiovisual archives in the United Kingdom', *Audiovisual librarian*, **14** (1), 1988, 19.

36 Brownlow, op. cit.

37 Ballantyne, J., 'Audiovisual archives: recent developments', *Audiovisual librarian*, **7** (3), 1981, 15–16.

38 Harrar, H. J., 'Photographs, pictures and prints', in Groves, op. cit. (in part 1), 173.

39 Bowden, R., 'IFLA 88', *Library Association record*, **90** (11), 645.

Part 3

MATERIALS

INTRODUCTION

According to some futurologists, the world is now becoming the information society, and if that means that there is a deluge of information being produced and distributed, there is a great deal of truth in the notion. The constant acceleration in the production of information is combined with an increase in its accessibility, for it is not only being created in large quantities but being made more readily available. Techniques like desk-top publishing and computerized typesetting have made it much easier for cheap printed publications to be produced and distributed, and the use of satellites and cable television has greatly increased the availability of visual information. A further development has been the growth of access to information prepared in and distributed from other countries, which has added to the mountains of information to which people now have access.

Selecting from all this information is now a major issue for most people. Storing it is even more of a problem. One hope that has been widely promulgated is the paperless office, but progress towards this remains slow. The difficulty is not so much running one's own office in a paperless way but the vast amount of paper that other people keep sending to it! There is still much to be done before this state is reached, if ever. However, it is a principal target for much of the technological development that is currently taking place.

One of the outcomes of this growth in information has been the growing importance of NBM as a major storage system. There is little doubt that this will prove to be the dominant system in the future, though the forms that it will take are still uncertain. One of the features of the last decade has been the rapidity of technological development, and there is no sign of this reducing. Outcomes are not easy to forecast as each new development seems to breed its own set of original ideas for the next stages, but certain trends are evident.

Because of the enormous growth of information, there is a need to compress the space in which it is stored. Filing cabinets are emptied into a microfilm, a 16-volume encyclopedia into a CD-ROM. Such compression must be accompanied by the ability to find the relevant items of information quickly, so the accompanying need is to develop fast search and access systems. Because users usually have difficulty in formulating what they require in the terms which the cataloguer used, these search systems need to be initiated through language that is as close to natural speech as possible.

A second trend is to increase the capacity for the user to manipulate the information; to compare readily different texts, images and sounds; to edit and rearrange them into new, relevant and more interesting orders; and also to produce his or her own versions. Thus an essay could contain extracts that are not retyped but directly transferred; a presentation of holiday snaps could be simply rearranged for different audiences; a publication can be a mixture of text, sound and moving pictures.

One of the problems with NBM has been the mass of different equipment and devices. To reduce this, there is a continuing effort to integrate them into fewer systems without losing the versatility and quality that the separate pieces of equipment provided. While versatility is rarely sacrificed, and on the whole is increased, there is much difficulty in retaining high standards of reproduction. Sometimes there is accompanying improvement, as with CD recordings over vinyl discs, but video still fails to achieve the same standards as film.

With the attempt to achieve greater compression, there is also the move towards portability, at least for some types of equipment. One difficulty remains the quality of screens, but developments in liquid crystal technology have led to improvements. This is most clearly seen in the increasing clarity and size of displays on portable computers. Portable equipment is dependent on batteries for power, and the current developments are being achieved because of the progress in designing rechargeable versions of them.

The final trend is more difficult to appreciate as it raises as many questions as it provides answers. As storage systems are able to hold more information in a smaller space, the natural inclination is to expect that more can be held in local systems adjacent to the equipment. However, at the same time, communication systems through satellites and cable connections are also improving, so that it is also easier to search and retrieve distant collections of information and download them where necessary or relay them to a personal receiving station. The choice made for any piece of information will tend to balance economics with convenience and need, but these are variable characteristics which change continually. Thus a response to this dilemma of either using a remote information bank or purchasing a store for local use is one that needs constant review.

All these developments are the result of continuing, almost unremitting technical progress. The trends indicate the broad direction in which developments are moving; but as they occur, the user is confronted with a growing variety of options. Some formats disappear − for example, the film loop − and in time some format within a form loses the competitive battle and is withdrawn − as, for example, the Beta system for videocassettes. However, as each new piece of technology emerges, a variety of manufacturers bring out their own versions, most of which are incompatible with those of their competitors. Each manufacturer wishes to corner a piece of the potential market, and in most cases feels that some characteristics of its invention are particularly advantageous for the user. Thus for a period of time, until one form becomes the accepted norm and *de facto* standard, the user is confronted with a wide variety of options.

Now that these NBM technologies are so important for the future of society, the number of significant multinational companies in each field is constantly increasing. In the middle of this century, when Kodak made an announcement about the quality and standards of film, this was as effective as announcing the world view. To a large extent this still holds true for this medium. The standard for the audiocassette was that decided by Philips, effective because it released the rights for all manufacturers to adopt it without paying any licence fee. With videocassettes, there was essentially a battle between two Japanese standards on the world stage, those adopted by European companies like Philips and Grundig never making a significant impact on the market. The computer-based market is very much more open. Although IBM was the mainframe leader, when the microcomputer developments occurred it was unable to dominate the market because other companies such as Apple had a significant proportion of the activity. Consequently, despite the widespread adoption of IBM's operating system in the business arena, it is clearly not the only dominating influence for the future. A large number of companies from a variety of countries are now important players, and agreements are likely to take a considerable time to achieve. The same is true in the field of broadcast television standards, although that debate does not have as many protagonists.

Such rivalries are naturally bound to occur in a developing field, and indeed the rigid application of standards can detract from progress and improvements. The need for compatibility is important so that the user can ensure that materials continue to be used, but it may hold back technical inventions that increase quality and versatility. The latter is the positive aspect of incompatibility; there is a negative aspect when a major manufacturer designs a unique system that, in effect, shackles users to that company's equipment. Sometimes this is the result of patents and unwillingness to pay licence fees. For example, manufacturer X develops a cassette system for, say, slides. That is patented, which means that other manufacturers can use it only under licence, which naturally requires payment to X. The public responds to the invention by welcoming it as a successful method of storing and retrieving slides. Manufacturer Y sees that X has produced a market that Y can enter in competition only if they pay X for the privilege by paying a licence fee. To avoid this, Y develops a system which, to avoid infringement of patents, must be different from X's, and the two compete. X's cassettes cannot be used on Y's machines and vice versa. For the unfortunate user, the situation is full of difficult questions. Should he or she use such a cassette at all? If the answer is affirmative, then which system should he or she choose? If X is favoured, is there any assurance that X will stay in business, or will X be forced out by the success of Y? Will X continue to have spare parts for their machines? Will the lamps, for example, remain available? Will X be so successful that they will improve their cassette and make their new versions in such a way that they will be impossible to use with the old equipment?

Pitfalls typified by these questions litter the pathway of developments of NBM and are part of the reason why some people shy away from them. It certainly has not always paid to be a pathfinder in the past, and yet in order to ensure that developments take place, it is essential that some users try to encourage manufacturers who are probing new territories, even though some will burn their fingers. To the prospective purchaser, the difficulties described above mean that very great care and often advice have to be taken when making selections.

The issue of compatibility is an important one for the user, who is now investing significant sums of money in materials to go with the equipment. New advances from the same manufacturer are expected to be able to use the same materials that were published for previous machines, a situation commonly referred to as 'upwardly compatible'. Regrettably, this is not always so. Many items are not usable. The most obvious case at the present time is reflected in formats for playing music. The old music centre played audiocassettes and vinyl discs, the latter at one of two speeds and one of three sizes. Now there are compact discs (CDs) which require laser players, and to come shortly are digital audiotapes (DATs) which will require a different player again. Anyone who purchases CD and DAT players will not be able to use audiocassettes and vinyl discs with them, unless appropriate facilities are incorporated.

This is obvious as the materials look different, but with computers visual information like this does not apply. The 3½in. disc looks the same for every machine, but the form of its recording and the arrangement of the information on its surface make it possible to use it with some equipment and not with others.

To overcome some of the basic incompatibilities, some standards exist. As described above, many of these come from manufacturers themselves, particularly those that dominate particular markets. Others, especially those that relate to safety and the dimensions of equipment and materials, are accepted by international agreements through organizations like the International Standards Office and the International Electro-Technical Commission. These are largely responsive to decisions made by countries in Europe, America, Australia and Japan through their own various standards organizations, the British Standards Institute (BSI) and the American National Standards Institute (ANSI) being important members. Other countries usually agree to support them. Standards for interconnections between computer-based equipment are also gradually emerging and being accepted through Open Systems Interconnection (OSI). At another level of international agreement, the standards and interrelationships for broadcast television in Europe are maintained by the Council of Europe, and this process, therefore, often incorporates political decisions as well as technical and manufacturing ones.

Such movements towards forms of international agreement and standards do provide some basis from which the user can gain confidence and reassurance about the quality and continuing support for equipment that is purchased. Nevertheless, there remain many quandaries to be faced in making choices and selections. Given a variety of alternative incompatible pieces of equipment, which should be purchased? One option is to buy a selection of each, which means that all the available materials can be made available to users. However, this is an expensive choice. Another option is to purchase just one model of equipment and keep to that. Materials made available only on other systems are excluded from the user, who may go elsewhere or remain without access to them. Some may be obtained on loan from other sources, but use would be confined to the user's own equipment if that were possible. For a library or information centre, making such a choice diminishes the comprehensive coverage that their users may expect from the service. If later a different system is purchased, perhaps because the first one is superseded, it may be possible to transfer the materials acquired for the first one on to the new equipment. However, there is no guarantee that this will be possible, and it may prove an expensive exercise.

Making decisions like this may be considered invidious, and so it may be considered better not to purchase any of the equipment until it is clear which is the winning system. Such a decision may lead to a long wait until one format emerges as the *de facto* standard. For example, it has taken some 12 years for it to become clear that the accepted standard for videocassettes is the VHS system, and taking the route outlined would have prevented users from having access to any videorecordings during this time. Some items may no longer be available as they are 'out of print' and so will never be purchased.

Any decision to buy equipment for use with NBM at this time has to be taken with an acceptance of potential obsolescence. When the equipment is for use with widely accepted standards like slides and audiocassettes, then the viability of the machines is likely to be for a substantial period of time. However, in areas where the standards are more ephemeral − for example, with television, videorecording and computer-based equipment − the potential life should be considered to be three years or less. Technical details and facilities will change and create new environments, and while old equipment may be retained to provide access to earlier formats of materials, only by investment in the new equipment will the new materials and use of their facilities become available to users. With the trend towards increasingly tight budgets for information storage and handling, this is an unfortunate necessity that has to be built into any long-term financial planning.

In spite of all the different pieces of equipment, essentially users are looking for only four different types of presentation of the information they require, either independently or in combination with others. These are printed items, which can be writing, graphics, photographs on material or on a screen; still pictures, which can be transparent for projection or viewing, or can appear on a screen; recordings of sounds; and moving pictures. In addition, for tactile stimuli, artefacts and realia may be of value. All information carriers can be sorted into these four basic groups. Through the technology, however, users have been provided with a wide range of different means of organizing and distributing them, hence the confusion of formats and equipment that has followed. Nevertheless, within all these developments and variations, manufacturers are making use of only four basic types of physical material: paper, which may carry photographic emulsion; film, a celluloid-type base with photographic emulsion or diazo dyes; magnetic material fixed to a base of either tape or a flat disc; and plastic, flat and transparent, opaque with grooves, reflective with pits or covered with photochromic chemicals. Different forms, sizes and configurations of these four materials are organized to provide the different formats in which the four basic media groups are presented. In addition, users can obtain direct access to other information through cables and telephone lines or from broadcast sources, but if they are to be stored locally, the same four types of material are used.

Worked with the appropriate equipment, these information carriers should offer the following facilities to users: they should support individual use; be capable of broadcasting the information to a large group; store information prepared by national producers; store information prepared and arranged by a private user or a local producer with minimal processing; and secure the information to prevent accidental loss or replacement. Most of the formats that will survive have most of these characteristics, the main area of contention being whether or not the individual user can prepare and arrange his or her own material or whether it is only available from a national producer. Much effort is devoted to resolving this problem, which is reflected, for example, in the considerable amount of research that is taking place to produce optical discs that can be prepared by individual users and even erased. Pressure from users demanding this facility, for example, can be significant in the final appearance of a format. It was that pressure that encouraged the development of cassette-type packaging for microforms, sound and videotape because storage, retrieval and utilization are made so much more convenient in this way. However, as a result of the individuality of manufacturers and their separate innovations, there are many different and incompatible types of cassette formats still available.

The remainder of Part 3 is organized under the headings of the different physical materials utilized in NBM. The physical properties of each will be discussed, together with the appropriate care and maintenance. Then there is a section describing the various formats into which these materials are made. This is followed by a description of the equipment necessary for each format, with a final section giving simple guidance on operation − a manual of practice.

THE MATERIALS

Paper

Care and maintenance of paper collections require the following points to be considered:

1   Poor quality paper, such as that used for newspaper, deteriorates rapidly in sunlight. At all times when they are not being used, extracts on paper should be kept out of the light.

2   Paper surfaces and edges damage easily with handling. They can be smudged by fingers, and edges will tear unless protected. Punch-holes made through paper for storage purposes often tear farther. Various protective devices, such as lamination, edge binding and hole protectors, can reduce these problems.

3   Printed sheets produced by spirit duplication fade in light. Copies that are stored should be kept out of direct light. If master stencils for duplication are preserved, they should be stored with separating sheets between them. Ink stencil masters should be suspended.

4   Paper that is rolled retains the curvature. Reverse rolling cracks the surface veneer and encourages deterioration. It is preferable to hang such rolls with weights at the bottom to keep them flat.

5   Dirt on paper can be cleaned off with an ordinary eraser. Unless a special washable surface has been applied, washing is more likely to destroy paper than to clean it.

6   Photographic paper has a layer of photographic emulsion on the surface. Although this has been fixed chemically, it will deteriorate with misuse. Sunlight bleaches photographic colours, including black, and also causes a tendency towards yellowing of the paper. Scratching the surface will scrape away the emulsion. Dirt may be washed off the surface with a damp cloth, but drying in an oven or over a radiator should not take place. Unless great care is taken to weight the corners the paper will curl as it dries. Dust should be removed gently, using a soft brush or a puffer. Blowing by mouth is not recommended because of the effects of dampness.

Film

Photographic film has a layer of emulsion attached to a polyester base material. Careful observation will show that the backing is shiny whereas the surface with the emulsion is dull. Another way of identifying the surfaces is to hold the transparent film to the light. When the picture is the correct way round, the viewer is looking at the base surface, with the emulsion on the reverse towards the light.

The image is created in the emulsion by chemical response to light, and is fixed there by processing with other chemicals. Any holes along the edge of the film are used to pull the film through the camera or projector. On cinefilms that have optical sound-tracks, a white line of varying width or with cross-hatching can be seen on the side. A brown stripe in a similar place indicates that a magnetic sound-track is being used.

Some microfiche are produced on non-photographic film. This may be diazofilm, usually black, blue or sepia in colour, and evident because the writing is normally produced in white against a coloured background. The base is again a polyester plastic film with the diazo dyes attached to it. They are produced by a photographic original being contacted with the diazofilm, exposed to ultra-violet light and processed by ammonia and heat. Another type of film used for microfiche is called vesicular film; on this the writing appears black with a white background. This is also a diazo-type film for which processing is similar though not identical. In producing a microfiche, a negative of the original is used and the result from a single process is either a negative-type diazofilm or a positive-type vesicular film, as described above. Some graphics on slides are occasionally produced on diazofilm as well.

Good care and maintenance of film material should be concerned with the following points:

1 Storage out of sunlight is important as all chemicals bleach. Colours fade only with prolonged exposure, however, and short duration viewing will not lead to deterioration. Diazofilms and vesicular films are less stable and should not be used for archival purposes.

2 Abnormally high humidity encourages bacterial and fungal growth in photographic emulsions. This is difficult to remove when established and advice should be taken from photographic specialists. Diazofilms and vesicular films do not suffer from this problem.

3 All emulsions are very easily scratched. The polyester bases are more difficult to damage in this way, but the emulsion is comparatively soft. Once scratched, there is no method of repair.

4 Grease marks from fingers, often with accompanying dirt, readily adhere to both surfaces of the film. Careful rubbing with lint-free tissue

or photographic cloth may assist in removing such damage. Ensure that the film is dry before storing.

5   Both surfaces, but especially the polyester base, attract dust. This is an electrostatic reaction, and can be discouraged by using cleaning cloths that are described as 'anti-static'. Dust can also be removed with a soft brush or puffer.

6   If paper is used to cover film material − for example, sleeves around microfiche − it should be sulphur-free to prevent chemical reaction with the silver salts in the emulsion.

7   Glass covering over film may induce the formation of Newton's rings if a trace of water is trapped between the two materials. The rings are rainbow-like effects which change shape with the heat of projection. Anti-Newton glass which inhibits this reaction is available.

Magnetic materials

Tape
The tape is made of a polyester base to which oxides of iron and chromium are attached. Examination of the tape shows that one surface (the polyester base) is shiny, and the other (the layer of oxides) dull. By magnetization and rearrangement of the magnetic fields borne by these oxides, a message is recorded on the tape which can be 'read' by a device in the playback machine. The quality of the tape depends on a number of factors: non-stretching of the polyester base; the adhesion of the oxide to the tape; and the density of the oxide. The finer the 'grain' of oxide, the better the quality of the recording.

The formulation of the oxide has developed and changed with technical advances. Improved recording quality is claimed for tapes using chromium dioxide (CrO_2), as it is for metal tape which uses a combination of metals on the same polyester base. Both these types of tape require an electronic change in the recorder and playback equipment, sometimes performed automatically, sometimes by a control button. Use of these tapes is inadvisable with equipment that is not prepared in this way. Metal tapes are used for 8mm video and digital audio recordings.

Most tapes, however, make use of either ferric (iron) oxide or a mixture of this and chromium dioxide. To assist in identification and to help standardize the manufacture of audiocassettes, the International Electrotechnical Commission (IEC) has agreed to a numbering system which should be marked on all of them. These numbers reflect the magnetic characteristics of the tapes and not the quality of the product.

IEC type 1 is the ferric oxide tape, type 2 is chromium dioxide, type 3 is ferrochrome and type 4 is the metal tape.

In use the oxide surface of the tape is pressed very closely against the recording and playback heads within the machine, and this is important in determining the quality of the reproduction. Any dirt or grease (which collects dust) is transferred from the oxide layer to the heads and produces a barrier between them, so it is important to keep this layer free of foreign matter. Any handling, marking or repairs should be on the polyester surface and not the oxide layer. When the tape is wrapped around an open reel or in a videocassette, the polyester layer is outermost and protection is relatively simple. However, in an audiocassette, the oxide layer is outermost and therefore easier to damage.

The care and maintenance of magnetic tape is concerned with the following points:

1   The tape must be quite flat on the reel. No part of the tape should be twisted, bent or creased. Tapes should ideally be tightly rewound when not in use to prevent this type of damage. Storage on edge, rather than flat, discourages any tendency to sideways slippage of the layers.

2   All tapes should be played periodically to prevent the magnetic print-through of the message from one layer to the next.

3   Dust and dirt readily accumulate on and between the layers of tape, partly as a result of electrostatic attraction. Tapes should be kept in as dust-free an atmosphere as possible.

4   High humidity causes dampness to form between the layers of tape. Fungal growth is encouraged and the tape layers tend to stick together.

5   Because the recording on the tape is the result of a magnetic process, it is important to store tapes away from the influence of magnetic fields. These can be caused by electric motors and dynamos, but to be really damaging the fields must be very strong. Vacuum cleaners, for example, are harmless, but some metal-detection devices as used at airports can cause problems.

Discs

Used for recording digital data for computers, the discs are thin circular plastic sheets, usually covered with ferric oxide, like tape. The density of information that is packed on to the recording surface is very high and so considerable effort is taken to protect it from damage. Thus the discs are supplied in card or plastic covers from which they should never be removed. Some are in completely sealed containers. Various slots are present in the card covers or mechanically revealed in the plastic cover, and it is through these that the head that records or reads the data coded magnetically there is applied. As with magnetic tape, the degree of proximity between the head and the disc is crucial to the accuracy of the reading, and so dust and dirt can have a serious effect. It is therefore essential that the magnetic surface is not touched and is kept covered as far as possible.

Care and maintenance of these discs should be concerned with the following points:

1 The discs must not be bent or distorted, as if they are they will not rotate efficiently in their covers or make contact with the head in proper alignment.

2 Dust, grease and dirt seriously interfere with use and the discs should be protected from these hazards as far as possible.

3 High humidity causes dampness and encourages fungal growth. Excess temperature, including exposure to the sun, causes the discs to bend.

4 Pressure on the disc can damage the surface. This can be caused, for example, by writing with a ball-point pen on a label on the cover or by packing the discs into a container too densely. Discs are preferably stored in a vertical position to prevent such damage occurring.

5 Because the recording on discs is the result of a magnetic process, it is important to store them away from the influence of magnetic fields, as described under tapes. One corrupted piece of data on a disc can prevent a program being used.

Plastic materials

Transparent acetate or polyester sheets
Flat transparent acetate or polyester sheets are used as the base for overhead projector transparencies. The material can be written on them by using special quick-drying inks; some are water soluble for easy erasure, some are spirit-based and can be removed with difficulty only by using special solvents. In addition, self-adhesive film and letters can be attached to the surface, and the plastic can be printed on by many photocopiers, laser printers and other standard processes.

Vinyl discs
The recording on plain vinyl discs is created by the curvature of the

bottom and sides of the groove through which the stylus travels. Produced by pressing from a master negative of the final disc, the accuracy of reproduction can be seriously impeded by the presence of foreign material in the groove or damage to the sides, which causes the stylus to alter its path.

A form of videodisc, the VHD format, uses a vinyl disc in which there are tiny pits. As the reading head is guided over the surface, so it registers the capacitance from these pits, which provides the information for the video replay. This format is unlikely to continue and is not dealt with any further in this book.

Optical storage systems
Most commonly seen in compact discs for music, this technology is beginning to provide an extensive range of storage systems. The disc consists of a plastic material indented with a spiral of pits backed by an aluminized reflective surface, which itself is protected by a strong transparent lacquer. The pits vary in length, the recording reproducing either an analogue or a digital version of the original. In each case, the presence or shape of the pits is 'read' by a laser beam being reflected from this mirror-like surface. As there is no physical contact with the surface of the lacquer, no damage can occur through using the disc.

It is suggested that these discs are almost indestructible, but they have not been available for long, and so time will tell. Handling them and even scratching the surface cannot interfere with the quality of the recording as only the protective layer of lacquer is affected. The laser beam itself focuses through this and therefore is not affected by anything on the external surface. Because of the strength of the plastic used, breakage is also difficult.

Care and maintenance of these plastic materials includes the following points. Only 2, 3, 5 and 6 apply to optical storage systems.

1   The material readily bears a strong electrostatic charge which attracts dust. Wiping with an anti-static cloth is helpful. Various other devices, like an anti-static pistol, are available.

2   The materials must be flat in order to operate efficiently. Warping and twisting under excessive heat or distorting pressure should be avoided as this kind of damage is irreparable. Because of the danger of distortion being introduced through pressure, the disc should be stored on edge rather than flat.

3   Surfaces are easily scratched, and the marks are permanent.

4 Dampness encourages fungal growth, and may arise in conditions of high humidity. Surfaces may adhere together through water tension. Specialist help should be sought if this occurs.

5 If dirt gets into grooves, various liquid cleansing agents may be used to loosen it. However, it is important that this liquefied dirt is removed by a powerful vacuum; otherwise it will solidify again. The disc must be thoroughly dried afterwards. For optical storage discs, it is advisable to keep the surface clean and dry. Any agent used should be applied and rubbed off in a radial and not a circular direction.

6 Storage in protective sleeves or between sheets of inert material such as paper can help to protect the materials.

THE VARIETY OF FORMATS

Paper collections

Little need be said about collections of paper materials. Charts and folders containing loose sheets are commonplace, the size and quantities of paper being variable. It can be expected that these formats will continue to be popular, both for educational and domestic use. A change in the structure of the textbook has occurred. Some are now published in a loose-leaf format, the pages held in a ring or lace binder. All the pages can be removed individually and extra ones can be added. Diagrams and photographs which are referred to frequently need be printed only once, and extracted for repeated study. Novels and reference materials are also now printed and punched for insertion into the ubiquitous personal organizers that many people use.

A combination of books and loose-leaf pages inside a folder is also a format that is being used. Because most of the other media require the intervention of a machine in order to see the contents, they are usually accompanied by booklets and paper inserts. Some textbooks are also published with slides or computer discs inserted into pockets within the covers. The standard book is not a static format, but one which will evolve in combination with other arrangements and media.

Film

Transparent film is used in a number of different formats.

The filmstrip

The filmstrip is a collection of images organized in two different forms, the single- or half-frame and the double- or full-frame. The differences between them are illustrated in figure 1, which shows the relevant dimensions also. The single-frame filmstrip is usually passed through the viewer or projector vertically, the double-frame strip horizontally. At the beginning and end of the strip are lengths of black film, the leader and trailer respectively, which are used for attaching the filmstrip to its carrier.

Filmstrips are usually supplied in small circular canisters and accompanied by notes explaining the content of the pictures.

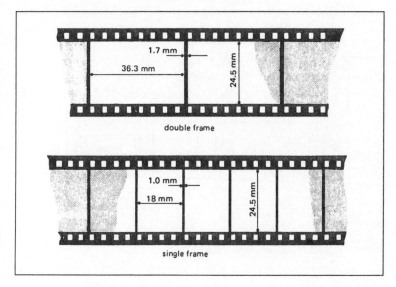

Figure 1. Filmstrips: double and single

Slides

The photographic slide, sometimes referred to as a transparency, is a single frame of transparent film, usually held within a mount made of cardboard or plastic. Glass is sometimes used to cover and protect the film within the mount. There are two common formats, the dimensions of which are shown in figure 2. The 35mm format has the same dimensions as an individual frame of a double-frame film strip, and is the one most widely available commercially. The 110mm format is almost exclusively for domestic use. In addition, there is a 60mm square slide, which can be mounted and used in major lectures, but is more widely used as a master for large colour prints.

The dimensions of a slide may be increased to 250mm square, suitable for use with an overhead projector.

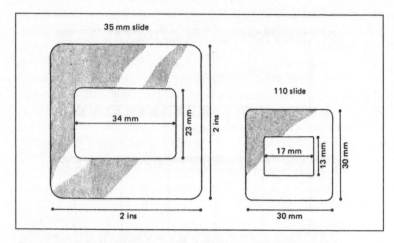

Figure 2. Slides: 35mm and 110mm

Cinefilm

The cinefilm is a sequence of images arranged vertically, which gives the appearance of movement when projected on to a screen at the correct speed. A variety of formats are available; their arrangements are illustrated in figure 3.

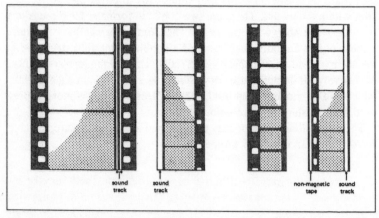

Figure 3. Cinefilm: from left to right — 35mm, 16mm sound, 8mm standard and 8mm super sound (note: diagrams are not in proportion)

1   *35mm with sound-track*   This format is almost exclusively used
in public cinemas. A double-sized frame, 70mm, is also used for major
productions.

2   *16mm with sound-track*   This is the common format for distributing
films to small clubs, schools and businesses. The film should be projected
at 24 frames per second, a reel of 400ft (120m) lasting about 11 minutes
(36ft or 11m per minute). The sound-track is usually optical, being a
white stripe down the side, but in some films this is replaced by a brown
stripe, which is the same as a thin piece of sound tape. This carries a
magnetic sound-track with all the properties of magnetic tape, and it can
usually be erased. Optical sound-tracks cannot be altered in this way.

3   *16mm silent*   This is now almost exclusively restricted to copies
of old silent films. The film has sprocket holes on both sides and should
normally be projected at 16 frames per second, a reel of 400ft (120m)
lasting about 16 minutes (24ft or 7m per minute).

All types of cinefilm are usually stored on open reels, each end having
a long blank piece of film acting as leader or trailer for attachment through
a projector. Obsolete film stock such as 8mm can be transferred to
videotape. Many companies undertake this transfer, and will even record
collections of slides in a similar way. Cinefilms should be checked for
breakages and tears. The latter are usually found around the sprocket
holes; these may be extended or the film in the region ripped. Sometimes
holes are also found in the sound-track where the user has threaded it
the wrong way. Wherever this occurs, the torn film has to be cut out
and the two ends stuck together. While thin self-adhesive tape is available
for this purpose, it is better to splice the ends together with special cement,
which is stronger. It is important to realize that the continuity of the film
will be broken and that the image will 'jump' on the screen. Because
the sound-track runs ahead of the image, the piece of sound excised in
this process will refer in part or completely to frames of film that will
be seen after the point of repair.

Microforms
Various configurations of microform are available:

1   *35mm roll film*   The film has no sprocket holes, and may be in
an open reel or, very rarely, a cartridge. The images in the frames are
arranged horizontally, as in a double-frame filmstrip, which has the same
dimensions.

2   *16mm roll film*   The film has no sprocket holes, and is supplied

in open reel, cartridge or cassette formats. The images may be arranged in comic-mode (often referred to in other formats as portrait shaped) or in cine-mode (often referred to in other formats as landscape shaped), as shown in figure 4. There may be a single strip of images, the simplex format, or a double cine-mode line of images, duplex in the same direction or duo in opposing ones. Roll film is used on open reels, in closed cassettes or in cartridges. While open reels are usually interchangeable between those machines which accept them, both cassettes and cartridges are made with different mechanical configurations and may be used only with equipment specifically designed to accept them. They are therefore not necessarily interchangeable between machines. A cassette contains two reels, the film passing from one to the other in either direction: a cartridge contains one reel, the film being withdrawn from the cartridge and wound on to a receiving open reel. The important advantage of them both is the protection from handling and dust that is given to the film, and the cassette has the added value that it can be withdrawn from the equipment without rewinding back to the beginning. In the open reel format, removing the film part way through its projection is very cumbersome. With a cartridge, this is impossible and the film has to be totally rewound before it can be removed.

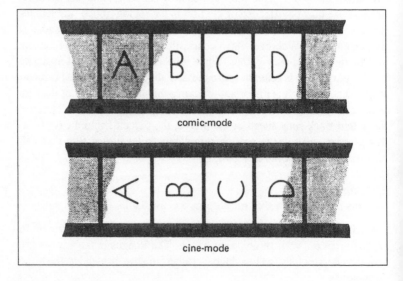

Figure 4. Microform: comic-mode and cine-mode

3 *Aperture cards* These are pieces of card with a window into which the microfilm is inserted. The card is usually approximately 187 × 82mm. It can be written on for reference purposes and notched for mechanical sorting or computer information and retrieval. The latter can also be performed through machine-readable marking. The microfilm is usually directly affixed to the card or it may be inserted into a thin jacket (see below) which is itself fixed to the card. Commonly one 35mm frame is inserted into the window, but a number of 16mm frames may be used instead.

4 *Microfiche* The microimages are arranged in a grid formation on a transparent film, 148 × 105mm (the A6 dimensions, approximately 6 × 4in.) A strip of eye-readable writing is placed along the top edge for identification. The number of frames may be varied with the reduction ratio used, but the standards are 60- and 98-frame formats, the latter being more common, using a reduction ratio of 24× from the original.

The recommended arrangement of frames is in the portrait shape (comic-mode) and the microfiche should be read in this orientation. Where the original allows, the page may be spread over two adjacent frames. Regrettably, some publishers intersperse images read this way with ones read horizontally although printed in the same fashion, so that the user has either to turn his or her head sideways, reinsert the fiche sideways, turn the machine on its side or use an image rotation control, if available.

The commonest arrangement for COMfiche (computer output on microfiche) is 270-frame format, using a reduction of 48× from the original. The images are printed in landscape shape with the long side horizontal, parallel to the top edge of the fiche. Reduction ratios up to 150× (ultrafiche) have also been used by particular businesses or for unique purposes.

Microfiche can also be presented in jacketed formats. A jacket is the same size as a standard microfiche, usually with a strip at the top for labelling, and has a number of double-layer plastic channels into which lengths of microfilm are inserted. The common form is a 5-channel jacket which accepts non-perforated 16mm film, but other versions exist for 35mm film. The jacketed fiche, which is the do-it-yourself version, is easily amended and rearranged, and of course can accumulate frames as they are filmed, the 5-channel variety achieving a maximum of 60. Copies in standard format can be made from the jacket, which can act as a master. In filling the jacket, it is usually advisable to use a mechanical inserter as the two layers of plastic forming the channel are necessarily difficult to separate. Illustrations of microfiche are shown in figure 5.

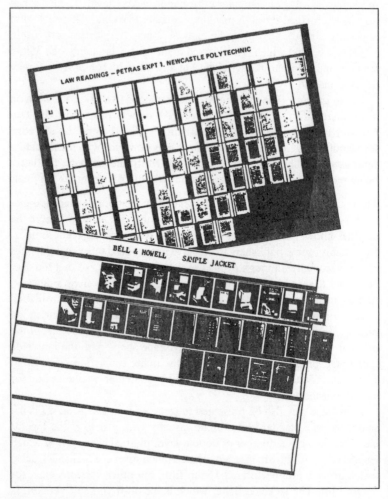

Figure 5. Microfiche: standard and microfilm jackets

Magnetic materials

Magnetic tape will be considered under two main divisions, sound and video.

Sound tape

This is commonly available in two formats, open reel and cassette. Tape may also be glued to 16mm and 8mm cinefilm to provide the base on which sound-tracks may be magnetically recorded, referred to above. It is important to note that stereo, quadrophony, 2-track, 4-track etc. are functions of the tape recorder/player and not of the tape or its mechanical arrangement.

1 *Open reel* This format is now rarely used for the dissemination of copies of recordings, but it is still widely used for the preparation and storage of masters or originals. Mainframe computers often use open reel tapes to hold large volumes of data, but these are not described here.

While wider tapes are available for such purposes as studio recordings, the usual width of tape is 6.3mm (¼in.). The tape is supplied wound on a reel, the magnetic surface on the inner side, the reels usually 8cm, 13cm, 18cm or 26.5cm (3in., 5in., 7in. or 10½in.) in diameter. The amount of tape and the playing time available varies within two parameters, the thickness of the tape and the speed at which the recording is made. The thinner the tape, the more there is on the reel, but also the more likely it is to stretch or break.

There are no standard codes to identify which tape is which, so the user has to identify this at purchase. Tables 1 and 2 give playing times for lengths of tape of different thicknesses recorded at different speeds, measured in centimetres per second or inches per second (ips). Using both tables, it is possible to calculate how long a particular tape will play or record passing once through the recorder at a certain speed. For example, an 18cm (7in.) reel of standard tape (360m) at 9.5cm/s (3.75ips) speed lasts 60 minutes. It is very important to store tape indicating the speed of the recording and its duration − usually as a function of time, but tape length may be given also.

Tapes are supplied with coloured leaders and trailers, which are lengths of coloured plastic tape at the beginning and end without the magnetic surface attached. On these may be written the information concerning the recording, but their primary purpose is for attaching the tape to the plastic spool. This is usually done by slotting a short length of the leader (or trailer) through the notch on the spool (see figure 6). Sticky tape may be used with care, but is not the recommended method.

SPOOL SIZE   TAPE TYPE

	standard		long play		double play		triple play	
	m	ft	m	ft	m	ft	m	ft
8cm reel (3in.)	54	150	62	210	90	300	135	450
13cm reel (5in.)	180	600	270	900	360	1200	540	1800
18cm reel (7in.)	360	1200	540	1800	730	2400	1080	3600

Table 1. Spool size related to tape type and tape length

TAPE LENGTH   TAPE SPEEDS

		19cm/s (7½ips)	9.5cm/s (3¾ips)	4.75cm/s (1⅞ips)	2.4cm/s (15/16ips)
m	ft				
45	150	3.9	7.8	15.6	31
65	210	5.5	11	22	45
90	300	7.5	15	30	60
135	450	11	22	45	90
180	600	15	30	60	120
270	900	22	45	90	180
360	1200	30	60	120	240
540	1800	45	90	180	360
730	2400	60	120	240	480
1080	3600	90	180	360	720

*Table 2. Minutes of playing time for one pass through the tape recorder
for different lengths of tape at different speeds*

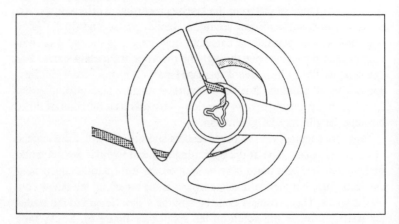

Figure 6. Attaching open reel tape to empty spool

Between the leader or trailer and the magnetic coated tape is sometimes found a short length of silvered tape. This affects the tape recorder as it passes through the record/playback channel and in those machines with the appropriate facility causes the machine to stop. This is useful in preventing the tape flapping around on its spool after it has finished recording or playing.

When stored, the loose end of the tape should be fixed into the reel, using either a special plastic clip or a piece of adhesive tape. In this position there is no danger of damaging the recording as the adhesive should be attached to a leader, or in its absence to the plastic backing of the tape and not its magnetic surface.

2 *Cassette* First developed by Philips during the 1960s, the audiocassette is now an international standard. Indeed, Philips released the patents at the beginning in order to encourage universal acceptance, and the other formats being developed at the time on a more restricted basis have now disappeared. There are also small cassettes designed for dictating machines which are not considered here.

The audiocassette has standard dimensions (10.2 × 6.4cm) and features. The tape is 3.8mm (0.15in.) wide, and in the cassette the magnetic coated surface is on the outward or exposed surface. All cassette recorders and players run at a standard speed (4.75cm/s, 1.875ips), and this means that cassettes are sold with predetermined playing times. Commonly these are C30 (15 minutes each side), C60 (30 minutes each side), C90 (45 minutes each side) or C120 (60 minutes each side); the sum of the time produced by playing the tape through one way, turning it over and playing it through again is the number given to the tape. The thickness of the tape decreases as the length increases; C30 and C60 are approximately that of triple-play open reel tape, C90 and C120 becoming progressively thinner and less robust. Prerecorded tapes are cut to an appropriate length for the content and do not abide by these standard length dimensions.

Tapes for computers are generally shorter and of lower quality. The common lengths are C10, C12 and C15. While longer tapes may be used, it takes such a long time to find the program that the shorter length is more suitable. Prerecorded tapes for computers are mainly confined to games, and as they are an unreliable form of storage they are gradually being replaced by discs.

The inside of a cassette is shown in figure 7. As will be seen, the tape passes from one spool to the other, both of them within the cassette, so it may be removed from the machine at any point without any necessity

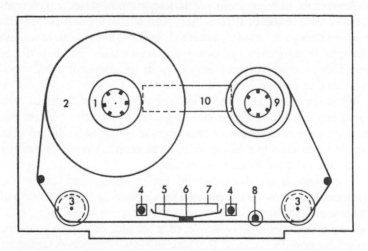

Figure 7. Diagrammatic view of the inside of a cassette: 1=gearing of the left-hand supply reel; 2=left-hand supply reel; 3=guide roller; 4=guide pin; 5=pressure spring; 6=felt pad; 7=baffle; 8=capstan; 9=gearing of the right-hand take-up hub; 10=inspection window

for rewinding. Within the cassette, the tape is kept in position by a series of guides, and is attached at each end to the respective spindles by strong adhesive tape. When fully wound to one side, the user will notice that a leader or trailer of transparent or coloured tape is visible. Storing fully rewound in this way prevents any damage to the magnetic coating, as this is protected within the cassette. The leader or trailer takes between 5 and 7 seconds to pass, so no recording can be made during this period. In early cassettes a silvered portion of tape was inserted between the trailer and the coated tape to provide an automatic stop, but this facility is now handled by a sensor which determines the different thickness or density of the coated and trailer sections.

The quantity of tape within the cassette may be seen through the window on its surface. Most cassettes are held together by screws, and this has the advantage of providing easy access for any necessary adjustments and repairs. At the rear of the cassette are at least two lugs, pieces of plastic covering a hole (see figure 8). When present, the cassette can be erased or recordings made. If they are snapped off, recording is not possible and accidental erasure is prevented. Therefore, if a cassette

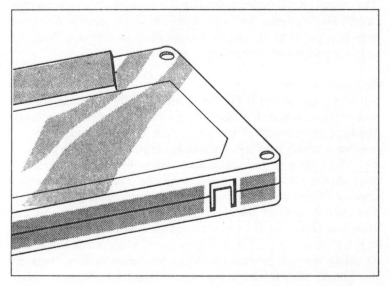

Figure 8. Lug at back of cassette to prevent accidental recording

with the lugs removed is returned by a borrower with the recording
tampered with, the tampering can definitely be established as deliberate
interference. As the cassette has two playing sides, there are two lugs;
with the cassette flat on the table and the exposed tape facing you, the
lug referring to the upper side as per label is the one at the back on the left.

Other important features to note on a cassette are the pressure pad
behind the tape, usually a small piece of sponge rubber which is supported
by a spring and used to keep the tape in firm contact with the
recording/playback head of the machine; the notched rings in the large
holes which engage the spindles on the machine and help to keep the
tape properly wound in the cassette; and the four holes at the front, the
inner pair providing access for pins to hold the cassette rigid, the outer
ones allowing access for a rotating pin which with the wheel in the
machine actually propels the tape at a constant speed from one half of
the cassette to the other.

Digital audio tape (DAT) cassettes are much smaller, 7.2 × 5.4 ×
1cm (2.8 × 2.1 × 0.4in.), although the tape itself is the same width,
3.8mm (0.15in.). They are available in 60, 90 and 120 minute lengths,
although at long-play speed they can last twice as long, i.e. up to 4 hours.

The cassette itself is enclosed, completely covering the tape, and insertion into the machine pushes back a cover and lifts a lid to reveal it. Accidental erasure is prevented by moving a small slider on the back. When the hole is open, no recordings can be made.

Splicing sound tape
All sound tape, except DAT, can be mechanically edited and repaired with very little noticeable effect on the sounds being recorded or replayed. Clicks or other sounds of interference are hardly distinguishable.

When a tape is recorded, the message is passed on to a segment of tape which varies in dimensions according to the size of the recording head and more especially the speed of the tape. The faster the recording speed, the longer the space between the different elements of the message. For a tape to be edited, therefore, it is an advantage to have the original recording made at as fast a speed as possible. When splicing the tape, it is helpful to use a commercially produced block which will hold it in exactly the right position (see figure 9). Before starting, check the exact points that you wish to join together; mark the shiny rear surface with a chinagraph pencil to make sure they are not missed. Place the two ends to be joined on the block so that they overlap, the marked points being exactly on top of each other over the cutting groove with the shiny surface uppermost. With the tape fixed in this position, it is cut on a diagonal by passing a sharp blade through the groove. The two ends will now be accurately butted against each other. Adhesive splicing tape is then attached to the surfaces, and any overlapping edges are trimmed either by a slicing mechanism on the block or by a sharp blade.

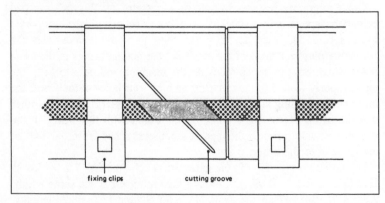

fixing clips   cutting groove

Figure 9. Tape on editing block

All widths of tape may be edited and spliced in this way, but it is easier to do this with the wider ¼ in. tape than with that in cassettes. Not only are the possible recording speeds faster with the wider tape, it is also easier to handle and manipulate than the thinner cassette material. Appropriately sized blocks are available for each width of tape.

Videotape
Almost all videotape is now made with chromium dioxide or metal as the major constituent of the magnetic coating. Before discussing the arrangement of the tape in its various carriers, a brief description of the recording mechanism may be helpful.

The tape is passed across the heads in the recorder at a certain speed. The heads are revolving at a high speed as well. The product of the two gives a 'head-to-tape' speed, the general rule being that the higher the rate, the better the recording. Tape writing speeds vary between 2cm/s and 3,800cm/s, depending on the quality of the recorder. With such high speeds between the head and the tape, the magnetic coating suffers considerable wear from friction, and it is rare that tape manufacturers recommend a longer life than about 1,000 passes. These are passes in which the heads are in contact with the tape, so they include both recording and playback but not rewind or fast forward when no picture is seen. When videorecording started, manufacturers designed machines to fit their own specifications, and such parameters as the 'head-to-tape' speed varied between them. Thus, although the tapes fitted different pieces of equipment, the pictures could be unstable even if they were playable. This incompatibility still exists in machines that use open reel tapes, but the cassette developments have been such that each format is now an internationally agreed standard.

Videotape does not have a different material forming a leader or trailer. That carrying the magnetic coating is continuous from beginning to end. Behind the decision to produce videotape in this way is the problem that the recording heads are very delicate and easily destroyed, so any changes in the physical surface may damage them. For this reason also, broken or damaged videotape should be destroyed rather than repaired. Adhesive tape may be used to mend a tape temporarily after it has passed the heads in order to complete a playback, but the material should then be discarded. Information is usually recorded by the helical scan process, and this makes it impossible to edit by cutting and joining the tape. Instead, editing is undertaken electronically; there is no potential for damaging the heads from this activity.

Like audiotape, there is no surface difference to indicate whether a recording is present, or whether it is in colour or monochrome, how long it runs for and for which television system it has been prepared. External labelling with such information is therefore very important. Unlike audiotape, videotape is recorded in only one direction as the information covers the whole surface.

Like all magnetic tape, videotape can also be used to record digital information for computer-related equipment. This is not commonly done, but it has been used as a major storage system on occasions. Videotape is normally available as either open reel or in cassettes as described below.

1   *Open reel*   The use of open reel tape is now restricted almost entirely to professional production units where high-quality masters are prepared. In some collections of old recordings, other forms of open reel tape may exist, for example ½in. EIAJ reels, but these are not dealt with here.

The highest quality tape remains 50mm (2in.), but its availability is restricted, even in professional studios, to some broadcast recordings only. Two tape speeds are usual, 39.7cm/s and 19.85cm/s. More widespread is 25mm (1in.) tape, which is used for most professional recording and also for many broadcast purposes.

Open reel tape is wound with the magnetic surface on the inside and the polyester base layer outwards. As there are no leaders or trailers and adhesive tape is not recommended, the tape end is fixed to the centre of the spool and to the other coils with plastic clips.

2   *Cassettes*   Within the container are both the delivery and take-up spools, so a cassette is a self-contained system which may be stopped at any time and withdrawn from the machine without rewinding. In contrast, cartridges contain only one spool and are fed into the machine. To remove them, the tape has to be rewound. Videotape used to be available in cartridges, but this is now a defunct system.

The present cassette is the result of a series of developments and conflicts between manufacturers, and other systems may be found in collections which are not mentioned here. With the decline of the Beta format, only three systems are now in active use: U-Matic, which is mainly confined to professional use; VHS, the common system; and 8mm video, which is used in a number of semi-professional cameras (sometimes described as camcorders).

U-Matic cassettes use 19.05mm tape at a tape speed of 9.5cm/s in containers, 221 × 140 × 32mm. They are available with varying lengths of tape providing recording times of 10, 15, 20, 30, 40, 50 and 60 minutes. Accidental erasure and recording is prevented by a removable plug on the underside of the container.

VHS cassettes use 12.65mm tape at a standard tape speed of 2.34cm/s in containers, 188 × 104 × 25mm. They are available with varying lengths of tape providing recording times of 30, 60, 90, 120, 180 and 240 minutes. Some machines offer a long-play facility in which the tape speed, 1.17cm/s, means that each of the tapes can last twice the time given. This speed should not be used for archiving as the quality of sound is not dependable. Accidental erasure and recording is prevented by breaking the plastic lug, similar to that in an audiocassette, at the rear of the cassette.

In cameras, a much smaller cassette, VHS-C, can be used to make the recording. For playback purposes, this can be inserted into a special container the size of the standard cassette and then used with a normal VHS player.

S-VHS is a new development to improve the quality of the recording and playback. The cassettes for S-VHS contain tape with an improved specification for the magnetic coating, and carry another notch which will identify them to the machine. These cassettes will not play on a conventional VHS machine, but a recording may be transferred to a standard cassette to play in the normal way. It is worth noting that these standard cassettes will play on the S-VHS players, but there will be no significant enhancement of quality.

Cassettes using the small 8mm tape are 9.2 × 6.2 × 1.4cm (3.6 × 2.4 × 0.6ins.). The tape is totally enclosed when not in use, the flaps at the front of the container parting to reveal it when placed in the equipment. Accidental erasure is prevented by closing the gap at the rear of the cassette, not opening it as in audiocassettes and VHS videotapes.

Playback of 8mm cassettes is generally either through a television set attached directly to the camera or through dubbing (i.e. transferring the picture and sound through a cable) to a conventional videorecorder. Separate 8mm recorder/players are available, but there are not many of them.

All cassettes should be stored in their own or specially purchased boxes. While the cassettes themselves provide some protection from dust and other hazards, and are a very convenient way of handling videotape, they should nevertheless be treated with care.

Discs

Magnetic discs are used with computers as the backing store for recording information or data and programs. The slower alternative is the cassette, almost wholly restricted to games for the less expensive microcomputers, and referred to under that heading above.

Mainframe computers use disc packs, but these will be stored within the computer service area and are not considered here. More common, and increasingly available at relatively inexpensive prices, are 'hard' discs or Winchesters. These are 7.5 to 20cm (3 to 8in.) discs, kept with the reading heads in sealed, dustfree containers. They are usually attached to or part of the computer itself, and under various conditions are able to store up to 300 megabytes of data. As these are not normally transported to and from the computer like books etc., but remain attached to it, they do not require cataloguing and storing systems. The delicacy of the mechanism needs to be noted, and they should be treated with care, making sure that the reading heads are 'parked' before they are moved.

This section concentrates on the 'mini' or 'floppy' discs which are filed separately and used with microcomputers. At present they are supplied in three sizes: 203mm (8in.), which now has a very restricted use; 132mm (5¼in.); and 90mm (3½in.). A few machines use a 76mm (3in.) disc, but these are of limited application. The main parts of the discs are shown in figure 10. Note that these are the protective covers, the disc itself being stored, untouched, within.

When a new blank disc is received, it first has to be formatted for the machine with which it is going to be used. This divides the disc artificially into concentric tracks, each track being sub-divided into sectors and each being assigned a separate code so that it can be quickly located by the computer. Some discs have hard sectors; that is, the divisions are permanently assigned and the formatting merely appoints the addresses. Most, however, are soft sectored so that the arrangement of these divisions can be altered. The program to format the discs is provided by the equipment manufacturer, either on a separate disc or built into the permanent memory of the computer. Any visual examination of the formatted disc will not reveal any obvious changes, so correct labelling is very important. Hard discs also need to be formatted. Because of the technology of coating them, these discs are never perfectly made, and at the end of the formatting process the computer will store a list of damaged sectors which will never be used for storing data. Used discs can also be reformatted, but this will remove any information stored on them.

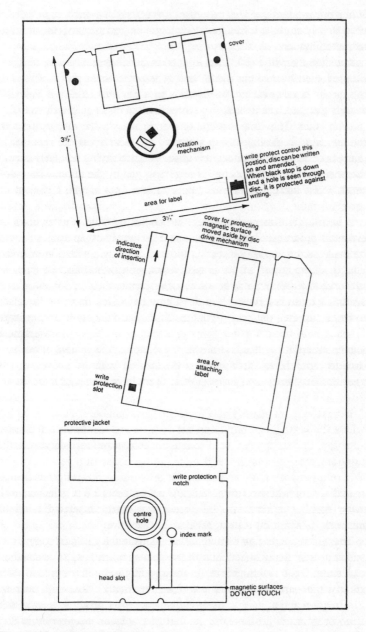

Figure 10. 'Mini' or 'floppy' disc

When information is stored on a disc, it is placed in a sector, the address of which is stored in the disc's catalogue and is instantly identifiable to the computer.

Accidental erasure or overwriting of an existing program or data can be prevented by making use of the write-protect slot on the disc. On the larger disc, covering the notch with a piece of adhesive paper − readily available commercially − prevents the disc being written on by the computer. The same is accomplished on the smaller disc by moving the tab to open the hole. Both activities are clearly easy to reverse. If data are to be saved on a disc, it is wise to do this saving regularly during the operation. Many users have been frustrated by the disappearance of much work through a power supply failure or a simple technical or program fault.

It is important to maintain back-up copies of data. Master discs of essential programs should not be used; instead back-up copies should be made as the working discs. At the end of a day's collation of saved data, back-up copies of the stored information should also be made to preserve it. From mainframe discs, either further discs or copies on tape are made and preserved. Hard discs may be copied on to floppy discs to make sure that the data are not lost if the hard disc fails or a mistake is made with the computer. This is a tedious process. More efficient is tape streaming − that is, transferring a copy of the content of the hard disc to tape. Many professionals do this on what is known as the grandfather, father, son system. Wise users have copies of their floppy discs as well.

Increasingly, in places where there are large numbers of users working with a similar range of programs, networks are in use. In the stand-alone situation, the user places the disc in the machine and loads and runs the program, storing appropriate data on the same disc or a personal copy. Where a network is in operation, the user draws the program from a hard disc somewhere on the system and out of the user's personal control. After running it, data may be stored back on the master disc of the network or again on a personal disc to take away.

There is an increasing number of variations in the world of computing, and at present many incompatibilities between machines, discs and their operation. Good labelling is therefore very important in order to identify clearly the parameters within which a particular disc will operate. Information about the disc itself includes whether or not it is formatted if no program is present, the number of tracks or the maximum data size (in kilobytes), and whether it is single or double sided. If data are stored on it, then the label should state the disc operating system used with its version number, and probably also useful is the model number of the computer used to record it. Should a program be present, its version number should be noted in addition to its title. Only with such information available is there any certainty that an intelligent user could determine whether the disc could be used with his or her equipment.

Discs should be kept in their protective jackets and also in paper or static-free plastic sleeves to protect them from dust and grease. Like all discs, they are stored most conveniently and safely in an upright position and should not be subjected to undue pressure or extreme conditions. They do wear out from use, and even if only a part is worn, it is better to replace a disc as the worn area may affect the delicate mechanisms of the disc machinery.

As must be clear from the above, discs require machines which may have mechanical problems. Alternatives have been suggested, like cards the size of credit cards and suitably coated, as future storage systems in machines without moving parts. This is not the 'smart card', already available, which has a small microprocessor or EPROM built into it as the storage system; but it is probably more versatile and easier to handle than the cartridge with a ROM (Read Only Memory) inside, which is inserted into the computer when the program it carries is required.

Another form of disc, about 5cm (2in.) in diameter, has been developed as a recording medium for still photographs shot with special cameras. About 50 pictures per disc can be photographed, playback being through a television set.

Plastic materials
These are divided into three sections.

Transparent plastic
This material is for use with the overhead projector and is available in various thicknesses, commonly ranging from 0.05mm to 0.25mm, either as single flat sheets or as rolls. The rolls are 25.4cm (10in.) wide and of varying lengths. Attached by self-adhesive tape to a central core of cardboard, to the ends of which are attached light metal hubs with key slots to align with the winding arms of the projector, the material can be used repeatedly. However, there is a tendency for the edges of the roll to tear or crack.

Flat sheets are usually supplied in three sizes, 26.7 × 26.7cm (10½ × 10½in.), 26.7 × 20.3cm (10½ × 8in.) and 29.7 × 21cm (11¾

× 8¼. or A4). Different manufacturers supply slight variations on these figures. While some are stored loose in folders, others may be attached to a frame, the common external measurements being 30 × 30cm (11.8 × 11.8in.). If sheets are kept against each other, paper should be inserted between them to reduce the natural adhesion between plastic. Because they have a natural tendency to bend and warp, it is wise to store them sufficiently compressed to maintain some rigidity.

Vinyl discs
Discs are marketed in 17.8cm (7in.), 25.4 cm (10in.) and 30.5cm (12in.) diameter sizes, the central hole for the spindle being about 7.5mm in diameter. This spindle need not be a tight fit, acting as it does as a centring device and not as an aid to the disc's rotation. The rotation is done by the turntable itself.

Recordings on discs are made at 33⅓ and 45 revolutions per minute. The 78-revolution discs are now obsolete, although they may be found in some collections. Recordings at 45 rpm are restricted almost completely to 'singles' of popular music. The length of time that the recording lasts is determined by the length of the groove, but it is unusual for a 12in. disc to carry a recording which lasts in excess of 25 minutes per side.

Although the plastic from which the disc is pressed is fairly strong, the groove itself can be quite easily damaged. It is inadvisable to place one disc directly on another, for this sort of stack playing will increase wear. Because the pick-up stylus physically vibrates along the groove as the disc is played, the plastic material becomes gradually worn away. However, no rule can be laid down for the life of a disc; it depends on the weight of this contact between stylus and groove, and this varies between record players.

To play accurately, discs should be as level as possible on the turntable. Bending and warping from exposure to heat and damp are common, or are the result of distorting pressure. Discs should be stored vertically, not leaning in either direction. The disc's wrapping is also important as it is needed to exclude dust. The disc should be placed in the paper sleeve, the opening of which should be against a sealed edge of the cardboard sleeve.

Optical storage systems
These storage systems are becoming increasingly imporant mechanisms for the future. Improvements in the control of laser technology enable

pits of ever-decreasing size to be accurately located and 'read', and thus an ever-increasing amount of information can be stored within the various devices without requiring more space to be used. In addition, the materials have proved very resistant to damage under normal conditions. Wear and tear appears to be an insignificant factor; it seems that a considerable quantity of information can be held in these optical formats with very accurate reproduction on virtually indestructible material.

As this has become more apparent, so the number of formats has increased, and this is likely to be only the beginning. In order to understand the complexities of the different recordings, it is necessary to be clear about the difference between analogue and digital signals. An analogue is a close and continuous representation of a variable characteristic, for example the wavy line of a sound signal with its frequency and amplitude. When copied, the accuracy of the representation is often reduced − that is, the waves tend to be flattened and some bumps are lost entirely. In contrast, a digital recording is a very frequent sampling of the signal, indicating at each sample point whether the wave is present and what its amplitude is. When this is copied, any tendency to reduce the size or interfere with its accuracy has no effect, for if any of the signal is present, it is reproduced as present in its entirety. If it is absent, then nothing is recorded. Consequently, copies of digital recordings are always exactly the same as the original, however many generations of copying they may go through.

If the user requires the most accurate reproduction of an original, it is clear that a digital recording with a very high sampling frequency is the most effective; but the drawback is that it occupies very much more space than an analogue version. Also, to replay the record in real time the data have to be retrieved and processed at much higher speed as there is so much more of them. With optical storage systems, such a density of recording is available for sound, and the improvements in the processing power of the computer-based systems that operate them make it possible to use the data gained to provide an accurate reproduction. At present, there is continuous development to create similar stores for digital versions of pictorial information, but as each dot on the screen needs several pieces of information to describe it, the storage of even one television picture demands a very large amount of space.

The other major strand of development is to make it possible for ussers to create their own recordings in these systems, firstly as a 'once only' process, then as a recording that can be erased and replaced by a new one. Much has already been achieved, and it is likely that a certain measure of success will occur. This is commercially important in order that CD audio can combat the competition from digital audio tape (DAT), for the problems outlined do not exist with the magnetic surface.

Various configurations of optical storage systems are available.

1 *Laservision* These have been produced in two forms: those carrying a continuous moving picture of an hour's duration each side and no still picture facility; and those capable of carrying a continuous moving picture of 36 minutes' duration each side, but in which each individual frame is identifiable and capable of still picture control. Two audio channels are available on each: in the first providing stereo sound; in the second offering selectable options such as two different languages, or sound effects on one with voice on the other. The discs are usually coloured silver, 30cm (12in.) in diameter and 3.4mm thick and have a centre hole of 35mm diameter. The player automatically recognizes the difference between the two types of disc. On each side of the second variety, there is the capacity for 54,000 individual frames or pictures, so the potential for storage is very large. In addition, a teletext analogue is also possible, providing the option for further information.

An extension of the laservision principle is known as AIV (Advanced Interactive Video), the best-known discs using this being the Domesday discs from the BBC. In this system, extra digital computer data − for example, the statistics and charts − are stored on the disc for recall as required in the viewing. Playing these discs on the conventional laservision players means that these extra data are not available. Non-AIV laservision discs will play normally on AIV equipment.

With the exception of these data on AIV discs, both the visual and sound information on laservision discs are recorded in analogue form.

2 *CD audio* These are now very popular formats for distributing recordings of music. The discs are coloured silver, 12cm (5in.) in diameter and 1.2mm thick and have a central hole of 15mm diameter. Maximum playing time for one disc is approximately one hour. A smaller version, 8cm (3in.) in diameter, is now gaining popularity for popular music. The recording is on one side only, the label usually being on the other, and is digital.

3 *CD-ROM* ROM translates as Read Only Memory. Similar in size and appearance to CD audio, this disc is used to store information for retrieval through a computer, and thus is entirely digital. On one disc, there is capacity for about 600 megabytes of information, equivalent to about 250,000 pages of text. However, the data need not be text only.

Graphics and sound may also be recorded. Just like all the CD series of formats listed here, the recording is made by the producer and is unalterable by the user. However, there is much research going on in developing versions of these discs on which users can etch their own recordings, and the first versions of these are becoming available. One type is called a WORM, translated as Write Once, Read Many times, and this describes the principle behind such discs; that is, that the user's etching is a once-and-for-all inscription of data. Rewritten discs are also available.

4 *CD V* The V stands for Video. These discs are being prepared in a number of sizes, are coloured gold to differentiate them from the other CD discs and will carry audio in a digital recording, video in analogue. The sizes are: 12cm (5in.), carrying up to 6 minutes of video with sound and a further 20 minutes of audio, all recorded like CD audio on one side only; 20cm (8in.), carrying up to 20 minutes of audio and video on each of the two sides; 30cm (12in.), carrying up to 60 minutes of audio and video on each of the two sides.

5 *CD I* The I stands for Interactive. These are not yet available, but the agreed format will produce 12cm (5in.) discs similar in appearance to CD audio. They will carry mixtures of text, graphics, audio and still and moving pictures. The capacity is about 200,000 pages of text, 7,800 still pictures, an hour of stereo sound or nearly 20 hours of speech (which is always recorded at a lower level than music and therefore occupies much less space). The recordings will be entirely digital. A potential rival format is described as CD G, the G translating as Graphics. At the time of writing, neither of these formats is available.

6 *DVI* This translates as Digital Video Interactive. It is not yet available, but the research is at a stage when production is expected soon. The discs will be similar to the CD ones, and the recording will be made in the same way on the plastic material. As the title suggests, the pictures will be the first to be recorded digitally for a lengthy moving picture sequence, the proposed limit being 72 minutes on a 12cm (5in.) disc. Technically, the recording will be a very compressed form of the video pictures, reducing the number of bits of data needed for each picture to as low a level as possible.

Quality of reproduction

A range of storage formats has been described above, playback of pictures from most of them being through a television set. One measure of the quality of reproduction from such stores is the horizontal resolution of pictures. This is the number of vertical lines that can be reproduced from the format on the screen; the more there are, the better the quality of the picture in revealing detail. The following are the figures claimed for a selection of these formats.

Broadcast television	300–330
VHS/8mm video	230–250
Still picture camera	300–400
S-VHS	400–425
CDV/Laservision	425–450

EQUIPMENT: PRINCIPLES OF OPERATION

In this section, the various pieces of equipment required to view and listen to the different formats of material described in the previous pages will be explained in terms of the principles by which they operate. No attempt has been made to apply these features to a particular model. Rather, the section has been written in very general terms, and includes as many of the features that are likely to be present as possible. Important electronic parameters are also included, together with a simplified explanation of some of the figures given in commercial descriptions of equipment. The divisions follow those of the previous sections, dealing with paper, film, magnetic and plastic materials in turn. Lastly, there is a discussion of the issues involved in all aspects of maintenance.

Paper
Paper materials do not normally require equipment in order to be used. Magnifying glasses may occasionally be needed to view small print, but this is not often necessary. For charts and pictures, suspending devices may be used. It is preferable that these do not damage the material; if hooks or pins are used they should go through prepared and protected holes. Clips are available in a number of forms, from pegs to bulldogs. One successful form uses a plastic roller to trap the paper and hold it firmly.

Film
As film is transparent, it can be viewed only by means of light passing through it into the eyes. This light may be direct or may pass through a magnifying system, or may go through the system and then be projected on to a screen. Viewing directly — for example, by holding a piece of film up to the light — requires no further explanation (figure 11(a)). It is, however, worth noting that some light distorts the colour quality of the picture being viewed, fluorescent tubes being particularly liable to do this.

Direct viewing through a magnifying lens is a simple system, usually suitable for only a single user at a time (figure 11(b)). Some arrangements require the introduction of a translucent screen between the magnifying lens and the user. Such an arrangement is called rear projection as the image is thrown on the back and seen by looking at the front

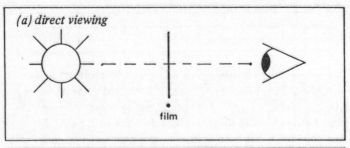

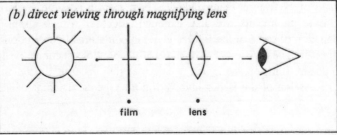

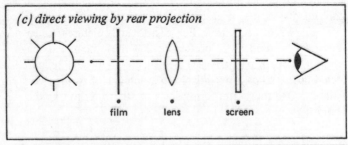

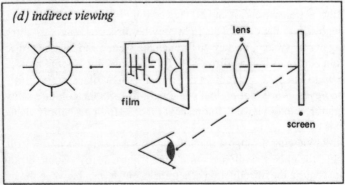

Figure 11. Various methods of viewing film

(figure 11(c)). With these systems, if the screen is made fairly large it is possible for several people to view simultaneously, but in practice the results are not very effective.

Indirect viewing via reflections from a screen is a more complex system, and is the one adopted for mass viewing. Because it is more restful to the eyes, it is also adopted in place of a rear projection system for individual viewing where long periods of study are involved (figure 11(d)). Unlike the other methods of viewing, this system has to have the film inserted laterally and vertically inverted before magnification rather than placed initially in the 'correct' alignment. In those rear projection systems in which light from the projector is reflected off a mirror before reaching the screen, similar inversions have to take place.

In essence, all film viewing and projecting systems operate in the same way. The film is placed between a lamp and a lens, the latter magnifying the image. If the eyes of the user are close to the lens − that is, within the focal length − the image is viewed as through a magnifying glass. If the eyes of the user are farther away than the focal length, the image is inverted vertically and laterally by the lens and can only be viewed clearly by casting the image on to a screen.

The size of the image seen is determined by the power of the lens (expressed as the focal length) and the distance between the film and the lens. Adjusting this distance fixes the place at which the image is focused. That is why focusing is controlled almost invariably by moving the lens in and out within its carrier.

The image cast on a screen by a lens increases in size the farther the screen is moved away from it. When the image overlaps the screen edges, a lens with a longer focal length is introduced instead. Thus, as a rule of thumb, the longer the distance between the lens and the screen (the 'throw'), the longer the focal length of the lens required. The appropriate lens can be selected by using the charts (figure 12), provided the distance of the 'throw' and the size of the screen available are known.

While the lens in a simple magnifying situation (figure 11(b)) is usually constructed in a single piece, those in projecting arrangements are normally made of a number of separate parts carefully sealed at set distances apart in the lens holder. This is referred to as a complex lens, and is used to eliminate distortion of the light as it passes through the glass. As there is no opportunity for dust or condensation to collect between these pieces under normal conditions, there is no reason why they should be separated, and it is most inadvisable to attempt to do so.

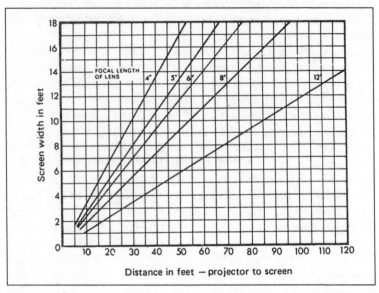

Figure 12(a). Lens selection: filmstrips and slides — single frame 24 × 18mm

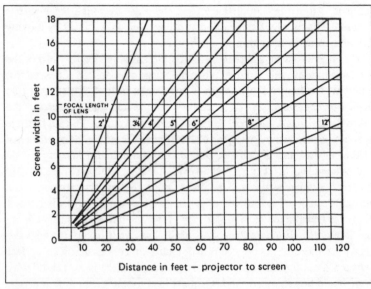

Figure 12(b). Lens selection: 2 × 2in. slides — horizontal 36 × 24mm

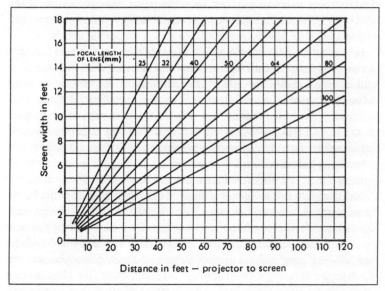

Figure 12(c). Lens selection: 16mm projector — millimetre range of lenses

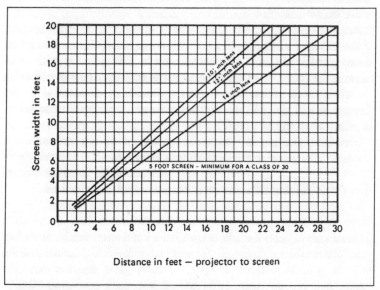

Figure 12(d). Lens selection: overhead projectors

The complex lens in its holder may, of course, be removed from the lens carrier to exchange it for another, for security reasons, or for simple maintenance.

Between the film and the lamp in many projectors may be found another series of lenses referred to as condensers. The purpose of these is to collect and marshal the light so that as much of it as possible passes through the whole area of the film. This is further supplemented by a concave mirror either behind the lamp or, occasionally, as an integral part of it. The separate mirror and the condensing lenses may be removed for cleaning, provided great care is taken in noting exactly where and which way round each piece is placed.

Lamps in projectors get very hot, and unless some method of reducing the temperature is available, the film and even the wiring may get burnt. In very small projectors or those in which the lamp is of low power, the case will have a number of air vents through which cold air can pass by convection currents around the lamp to cool it. These vents must be kept clear of obstruction. In larger machines, fans are incorporated into the equipment to drive the air around the lamp. Such fans must operate continuously while the lamp is illuminated, and care must be taken to ensure that the holes through which the air passes in and out are kept open and clear. Any blockage may result in overheating electrical parts and scorching the film.

Another result of the heat generated by the lamp is that the film may visually 'pop' — that is, go out of focus suddenly. This is caused by the centre of the film frame expanding with the heat and bulging forwards towards the lens. When this happens, it is no longer possible to focus the whole frame of the picture, and a weakness is created in that frame of the film so that it is likely to go out of focus on subsequent occasions, even at lower temperatures.

The foregoing points refer to all pieces of equipment used with transparent film, no matter what format that film is in. The principles behind the equipment used with each format will be considered next; first that involving still pictures, then that involving cinefilm.

Viewers

These are usually used for filmstrips, slides and microforms. Some are just light boxes, a strip light or several individual bulbs illuminating the material which rests on top of diffusion glass above them. No magnification is provided, but a general inspection is possible. Others are based on the system illustrated in figure 11(b). Frames of cinefilm can be wound through a few varieties, but as projection speed cannot be maintained, only casual inspection is possible.

The distance between the lens and the film is fixed; any increase in magnification can be obtained only by the user moving his or her head back from the lens. Some simple viewers make use of daylight or room lights as sources of illumination, and these work very successfully, particularly for casual inspection. For longer study, viewers with bulbs are preferable, powered either from the mains supply or by batteries. Because the light passes fairly directly into the eye, this is not a comfortable means of undertaking long-term study. It is also noteworthy that the edges of the picture are less clearly illuminated than the centre.

Viewers are usually made for one format of film only. Some models are available for both types of filmstrip or for two or three sizes of slide. With delivery and collecting chambers attached to the side, some slide viewers provide the user with the facility of running through a stack fairly rapidly. A lever is pulled and pushed, the movement ejecting one slide into the collecting chamber and delivering another into the viewing position.

Filmstrip projectors

These are very simple projectors, their particular feature being the method of holding the filmstrip. There are specialized machines which use a cartridge from which the strip is wound, and others with chambers inside the body of the projector into which it is coiled, but the majority work on the simple mechanism of winding the strip from one holding spool to another through a fixed position between the lamp and the adjustable lens. It is important to keep the frames rigidly in the correct position, for any movement causes the picture to blur out of focus. In one system, this is prevented by clamping the film between two pieces of glass, a method which also eliminates any possibility of 'popping'. However, it does introduce the danger of scratching if the strip is pulled sharply through its glass 'sandwich'.

The filmstrip is attached to the spools by either clips or adhesive tape, and by turning the spool, usually by hand, the film is wound from one to the other, each frame passing into the projecting position in turn. Variations on this introduce a further spool and make use of the sprocket holes on the edge of the strip to determine an exact movement from one picture to the next.

Not all projectors accept both formats of filmstrip. The key to deciding whether a particular machine does is to examine the size of the hole in the filmstrip carrier. If this is big enough for a double- or full-frame filmstrip, it is likely that the manufacturer also provides a masking mechanism which will cut down the size of the hole so that it is suitable for the other format as well.

Slide projectors
The complexity of slide projectors depends on the degree of automation. Hand-operated projectors are usually based on a simple rotation or lateral movement of slides behind the lens, usually replacing each one in the carrier alternately. Controls are limited to mains power, lamp brightness and focusing.

Semi-automatic projectors provide a system for reducing the problems of changing slides. Instead of feeding them in singly, they are carried in a magazine. A hand-operated lever is used to pull out a slide from the projecting position into the magazine, move it one place and push in the next slide. Normally they operate only in a forward direction, the magazine having to be pushed backwards by hand to allow a previous slide to be reshown. The commonest magazine is a straight one carrying up to 50 slides. Care should be taken in selecting them, for not all are interchangeable between projectors. Circular magazines, taking up to 100 slides, are also available for certain machines.

In automatic slide projectors, the changing of the slides is done mechanically. The changing mechanism can be similar to that on a semi-automatic projector, a lever carrying the slides in and out mechanically from a magazine held at the side of the machine or through a partial gravity feed mechanism. In this latter method a circular magazine is used, lying flat on top of the projector, with a hole in the underside immediately above the slot in which the slide fits to be in the projecting position. The slide drops into this position by gravity and is held there by light springs. When the signal is given to change the slide, an arm under it lifts it back into the magazine, which is then moved on to a new position by a lever. The arm then drops back into its bottom position and a new slide falls into place. During the movement which changes the slide in automatic and most semi-automatic systems, a shutter passes between the lamp and the lens to prevent light shining on the screen and showing the transfer action. In some machines there is a small hole in the shutter so that the black-out is only partial and therefore the contrast for the viewer is not so great.

The changing mechanism of an automatic projector may be operated in both forward and reverse directions, depending on the signal given.

Commonly the two signals are given by separate buttons, but in a few machines the difference between forward and reverse is governed by the length of time for which the signal is given. Automatic projectors have control buttons on the projector and a socket for a plug (usually of the DIN variety, see figure 13) which provides access for signals to be given remotely. The sources and effects of these may be:

(a) Slide change by a remote control attached by a cable, carrying forward and reverse buttons, and usually a control for moving the lens for fine adjustment of the focus.
(b) Repetitive changes at set intervals, a simple adjustable automatic timing device which gives slide change signals at predetermined intervals.
(c) Changes caused by signals from an audiotape player.
(d) Zeroing; that is, the projector automatically changing back to the beginning of the slide sequence after the last one has been shown.

All the signals are conveyed electrically to the socket, and therefore the device providing the signals must be attached to the projector.

Much use is now made of the multislide projector show in which two or more machines are used. While one slide is changing, another machine provides the picture, or several can be superimposed from different machines at the same time. Changes between slides may be rapid or may fade gently at a chosen speed. Controls for this are through computer-

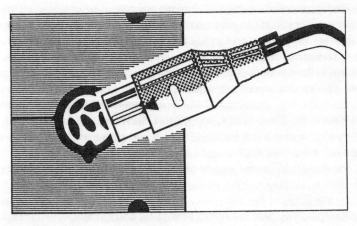

Figure 13. DIN plug and socket

based devices, and affect the brightness of the lamp as well as the slide changing mechanisms. Most of the systems operate on different signal arrangements and are therefore not interchangeable, so a programme made with one system must be replayed using that same type.

Microform readers

Although the film may come in rolls, in a cassette or cartridge or as a flat piece, the methods of enlarging or projecting it are essentially similar. The film is placed very close to the lens to ensure that the maximum light passes through the frame for magnification. Because the information is so small, the quality of the lens must also be good in order to achieve even magnification over the whole area of the image. The closeness of the film to the lens and the considerable magnification required also means that slight movements of the film cause abrupt changes of focus. It is therefore important that the film is kept rigidly in position, which may be done through a holding mechanism, as with microfiche. Paper copies of individual frames of microforms can be obtained by using specially modified equipment called reader-printers. The copy is an enlargement of the parts selected by the user. Such equipment is available for both roll microfilm and microfiche.

Although there are viewers for microforms, they are not very comfortable for extensive reading. The common arrangements of readers are front and rear projection. The latter is often considered less satisfactory because the optical and screen qualities tend to mean that the screen is unevenly illuminated, and the excessive brightness in the central area can cause discomfort to the eyes. With front projection, the light is bounced off a screen and this helps to reduce the bright spots. The front projection screen may be an integral part of the reader, but in a number of them it is separate and may even be a piece of paper placed in the appropriate position by the user. In this latter arrangement, because the lens to screen distance is variable, the user can increase the magnification by extending it without changing the lens. However, it should be noted that as the magnification increases, so does the size of the image, and therefore a larger screen is required to show the whole picture. Focus adjustment will also be necessary.

Various lines may be present on the screens. Some are introduced to provide a working outline around the edge of the image for particular magnifications. Where the reader is integrated with a printer, lines may be introduced to show the outline of the area which will be printed. Many screens are made for COMfiche with a fixed or mobile horizontal line, a cursor which assists the user in sorting through columns of figures.

While all front projection screens are white or slightly silvered, those used for rear projection are often tinted to reduce the problems of glare and visual discomfort. Blue, grey and green surfaces are available, and can be an assistance for reading passages of writing. However, users should be aware that coloured film will not be viewed in its original colours when these screens are involved.

Readers with both types of screen arrangement can frequently be altered for projection on to a room screen for mass viewing. While the equipment is usually designed for individual use, a simple adjustment can often be made to remove the screen or tilt a reflecting mirror or swivel the lamp-film-lens assembly so that the light can be made to fall on a big screen.

Microform readers are very simple projectors with few controls. Lamp brightness is usually fixed and remote control is not necessary. A control to alter the orientation of the image is present in some of the more expensive equipment. Operating by means of turning a prism placed between the lens and the reflecting mirror, this provides a method for turning the image 90° (sometimes 360° is available for roll film) in either direction; a portrait-shaped original can thereby be turned so that it can be viewed as a landscape image.

Most readers have the facility for changing lenses to give a variety of possible magnifications. Different methods have been adopted to do this. Some machines have to have the lens in position unlocked and then unscrewed before a different one can be inserted. Others incorporate a nosepiece to which the lenses are fixed, while others have them attached to a bar which is slid from one position to another. Selecting the most suitable lenses depends on the reduction ratios of the original material to be viewed. For 35mm film, it is likely that $10 \times$ and $20 \times$ are suitable. Microfiche and 16mm film will usually be viewed satisfactorily with $24 \times$ and $48 \times$ lenses, the latter being designed for COMfiche as well. Because of their threading and physical dimensions, lenses are usually not interchangeable between models of machines.

Focusing the image means moving the lens, usually by fractional amounts. Most frequently this is done by rotating the lens in its carrier by hand. However, this may also be accomplished by a remote mechanical connection to a control on the outside of the machine.

Readers for roll film
Cassettes and cartridges are made to fit particular machines, depending on the manufacturer of the container. When fitted to the reader, the film

is either placed directly in the appropriate position between the lamp and lens or it is automatically threaded into the correct place.

Open reel film is attached and usually threaded by hand through the 'gate' between lamp and lens, the pathway marked on the reader. Winding the film from one reel to another can be done manually by turning the handles attached to the reel carriers. Because very long lengths of film, holding perhaps 2,000 or more images, can be fitted on roll film readers, some machines have a motorized form of film transport. The speed of this differs between machines, and a manual override is essential finally to centre the image to be viewed. Incorporated also in many readers is a facility which enables the user to move the reflecting mirror up or down so that various parts of the image can be centred in the vertical plane.

With such a large number of images on a single roll of film, it is essential that the relevant ones can be located quickly and smoothly. There is no standard or universal system. Code line indexes on the film between the images are sometimes used, but more commonly a footage counter or odometer is used with motorized movement machines. Provided this is started from the beginning and the counter counts the same thing – in this case length in feet – the system is effective. Photomechanical methods which count blips or white spots on the edge of the film are also available.

Aperture cards
These can usually be read with equipment designed for microfiche, provided the carrier tray for the fiche is wide enough to accept the card. Some machines are made specifically for use with these cards, having a slot into which they are inserted. The readers have few controls, although a minimum of two lenses is essential.

Microfiche
Except in the case of the smallest readers, the fiche is always inserted into the machine inside a carrier. This may be transparent plastic or glass. It keeps the fiche in the correct position and protects it from damage as it is moved around. Usually the carrier opens automatically like an oyster shell as it is pulled towards the user, and the fiche is inserted into place. As the carrier is pushed back under the lens, it closes. In some readers, the carrier is opened manually, but before the user does so, the carrier must be withdrawn from under the lens.

Locating the correct frame is done on an assumed grid system. On some microfiche, the identity of each frame based on this grid is marked, but frequently it is not. The system assumes that every horizontal row has a letter, A being that immediately under the title strip; and every vertical column has a number, 1 being the one on the extreme left of the fiche. Thus each frame can be addressed by a letter and a number (figure 14).

Because there are some variations in the grids, position finding can be confusing. The common arrangements are: 18-frame microfiche using 35mm frames − rows A to C, columns 1 to 6; 60-frame fiche − rows A to E, columns 1 to 12 (this includes jackets although the vertical separation is slightly larger); 98-frame fiche − rows A to G, columns 1 to 14; and 270-frame fiche − rows A to P (omitting I), columns 1 to 18.

To locate the positions, one of three different methods is commonly adopted. Before describing them, however, it should be pointed out that each fiche grid requires the use of different scales. The machine scans the same distance from top to bottom whether the rows are from A to C or A to G, and therefore the scales have to be changed appropriately. The systems are as follows:

1   Two independent markers move along the letters and the numbers. Thus to find B3, the letter marker is aligned with B, the number marker with 3. Usually this system requires the use of two independent controls operating horizontal movements (for numbers) and vertical movements (for letters) of the fiche carrier.

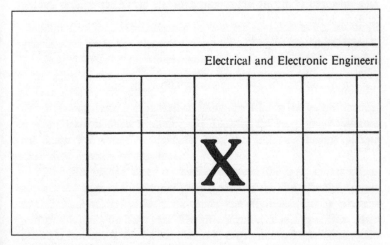

Figure 14. Microfiche 'X' in frame B3

2   The carrier is moved until the selected letter and number are adjacent to or superimposed on each other.

3   A pointer attached to the carrier is pulled over a map of the grid which is attached to the reader. When it is placed over the selected square, the frame is ready to be viewed. Some machines provide facilities for interchange of maps for different grids.

With the growing popularity of fiche, large numbers are used to store information, and finding the appropriate one can be difficult. Computer-controlled sorting systems are available which help to mechanize this process.

Cine projectors

The concept of movement produced by cinefilms is the result of a sensory phenomenon known as 'persistence of vision'. When an individual picture is seen, the details are registered in the brain and retained there for a short period of time. When another picture appears, that too is registered. Provided the frequency of the different pictures is above a certain level, they appear to represent a continuum, even though they are in fact rapidly changing. If there are slight differences between succeeding pictures, it appears that movement has taken place.

Cinefilm is a series of still pictures, separated from each other by a thin black band, and the projector shows each one in turn. The black bands between each picture should not be seen. To achieve this, the mechanism of a cine projector pulls a picture between the lamp and lens, projects it for a short time (for a twenty-fourth of a second in the case of sound films), covers the lamp for a moment while it pulls the black line past and places the next picture in position, and then uncovers the lamp. Thus the movement of the film between lamp and lens is in practice a series of rapid jerks and stops. In contrast, the film carries the sound track as a smooth continuous recording; if it were replayed as a series of jerks, the ear would detect some distracting noises. Therefore, the projector must be moving the film smoothly past the place where the sound is replayed.

Cine projectors are therefore designed to accommodate these two different types of movement on the same piece of film. Those which only project silent films operate on the 'jerk and stop' principle.

The pathway of the film through a projector is outlined in figure 15 and the points that follow refer to the parts labelled in that figure. In spite of outward differences between projectors, the principles are identical.

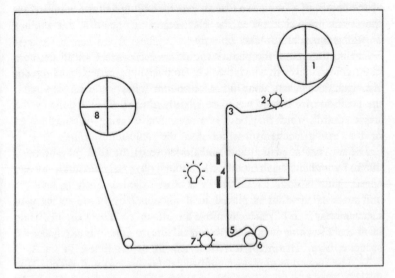

Figure 15. Stylized lacing diagram for 16mm projector (see text for interpretation of numbers)

Many machines incorporate an extra sprocket drive wheel between the lower loop and the sound drum or pick-up head, and also some free-running pulleys to change the direction of the film to the take-up reel.

1   The film should be attached so that the sprocket holes are on the right as seen from the projector lamp side. This is the starting reel.

2   Both sprocket drive wheels move at a continuous speed. The spikes on the edge of the wheels engage the sprocket holes, this one pulling the film into the projector.

3   The loop here is essential to allow the film to be jerked through the gate below without breaking. By keeping the loop, the continuous feed from the wheel is changed into the jerk movement without mechanical tension on the film.

4   The film passes along a channel between the lamp and the lens. Ridges at the edge of the channel keep the line of the film exactly straight, and a spring-loaded pressure plate on the rear of the lens carrier prevents the film from moving forwards. The film is pulled down by a claw which protrudes through a slot in the channel, engages a sprocket hole, pulls the film down and then releases it. Each pull down is the same distance

as the height of a frame, so that an intermittent movement is caused by the slight interval between the claw releasing the film and another engaging the next sprocket hole up.

During the pause, the picture should be exactly in front of the hole in the channel through which the light from the lamp passes to the screen. If a black line appears at the top or the bottom of the picture on the screen, the position of this hole has to be slightly altered. This is done by the frame control, which may be a lever raising or lowering the hole position or a screwing mechanism which does the same thing.

The movement of the claw and therefore of the film may be done manually with the drive motor off, although obviously not at the correct speed. This is done by turning a control called an inching knob or animator. If the film is placed in the channel by hand, rather than mechanically, it is advisable to move the film up and down slightly while turning the inching knob until the claw is heard and seen to engage the sprocket hole. This helps to reduce tearing of the film as it starts.

5   The second loop plays a similar part to that of the first (no. 3) in reverse. The film leaves the channel with an intermittent motion, jerks and stops, and is pulled on the next part of its journey in smooth motion by the second drive wheel (no. 7). In the absence of a loop, mechanical tension will break the film. In some projectors, there is an automatic loop former which senses the tension when the loop disappears and jerks sufficient film out of the channel to remake it.

6   To replay sound, one of two methods is employed, depending on the method of recording. Magnetic recordings are 'read' by a head similar to that in audiotape recorders. Optical recordings are 'read' by light from a lamp passing through the transparent pattern on the sound track, the dimensions of the light being translated by a photoelectric cell into the noises recorded. For both to operate, it is essential that the film is kept very tightly against the head or drum or else the quality of the sound will be defective.

7   The second drive wheel pulls the film continuously past the sound area at the set speed.

8   The take-up reel is driven by a belt at the same speed as the drive wheel and wraps up the film constantly. This contrasts with the starting reel, which runs freely.

Rewinding   Almost all projectors will rewind the film. Reverse wind through the projection path is slow, 24 frames per second on sound projectors. As the lamp can be turned on during this process, the amusing sight of backwards motion can be observed. All the sprocket drive wheels, including the claws, reverse their direction, the take-up reel freewheels and the starting reel is driven to wind up the film. When the rewind system is activated with the film outside the projection path, a gear has to be engaged if a high speed is required. After rewinding is completed, the gear must be disengaged.

Damaging the film   Poor projection is frequently the cause of film damage. The common points where this occurs are the following:

(a) Sprocket drive wheels damage sprocket holes or cut across through faulty lacing and attachment.
(b) The claws can cut the edges of the sprocket holes or cut across the film if it is not correctly placed in the channel.
(c) The loss of the loops causes mechanical tension, which will tear the film.
(d) The failure to disengage the rewind gear will in some machines allow forward and reverse to operate simultaneously, which will break the film.

Every instance of slight damage to a film will be a site of weakness in future projections.

Automatic loading   A considerable number of projectors incorporate a facility for automatic loading. The leading edge of the film has to be trimmed, usually by a clip which is provided. When the film is inserted on to the sprocket wheel drive, with the motor on, it is automatically threaded, two curved levers forming the loops. If the film breaks or has to be removed during its projection, it is sometimes awkward to withdraw it.

Still picture   Some projectors are supplied with a control which stops the film instantly. Unfortunately this action does not always coincide with the film being in the right position and the picture may not be seen because the shutter is covering the lamp. Turning the inching knob will clear this. A heat filter is automatically introduced to prevent the frame burning, and this may mean that some refocusing is necessary.

Amplifier   The sound from the projector increases in volume to audible levels by means of an amplifier, which is usually an integral part of the equipment. This is then connected to a loudspeaker which may also be within the projector or linked to it through a cable. Controls usually include an on/off switch and base and treble variables.

Lamps for all projectors
The power supply to projectors must be that for which the equipment

has been designed; if not, adjustment has to be made. The lamp must be that listed in the operating manual. Some projectors have adaptations to increase the life of the lamp by operating at a lower voltage, which means that the equipment includes a transformer. If too high a voltage is passed through such a lamp it will break. Another possible adaptation is a control which allows the lamp to be used at two different levels of brightness. If the lower brightness is acceptable, it should be used.

Changing the lamp is usually simple if the instructions are followed. Modern lamps should not be held by uncovered fingers as the grease from them causes a weakness in the glass cover.

Projection screens

The surface covering of the screen dictates the clarity of any pictures viewed. The brightness of the image is chiefly the result of the power of the lamp, but various factors concerned with the screen also have an effect. Principally these are the reflectivity of the surface, the amount of light which does not come from the projector that falls on it (called ambient light), and its position with relation to the viewers.

A matt white screen is a good reflector of light over a wide area. Other types − lenticular, beaded and high gain − have better reflective qualities, but these are appreciated only by viewers seated close to the centre line. Therefore, like rear projection screens, they are more suitable for small groups of viewers.

The reduction of ambient light is important. Where possible, it is advisable to use hoods or covers to mask the screen if no other means of reducing it is available. Screens are like mirrors, and can distort if they are not correctly positioned. The surface of the screen should always be at right angles to the centre of the beam of light from the projector (or mirror if it is being reflected from one). If the projector is tilted upwards, then the top of the screen should be tilted forwards; otherwise the viewer will see a picture that is wider at the top than at the bottom (called a keystone effect). This distortion also causes some parts of the picture to be out of focus because full focus of the whole image can be produced only if it is all in the same plane. Ideally, the edges of a screen should be slightly curved towards the projector so that the light rays on the outside of the beam also reach the screen at right angles. This is very important for the silvered screens that are used with projections of video and computer images because the light output from the equipment is poor and focusing is difficult to achieve.

Correction of a picture that is wider on one side than the other is simply brought about by moving the wider side nearer the projector or the narrower side farther away.

Magnetic materials

Messages are recorded by the magnetic realignment of particles on one surface. This action is brought about by changes in the magnetic flux on the head which rubs against the surface, the variations in that flux being caused by electronic translations of the signals entering the record circuits of the equipment, either from a microphone or from other electronic sources. As the flux alters, so does the alignment of the particles. In a tape recorder, before the tape reaches the ferrite metal piece on the head which conveys the signal to the magnetic surface, it passes a similar piece on another head which erases any sounds previously recorded on that part of the tape by transmitting a supersonic signal which realigns the particles. On a disc, the same action is brought about by reformatting or by a user's command to delete. In this latter case, the normal result is that the item is deleted from the disc's catalogue and therefore the sector referred to is considered to be empty. New messages then overwrite the old ones, which remain present until this happens.

During playback or retrieval, the tape rubs against the same head or another one; in this case inducing from the surface a direct replica of the flux that produced the signals, which can then be amplified or form part of a program. When the same head is used for both record and retrieval, there is electronic switching which causes it to operate in the chosen manner, and this is selected by the controls or commands given by the user. In tape recorders there are erase heads, record heads and playback heads, the latter two often being combined. In a computer disc drive, there is just one head. Because the ferrite material which makes up the heads is very delicate, great care must be taken not to break, scratch or knock them off the carrier. Friction between the head and the tape introduces wear which makes head replacement sometimes necessary; this should be carried out by a service engineer.

Digital recordings of the flux are simply alignments that represent either a signal or no signal, a typical binary notation. Analogue recordings are more complex representations of the wave and are therefore more dependent on the quality and more easily degraded.

Tape equipment

Recordings and playbacks occur only when the tape is moving from left to right. The tape moves from the left reel to the right one at a fixed speed across the front of the heads, a series of spring pressure pads keeping the magnetic surface against them. The erase and record heads are activated in the record mode, the playback head in the playback mode. Only a certain area of tape is in contact with the heads, and great accuracy in levelling their plane is required to ensure that exactly the right portion is rubbing against them. If the wrong portion is in contact, the message is either absent or distorted.

Although the spindle on which the collecting wheel rotates is driven round, this is mainly to keep the tension on the tape and ensure that it is wound up. The delivery reel usually runs freely. The movement of the tape is maintained at an even speed and pulled across the heads by the rotation of the pinch wheel and the capstan which grip it. Variations in speed distort the signal; on sound equipment slow speeds deepen the noise, faster speeds cause higher pitch.

Amplifiers are attached to or are an integral part of tape players. They may have separate on/off switches, but the usual controls are volume and tone. The latter may be one control, separate base and treble, or a graphic equalizer with separate control over different frequency levels. Slider controls tend to give a more sensitive response.

Open reel audiotape recorders
Open reel tape recorders usually have a choice of speed; the higher the speed, the greater the area of tape on which the message is inscribed and hence the more faithful the reproduction quality. Thus a wider range of frequencies of sound is recorded and played back when the speed is increased. Because the various elements of the message have been spread over a wider area, editing between them can be done more easily. The three common speeds are 19cm/s (7½ips), 9.5cm/s (3¾ips) and 4.75cm/s (1.875ips). As the use of open reel tape recorders is now limited to specialized applications, they will not be discussed further in this book.

Audiocassette recorders
Cassette tape runs at one set speed, 4.75cm/s (1.875ips) only. The number of tracks recorded on a tape depends on the type of heads used. On looking at the head, the user can see if there are two pieces of metal attached with a little separation between them or whether there is only one. Two pieces indicate that the machine is capable of stereo replay, one piece that it is limited to mono. The exception to this is the arrangement on the heads for tape-slide cassettes. This is described later (page 123).

The layout of the tracks is shown in figure 16. The very thin heads
and even thinner separation between them are worth noting. With the
exception of those used for language laboratories or in tape-slide
presentations, the heads record and playback either stereo or mono only.
When side 1 is playing, track 1 (mono) or tracks 1 and 2 (stereo) are
being used. When the cassette is turned over, the tape is travelling in
the opposite direction on the diagram, track 2 (mono) or tracks 3 and
4 (stereo) being used. An examination of the arrangement of the heads
will indicate that if a stereo recording is played on mono equipment,
both the tracks — for example, 1 and 2 (stereo) — will be covered by
the mono head and the whole recording will be replayed. Similarly, if
a mono cassette is replayed on a stereo machine, the two heads will cover
almost all the recording and it will be reproduced virtually perfectly,
although only in mono, of course. Stereo reproduction means that the
output from tracks 1 and 4 is transmitted through the left-hand speaker,
and the output from tracks 2 and 3 through the right-hand one, depending

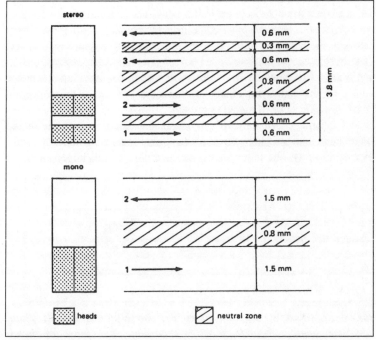

Figure 16. Audiocassette: track layout and dimensions

on the side of the tape being played. It is worth noting that the playing heads are on the bottom of the carrier, so that track 4 is at the top and track 1 at the bottom.

The layout of the recording and playback arrangements is shown in figure 17. When the cassette has been inserted, the heads are separated from the tape. Engaging record or playback modes causes the shift plate to carry the two heads and the pinch wheel to press against the tape, the pressure pad inside the cassette and the capstan spindle forming the other half of the sandwich. The pinch wheel can be moved in this way as it is a free wheel, the drive being provided by the capstan spindle.

Erasure of previous signals on the tracks selected for recording is performed by the erase head quite adequately, although there may be some background hiss. Total erasure can be done more thoroughly by using special equipment called a bulk eraser, which produces a strong magnetic field when switched on. Erasure is complete over the whole tape within a few seconds.

Recording can be from a microphone or from electrical sources like the radio, other tape recorders, record players or electronic boxes. Microphones are not discussed in this book, nor is it practical to describe the connections between other equipment and recorders as these will vary between models. The point to note, however, is the impedance values (a term referring to the resistance between interconnected devices, matching being achieved when the output impedance of one is within acceptable limits of the input impedance of the other) of the interconnecting machines. These must match to prevent distortion or, in extreme cases, potential damage. Manuals will provide the relevant answers. Care should be taken in matching impedance with external speakers and headphones. For user safety, the latter should be medium or high impedance.

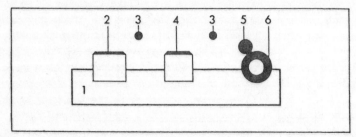

Figure 17. Cassette recorder/player: heads and pins − 1=shift plate; 2=erase head; 3=guide pin; 4=recording and playback head; 5=capstan; 6=rubber pinch wheel

The controls on the deck of a tape recorder which switch on the record mode should be noted, so that accidental operation is avoided. The usual system involves the simultaneous operation of two controls, record and play. If there are dials to indicate the record level, these will usually light up. In their absence, small indicator lamps may be illuminated. The level of the recording is shown on the dial, the optimum being when the needle just fails to cross into the red area. Recorders with manual control can have this level continually adjusted as the sound volume varies, but in most there is an alternative system known as AGC (Automatic Gain Control), which adjusts the recording level automatically to an even balance, based on the total volume of signals being received from all sources. Where the recorder has separate heads for record and playback, it is usually possible to listen to the quality of the recording being made just afterwards by monitoring the sound from the replay head. Of course, in the absence of the plastic lug at the back of the cassette, no recording can be made.

Some cassettes are recorded with the Dolby system, which is an electronic device to reduce the background hiss that is endemic with tape recorders, particularly when the tape speed is slow. It operates by compressing the recorded frequencies. Many cassette recorders have the Dolby sign marked on them to indicate that the circuit is present and the facility may be selected. If a Dolby recording is replayed on a machine without this circuit, the quality of sound is still adequate and some slight improvement is possible by increasing the treble control.

Digital audiotape (DAT) recorders
These work on a different principle. The recording uses the whole tape space as a helical scan, and thus can be used in only one direction. At a digital sampling rate of 48kHz, the tape travels at 8.15mm/sec (0.32ips). At the lower sampling rate of 32kHz, the tape speed is halved, which means that a tape of the same length lasts twice as long but the quality of recording is not as high. The lower frequency is satisfactory for the spoken word, but less so for music. Commercial recordings can be made at the same frequency as those for CD audio discs, 44.1kHz, and replayed perfectly at this level, but this frequency is not available for home recording.

Input for microphone, radio, other recorders and connections for computer data are available, and there are external links to separate amplifiers, speakers and headphones. Editing is done electronically, and not by adhesive tape as in a standard audiocassette. Rapid search and find facilities are also available, as on a CD system.

The cassette is pushed into a slot where the lower cover is pushed back, the flap lifted and the tape wound round the head automatically. The eject control reverses this procedure.

Computer cassette recorder
The use of cassettes for computer program storage is now limited almost entirely to popular games. Most of the equipment now has the appropriate cassette machine built into the system, but theoretically any cassette recorder could be attached to the computer. In practice, it is wise to use one that is recommended. The important factors are the volume control, the level of which is frequently critical for the effective transfer of data to and from the computer, and the capability of the computer to control the motor of the recorder. Signals from the computer can then start and stop the tape after a program has been loaded.

Tape-slide equipment
Signals from an audiocassette player can be used to control a slide projector so that the pictures can be accompanied by a prerecorded commentary. In multiprojector arrangements, open reel machines may be used to play the sound, but cassette machines could be used instead. The description here refers to the audiocassette version of tape-slide presentations as these are the ones in the most common use.

The system requires a fully automatic slide projector, the cable from the cassette recorder being inserted into the remote control socket. The head used for recording and replaying the pulses to activate the slide projector is on the same carrier as the sound record/playback head. In order that the pulses can be recorded while the programme is being heard, the head can be activated for record while the rest of the machine is in playback mode. The protection against accidental recording does not operate for pulse recording. The box controlling the pulses may be part of the recorder or a separate entity, and the operations are independent of the rest of the machine. From the recorder to the slide projector, the signals from the pulses go through this box, the final cable to the projector going from this part of the system.

Inspection of the heads of the cassette recorder will indicate whether it is capable of being used for a tape-slide system. The heads must cover both tracks 1 and 2 (stereo) or 1 (mono) and at least track 4. Tracks 3 and 4 are sometimes covered by a continuous head. The allocation of tracks is that tracks 1 and 2 are used for the sound, narration and sound effects etc., track 4 for cue tones (pulses for synchronizing).

The frequency and duration of pulses or cue tones follow an international standard and have the following characteristics:

- For slide change: a frequency of 1,000 Hertz (1 kiloHertz, 1kHz), the duration being 450 milliseconds.
- For automatic switch off: a frequency of 1kHz, the duration being 2 seconds.
- For tape pause: a frequency of 150 Hertz, the duration being 450 milliseconds.

Tape pause is a control which stops the tape automatically while the slide may continue to be viewed. Very useful in education, it gives the producer of the programme the opportunity to set the user a problem to be resolved, with the tape stopped for as long as the problem takes to complete. Usually a small red light glows on the recorder to indicate that a pause is operating, a restart button near to it is ready to be pressed when the user is prepared to continue.

Another international standard specifies the manner in which a tape-slide programme commences. This states that the first slide is shown on the screen by manual control of the projector before the tape is started, the first cue tone causing the first slide to be changed to the second.

One of the problems with tape-slide programmes results from the fact that at present most systems do not rewind in synchrony. When a tape is rewound the heads are usually withdrawn from the tape so that the cue tones cannot be picked up. Therefore they have no effect on the projector. Even if they were picked up, the signal they produce induces a slide change in the forward direction. The speed normally involved in rewinding in such that it would be unlikely for the projector to be able to complete a slide change before the next cue tone passed its signal.

Computer synchronized audio programmes

This is not really a format, but rather a kit of which the audiocassette is part. It consists of a computer program which is carefully timed to proceed with the commentary and instructions given on a prerecorded audiocassette playing back on a completely separate machine. To operate, the computer program is loaded and run, and the cassette recorder is started only when the instructions to do so appear on the screen. Thereafter, instructions may come from the playback of the tape or from the screen. Sometimes they require the tape to be stopped; sometimes an audible signal is used to indicate that the space-bar on the computer keyboard should be used to change the image on the screen. There is no electronic or physical link necessary between the cassette player and the computer equipment.

Control for audiocassette equipment

Some of the controls and features gain from a further explanation.

Fast forward and fast rewind   These operations permit a tape to be run forward or rewound at high speed. The tape is separated from the heads, the drive being by the collecting reel, not by the pinch wheel and capstan as in normal play and record modes. This protects the heads from excessive wear.

Pause   This causes an application of the brakes on the tape drive mechanism and during its use the tape should not travel forward at all. This should normally be used in normal play or record only, not when the tape is being driven at speed. A good way of making a recording is to prepare the machine for record and then stop it on the pause control. When the moment to record arrives, the pause control is released and a smooth and instant start is made.

Odometer   This is a feature that indicates the amount of tape that has passed across the heads, a form of revolution counter. One form consists of a 3- or 4-digit counter, operating like a milometer in a car. These are not standardized between machines, and so numbers noted on one machine do not necessarily equal those on another. They count the number of revolutions of the take-up spool − which, of course, is not directly proportional to the length of the tape. Some odometers indicate the time taken from the start to a particular point, and these can be used as reasonably accurate measures for identifying parts of a tape.

Radio switch   In future it is possible that radio signals will be used to switch on the record mode of a connected audiocassette recorder for a particular programme. This would be identified by a code number, and the radio would respond to the appropriate signal as it was transmitted and then control the recording.

Videotape

Recordings on videotape are currently all in analogue form, and this includes the sound as well. The pathway of the tape is similar to that on sound recorders, from the left-hand reel past the heads to the right-hand reel. However, there are important variations. The method of contact with the heads requires a tight winding against them rather than the use of pressure pads. While there is a capstan spindle/pinch wheel driving system, it is placed between the delivery spool and the heads, not after them, and is used to draw the tape from the spool. The drive on the take-up spool pulls the tape past the heads. Thus the tension over the heads and the position of the tape is dependent on the relative speed of the two drives.

The recording is made using the helical scan system. This means that the signals are recorded across a slope, higher at the front, lower at the rear, so that as large a surface area as possible is involved. The implication of this is that the tape has to move upwards over the heads, and this is accomplished by the heads being at an angle. When the cassette is placed in the machine, it is automatically opened, levers pull the tape out and wind it round the heads, and the tension is taken up to play or record. Not only does the tape move past the heads, the carrier which usually holds at least two heads also revolves at speed. The same heads are used for both recording and replaying the programme, depending on the mode being selected. The heads themselves are more delicate than those used in sound recorders and are easily destroyed through rough handling. In front of these heads is a stationary erase head which is activated when the record mode is in operation.

On VHS cassettes, the sound is recorded separately and horizontally along the edge of the tape, so that it is disentangled from the signals responsible for the pictures. This is an asset if the sound-track is to be recorded separately, either in its entirety or for a short section, using the audio dub system. On 8mm recordings, the picture and sound signals are interwoven, and thus later dubbing of the sound-track is very complex. However, the quality and signal/noise ratio are very good, and this system is being used by the latest VHS hi-fi recorders to improve their own sound output. Some 8mm recorders offer a further improvement in audio, the ability to record and play back digital sound using a sampling rate of 32kHz. This provides some of the best quality sound in videorecorders.

All tapes record in either monochrome or colour, depending on the signal being received. As in all magnetic storage systems, there is no external indication as to whether a tape carries a recording or not, and it is therefore important to have a good labelling system on the container. Just as radios can be signalled to turn on the recording of a particular programme, so it is technically possible for the same system to be available for videorecording. However, this is not yet operational.

Recordings can be created from broadcast, cable and satellite transmissions, from another videorecorder or from a camera, or they may be purchased already made. Most videorecorders contain a tuner so that broadcast transmissions can be made direct via an attachment to the aerial. The television set need not be switched on or may be used at the same time to view an entirely different programme. Depending on the method of relay, most cable transmissions can be recorded, but the input is usually taken through the video socket rather than through the aerial one used for broadcasts.

Recordings from satellite transmissions are made in the same way as those from broadcasts, that is through the aerial socket. Signals may be clear, scrambled − which means altering the synchronization − or encrypted, in which the code is changed. The decoder and any unscrambling devices needed for 'paid' transmissions are placed between the dish aerial and the videorecorder, so that the signal received by the equipment is a 'clean' broadcast. Note that the recorder can receive only the channel to which the dish aerial is tuned. The user cannot be viewing a different satellite channel at the same time, unless of course there is a second dish aerial. Links between videorecorders should be made through the video sockets, as there is less deterioration in the picture by using this method. However, as with all analogue signals, the drop in quality from generation to generation of recording is considerable. Signals sent in and out through aerial sockets are modulated and demodulated, so that they 'mimic' broadcast signals which are borne on carrier waves to improve quality and distance; each time this occurs, there is some deterioration in performance. Connections are therefore much better through video links, but these are not always available on television sets.

Output of the recording is commonly made through the aerial socket of the television set. The signal sent in this way is known as RF (Radio Frequency). Provided appropriate sockets on the set are available, signals may be sent as composite video or as RGB (Red, Green, Blue). The former, composite video, is a combined signal of all the visual information, including colour intensity and brightness. Because the signals are not modified before being interpreted within the set, the quality of this output for the viewer is better than that sent as RF. The other method of video input to the set, RGB, produces the best quality pictures. The signal is received as three separate pieces of information, one for each of the red, green and blue 'guns' inside the set that 'paint' the picture on the screen. Thus each one is individually controlled. Sometimes the information incorporates the colour intensity (chrominance) and brightness (luminance) information, but in the S-VHS system this is further separated and sent into independent sockets.

Sound is output as part of the RF signal and is replayed through the television set as if it came from a broadcast. However, most videorecorders provide the option of relaying the sound through the external socket of a hi-fi system and the quality can be improved in this way. Many prerecorded videocassettes carry stereo sound recording, and some television sets are provided with speakers on either side of the picture tube to give a representation of this. Most broadcast transmissions do not carry stereo, and therefore recordings of them are purely mono. However, experimental transmissions of digital stereo using the NICAM system are taking place in some parts of the country. When the output from the videorecorder is video, composite or RGB, the sound is passed to the television set through separate audio sockets or, of course, it can go through the hi-fi system.

The television set itself is designed to play back signals in a particular standard, and the user will need to specify this when acquiring a set. If no specific standard is requested, then it will be assumed that the one appropriate is that for receiving pictures from broadcast sources in the country in which the set is bought. There are three such standards commonly available. These are listed below, together with a selection of the countries that have adopted them:

- NTSC   Canada, West Indies, Japan, Taiwan, USA
- PAL   Argentina, Australia, Austria, Belgium, Denmark, Finland, West Germany, Italy, Hong Kong, Netherlands, Singapore, South Africa, Sweden, United Kingdom, Yugoslavia
- SECAM   Bulgaria, Czechoslovakia, Egypt, France, East Germany, Iran, Poland, USSR.

The important point to note is that broadcasts or recordings made on one standard cannot be played back using videorecorders or televisions of another standard. Either there is no response or sound, or picture quality is substantially impaired. Both the sets and recorders are designed to be specific to the standards. However, there are multistandard recorders available which can be switched to play back tapes of a different standard, but the user will need the appropriate set as well if he or she is to view and hear the programme. New PAL videorecorders are now available which can play NTSC tapes on modern television sets.

With the appearance of satellite broadcasts, it appears to manufacturers to be a suitable moment to introduce new standards in order to take advantage of technical improvements in picture and sound quality. In Europe, the MAC standard is being introduced, regrettably in two forms, DMAC and D2MAC. Both carry the same picture information, but D2MAC has a substantially reduced level of audio quality; the suggestion is that it is less expensive to relay through cable systems. Early satellite transmissions in Europe have been in PAL or SECAM, depending on the country of origin; but as MAC coding boxes become available, many of the channels will transfer to these standards. It appears that the attachment of these boxes may be all that is necessary to ensure that current sets and recorders will be able to use the information, but as the standards become more widely adopted, specially designed equipment will be prepared.

To receive satellite information, the user requires a special aerial, the so-called 'dish', mounted in such a way that it can point directly at all the satellites from which signals are required. Dish size is dependent on the strength of the signals being received, though all are weak compared with land transmissions. The signals are focused by the dish on to an LNB (Low Noise Block converter) which changes the carrier frequency to one that is more easily managed by the television set. For land transmissions of television signals in Europe by, for example, the BBC and IBA, the carrier frequency is in the range of 400 and 800 megaHertz, whereas European satellites transmit at between 10 and 12 gigaHertz (in America, the carrier frequency is between 3 and 4 gigaHertz). From the dish, the signal may be fed to a receiver in a single television institution, called TVRO (Television Receive Only), or into a cable network for distribution to many sets, called SMATV (Satellite Master Antenna Television).

The LNB is linked to a tuner, normally adjacent to the television set or videorecorder system, which selects the channel being viewed. If more than one satellite is to be used, it is better to have the dish arranged so that it can be turned vertically and horizontally, or just horizontally for polar mounts, by remote control. This can be done through a suitably expanded tuner. Also available on this box are controls to enhance the sound channels and remove some of the interference that frequently accompanies the audio signals. Between the tuner and the receiver and recorder system, it may be necessary to include decoder boxes which allow access to subscription programmes by removing the encryption. Sometimes these are electronic cards that can be placed inside appropriately designed tuner boxes. In the absence of such decoders, these subscription programmes are unusable as they are scrambled or encrypted.

Currently in Europe, there are two competing methods for doing this, and standards have yet to be agreed. Whether the satellite transmission is being used for programmes or digital data, a tuner box is an essential part of the equipment, and a turnable aerial is strongly recommended.

In the United States, there has been no attempt to change the transmission standards with the arrival of satellites. Any moves forward in the technical quality of sound and pictures from television await agreements on the development of high definition systems (HDTV). Currently NTSC uses 525 lines with a field frequency of 60 Hertz, the pictures changing 30 times a half-second. This compares with PAL and SECAM, which use 625 lines with a field frequency of 50 Hertz, the pictures changing 25 times a half-second. HDTV aims at the same field frequency (because this is dependent on the electrical power supply) but with a target of about 1,000 lines. At the same time, there is the prospect of changing the size of the picture from a 4:3 aspect ratio, as at present, to 16:9 ratio. Similar interest in HDTV is occurring in Europe, and the MAC standards are so designed as to make a change possible, as HDTV will almost certainly be transmitted by satellite only. Thus the apparently settled formats of television are about to be changed and developed, but present plans suggest that a continuing division between the standards adopted in the United States and Europe will remain. Users will continue to need multistandard equipment or converters if they are to be able to exchange programmes. However, they can be reassured that as the changes are introduced, manufacturers are ensuring that compatibility with the current standards is maintained, at least in the short term.

Alongside the changing standards are developments in connecting plugs between videorecorders and television sets. As the benefits of video – as opposed to RF – connections are accepted, so new plugs are needed to take advantage of the technical advances. Most will continue to be capable of connection through the RF input, but where possible users should make use of the video links. The Scart plug, a standard 21-pin connector, has been christened the Euroconnector, and it carries composite video or RGB signals, as appropriate to the set. Most advanced quality television sets now have suitable sockets. To reap the benefits of the S-VHS recorders, two different techniques are being used. In one, there are two Scart plugs: one for the standard signals which, to be of the highest quality, should be RGB; the other having separate chrominance (colour or C) and luminance (brightness or Y) signals. In the other method, the sets have so-called 'S' terminals to which the recorder is connected; these provide the same range of inputs to the television as the double Scarts.

As mentioned earlier, audio connections are separate.

Controls on videorecorders have also increased as the technology has developed and as users have appreciated the growing sophistication of the equipment. Commonly, all carry forward, record, fast forward and rewind controls (performed with the tape removed from the heads); fast search forward and backwards (performed with the tape in contact with the heads at up to 8× normal speed and with the user able to see a form of the picture without sound); pause and, usually, audio dub. Despite the technical improvements, users may still find value in the tracking control. When the picture appears distorted in the middle or at the top and bottom edges, adjustment of this control may correct it. It operates by affecting the relative speeds of the heads and the tape take-up spool by influencing the automatic corrections introduced by the sensors that usually maintain this accurately. Various systems are available to preselect programmes that the user may wish to record, some using clocks and the most sophisticated using bar codes in published listings to feed in the information. The system is becoming available in the United Kingdom, and is used in the rest of Europe.

However, the most sophisticated developments are those associated with the term 'digital'. Three main improvements are linked with this. The first is the significant gain in the quality of still picture viewing. The frame chosen by the viewer is stored in a digital memory and then sent to the television. Unlike non-digital still frame operation, the heads are not revolving against the tape and there is no wear and destruction of them, but the quality is constant and at a high level of accuracy. If still picture is engaged with non-digital sets, users should retain it as briefly as possible as both the tape and the heads will be progressively damaged otherwise. This facility has also improved the quality of slow motion playbacks.

The second advance that 'digital' may indicate is PIP (Picture In Picture), in which the viewer may see, usually as no more than a ninth of the screen size, a small picture of another channel while viewing a different one. Some very advanced television sets can produce this effect through having the necessary circuitry within them, but normally PIP is a function of the videorecorder. The recorder passes a picture from the second channel through the digital memory to the television, so that the viewer can see it without sound. This can be superimposed on a live picture as well as on one from the playback of a tape. The third useful advance associated with the word 'digital' is an improvement made in sound by removing some of the aberrant 'noise' from the tape.

Feeding the cassette into the recorder is through the slot, which then usually indicates that a cassette is present. Finding the recorded programme is more difficult, but new developments in indexing are being introduced to ease the problem. Cue tones are placed on the control track to indicate the start of a programme and, when located in either fast forward, rewind or search modes, may even present a short (say, 5 second) sample of the programme that is recorded there. Such tones can be placed automatically by the machine each time a recording is made, or with some equipment they can be superimposed later. Another possible facility is to insert a title, written using the control pad and usually in capitals only. Some users prefer to use the counter to find the programme. Counters used to vary from machine to machine, so that the figure noted on one recorder bore little resemblance to the same place on another. To improve matters, many machines now show the time of the programme from the indexing mark, so that the location of specific sequences can be found by using the hours and minutes record. Another improvement in the counter or odometer is the ability of the user to discover how much of the tape is left before the end, and thus to make better use of the storage capacity available.

Whichever system is adopted to organize and catalogue recordings, the use of these index markers and the new forms of odometer showing the time elapsed since the start of each programme can be very helpful and make better use of the space available on the tape. The need for accurate labelling on stored tapes is paramount as there is a potential of 8 hours (longest tape at long-play speed) to search through to find what is wanted; that could lead to an enormous waste of time.

Attaching computers to videorecorders is another, but expensive, way of indexing and locating sections. More commonly, such a link is used as a form of interactive video, but there is no reason why it should not be used to catalogue the tape and also to aid in the location of particular sections. As an interactive video device, the wear on the tape is considerable, and the reducing costs of various forms of videodisc, particularly CDV, make this a more attractive approach.

Discs
Computer-based systems are now an important and significantly large method of storing and manipulating information, not only as text but also as graphics, animations, sound and links to other sources such as video and film. Through the systems also, catalogues of other media can be organized, and with appropriate equipment can be retrieved. At the heart

of the computer-based system are the formats for storing this information, the two methods currently available being optical and magnetic discs. The former will be discussed later. This section concentrates on magnetic discs as well as on some basic aspects of computer-based systems.

On the disc, information is stored digitally, the various parts being identified by a catalogue of names devised by the user. The directory of this catalogue is defined differently according to the disc operating system (DOS) that is being used, and usually the user does not have to know how this works because the retrieval of the program being sought is undertaken automatically. As the software (computer programs) increases in simplicity − or, to use the jargon phrase, in user friendliness − much of the knowledge of how the computer works becomes unnecessary. The catalogue within a particular type of computer is similarly organized whether the discs are of the floppy or mini variety (see figure 10 on p.91)), or even whether the catalogue is held within a hard disc module.

These modules are normally permanently attached to the computer system, and should not be moved, particularly when the equipment is in use. At the end of a time in which they have been operating, an instruction to park the heads should be used so that the mechanism is kept as secure from potential damage as possible. Such care is not so necessary with separate floppy or mini disc drives. While reasonable care should be used, these can be moved while in use with little risk of damage. All disc drives are now built into the computer box itself, but in older kits that may still be in use they are merely connected by a broad ribbon cable. When the disc is inserted into the drive, it should be 'locked' in through the particular method provided. Sometimes this is done by pulling down a lid, sometimes by turning a small handle at the front or by merely clicking it behind a lip in the slot. Turning the handle or pressing a release button should partially eject the disc so that it can be easily removed.

When inserting the disc, the label side should be uppermost for horizontal drives, or on the right-hand side for vertical ones. The edge farthest from the label with the tiny notches or the metal cover should be inserted first − some discs carry an embossed arrow to indicate this. To operate, the disc drive requires power, which may come from the computer itself or through a separate mains lead. In the absence of such a lead, it must come from the computer. When the power is switched through to drives that are not built into the computer, an indicator light is illuminated. Each drive is labelled by the computer with a number, starting at 0 or A. In a few machines, each side of a disc is assigned a different alphanumeric name. It is worth noting that some computers automatically assume that the user starts with drive 0 or A unless it is informed otherwise, and that is where it will look for the program first.

When information is being drawn from or added to a disc, a light is illuminated on the drive and a whirring noise can be heard. No attempt should be made to remove the disc during this activity or the delicate heads and mechanism will be damaged. These heads act like those in an audiocassette recorder, either reading the information stored there (without creating any change to it) or writing new information on to the disc. The difference between these two modes of the head is created by the DOS system and by electronics, as required by the program. The DOS totally controls the links between the computer central processor and the drive as well as the organization of the data on the disc itself. When cassettes were used − and they are still commonly available for computer games − the control was by a cassette operating system (COS) and the information was transferred serially − that is, 1 bit at a time. In contrast, information on discs is transferred in parallel, that is at least 8 bits at a time.

Once the information is transferred from the disc into the computer, it is manipulated by the central processing unit (CPU). In most computers, there is only one of these, but current advances into parallel processing require several to be present, the work on the program being divided between them and all going on at the same time − hence the term 'parallel'. Whether there is only one CPU or several, the principles are the same. According to the instructions prepared within the program being used, the information is manipulated, shuttling backwards and forwards between the CPU and a temporary memory store as required. The CPU responds to external inputs as they are created by the user, and sends output signals as the program dictates.

When the computer is switched on, the basic information to make it operate is transferred to the CPU from the ROM (Read Only Memory) attached to it. This information is increasingly complex as computers have become more sophisticated. It may include instructions about presentation on the screen as well as the operating system for the machine and for its disc drives. Useful programs like wordprocessors may be stored in this way also, becoming instantly available on switching on or being called up by a simple instruction. ROM is fixed, ever present, and it is not affected by whether there is power in the machine or not.

In contrast, the computer also contains another store, RAM (Random Access Memory), which retains information only when it is receiving power. Switch off the machine, and the RAM becomes empty. Some RAM chips are now produced with tiny rechargeable batteries attached so that they can continue to receive power and therefore hold the information they contain, even when the machine is switched off. The principal use of RAM, however, is to hold the instructions and basic information for the program that is being used. Other information, such as the way in which the screen is mapped, is also held in the RAM, but the majority of the space is dedicated to holding the material required for the program. Much of this can be occupied by information to make it easier for the user to approach and understand the way in which to use the material; for example, various introductory diagrams and menus, often referred to as 'front-ends'. A simple equation that is becoming increasingly apparent is that the greater the user friendliness, the greater the quantity of RAM that the computer needs to have available.

Quantity of RAM is a common method of describing the size of a computer. The measures are arranged as follows: a byte is a collection of 8 bits of data, and a kilobyte (Kb or K) is 1,024 bytes, usually simplified as 1,000; a megabyte (Mb) is 1,000Kb. Computers with less than half a megabyte of RAM are now considered small, and at the time of writing – with the size of programs that are now in common use – 4Mb of RAM would be the average towards which users should be aiming.

One of the limiting factors on RAM is the operating system, for some systems are unable to make use of or to address large quantities of memory. This limits the size of the program that can be used at speed, although larger programs can be run by moving information stored on the disc around the different RAM banks. The maximum storage capacity on a disc varies partly with the DOS being used, but a mini-floppy disc can carry up to or nearly 1.5Mb of information, and single hard disc units are available with a capacity of 300Mb. As well as influencing the size of RAM that can be used, the operating system dictates whether a program can be used with the computer. The manner in which the information is written, organized and retrieved differs with the system and prevents some material being used with certain machines. Particularly variable between systems is the way in which they interpret information concerning graphics and colour. As machines improve, so the operating systems of machines from the same manufacturers should become increasingly compatible, thus allowing the same programs to continue to be used. Unfortunately this has not always happened.

Most machines can now be linked in networks. These have a controller/server machine which ensures that the interconnections work effectively. For the user with a large store of programs, a central database on a hard disc with all programs downloadable to individual machines in a network is a sensible method of distribution and security. The crucial feature is to ensure that the distribution is fast and that the user does not have to wait long before the program is under the control of his machine.

In order to use a program, the user has the choice of a range of input devices and systems. The commonest is the keyboard, which increasingly is separate from the box containing the circuit of the CPU and disc drives. Some are linked by an extendable cable, while others send information to the box by infra-red signals, similar to many handsets for controlling a television set. In portable computers, all the various parts of the equipment are kept together in one container, but those used on desk tops with television-type screens are more usually supplied with separate parts.

One form of keyboard is a flat sheet of pressure-sensitive material over which different printed layouts of response areas are placed. Known as a concept keyboard, this reacts to touch on the designed area, sending an appropriate signal to the computer which has been programmed to accept this. The requirement for such a keyboard is part of the package of the program. Such a device has proved particularly useful for the physically handicapped. For them a variety of other input devices have been produced, based on subtle combinations of switches that provide them with means of using any movement they can control in order to communicate with the computer.

Input can be made to some computers by touch. The most efficient method of doing this is to use an array of infra-red lights on two sides of the edge of the screen surround and equivalent receivers on the other two. This forms an invisible grid of light across the front of the screen so that the exact point at which a finger interrupts it can be identified. When this corresponds with a recognized item on the screen display, an appropriate response or input can be made to the program. For some programs, the input may be a voice command, a facility which will become more common with further technical developments. Musical input can be provided through piano-type keyboards, and data from other equipment and devices can be used to provide signals to a program if the computer is equipped with the relevant sockets.

Recently, there has been widespread adoption of the WIMP environment to manage a program. WIMP stands for Windows, Icons, Pointers and Menus, and describes the screen appearance of the system. Windows are boxes of varying sizes that can be arranged adjacently or superimposed on each other, the one in which the user is working being 'live'; the others may be responding or, more likely, being used as references for information. Icons are small ideograms used to indicate various potential actions – for example, a drawing of a small waste-paper basket can indicate 'get rid of' or 'wipe'. Pointer is a moving arrow or indicator (it can be any shape that the manufacturer or even the user chooses) which can be moved to an icon or heading area to show that is the one to be used. Menus are lists of possible attributes or actions that can be taken which can be called from icons or the heading areas that have them.

The input device for WIMP environments is usually the mouse, a small box with up to three buttons on the top and a ball underneath. As it is moved around, so the pointer roves around the screen. When it is on top of an icon or a heading area, pressing a button causes the action to occur – a program to be 'wiped', a menu to appear or a particular item to be highlighted. The rules for the different buttons vary with the equipment and program being used, but the principles are the same. An alternative input system is a tracker ball, often referred to as a 'dead mouse', a box with up to three buttons and a large ball which is on top and controlled by the hand. It operates in the same way, except that no space is required to move it around. The various input systems are the means by which the user controls and manipulates the program, responding to any requests and feeding in any information. With the WIMP environment, it is usually possible to do nearly everything without touching a keyboard, although entering letters and numbers is usually quicker that way. To provide a further range of input signals, keyboards have keys in addition to those present on a standard typewriter: for example, 'control' and 'alt' keys which combine with every other key to provide the capacity for about 60 extra signals each; 'escape' and 'break' which can sometimes be used to stop a program or interrupt it; and a collection of function keys, each of which a programmer can design to represent the total instructions for an important action such as creating italic text in a wordprocessed article, and for which a printed guide should be available with each program.

Once the information has been manipulated as the user requires, it has to be output in some way. The screen is one such output system. In the early days of microcomputers, the standard home television set was used, and much difficulty was encountered because the computer signals from machines manufactured in the USA expected an NTSC receiver whereas UK homes had a PAL one. Most computers are now acquired with screens as part of the package, and this problem is not so apparent. However, if the computer is to be used with other sets, or the pictures from television or videodiscs mixed with the program output, note should be taken of the television standard so that they match.

Output is often made to a printer. Desk-top computers almost universally prepare alphanumeric characters and standard punctuation marks according to the ASCII code (American Standard Code for Information Interchange), which provides a standard for exchanging data directly between computers as well as for transferring information to a printer. Provided the computer contains the relevant instructions (printer driver) for the particular printer to be used, output to a printer can be successfully provided. Descriptions of different types of printers are not relevant to this book.

Instead, the output may be to a disc to store the information for further activity. Such an action would be part of the instructions provided within the program. For some users, such information may be more appropriately stored on their own disc, which they then remove to their own personal environment. In games, such an information store may relate to the position the user has reached within the activity. Many are provided with an option to 'store position' so that the game can be left and returned to later without the user having to start from the beginning again.

Thus a computer system consists of a box containing the circuitry, CPU, ROM and RAM, and operating system; an input device such as a keyboard; a storage system such as a disc drive; and an output device such as a screen. Normally purchased as a total system from one manufacturer, the various interconnections are those provided with the instructions. If items are purchased separately, it is important to ensure that they operate with each other as the various parts are not always interchangeable. Signals are not necessarily the same, and the wiring of plugs and sockets is often different. Extra pieces of equipment – such as further disc drives, modems for connection to telephone lines and connections to scientific equipment – may be attached if the appropriate sockets are present, but the wiring needs to be undertaken by people with the appropriate professional knowledge. All connectors should be screwed together where this is possible as that improves safety and prevents accidental detachment. Some equipment becomes hot with use, and fans may be needed within the computer box to reduce this. Extra cards carrying special circuits or ROMs may be inserted into the computer box in appropriate places to extend the facilities or introduce a standard program, such as a wordprocessor. While these can usually be introduced by an average user, the services of a professional engineer may be more appropriate.

The range of programs for use with a computer is constantly increasing, but those available can be divided into two main groups. First, there are those which provide a framework for the user to insert his or her own information, often referred to as generic programs. These include wordprocessors, spread sheets, graphical and painting programs, music generators and programs offering compiling or interpreting facilities for particular computer languages. In each of these cases, the program provides a controlled space and facilities within the parameters of which the user creates his or her own material. Frequently, this can be saved on a disc without the generic program itself, although it can be recalled only by loading it with that program present in the computer. Thus, a user can frequently carry away, say, a wordprocessed document on his or her own disc without having to copy the wordprocessor program itself.

Another important generic program is that used for storing, searching and retrieving a database. Again, the program can be held separately from the database itself and, further, the result of a search from the database can itself be filed on a separate disc. Thus a user can use a database program to generate his or her own database of relevant information on his or her own disc. For further use of that database, it will be necessary to ensure that the database program is loaded into the computer, but then manipulation can take place and outputs can be stored on the user's own disc. Alternatively, a published database can be searched and manipulated and the results can be retained in the user's personal store. While on the subject of databases, it is important to note that difficulties may be met in trying to manipulate data stored using one database program by making use of a different one, but in many cases conversion routines are available.

The second group of programs is those with particular content with which the user interacts. Most teaching/learning programs fall into this category, as do games and adventures. Like generic programs, these are written for particular machines and are not interchangeable between them. If an institution has several different computers, then versions for each of those on which the program is to be used will have to be purchased. This lack of interchangeability and the current state of non-compatibility between machines means that comprehensive labelling of all stored computer material is essential. Information should include the operating system of the computer and its version number as well as the storage capacity of the disc or its number of tracks and density.

Care should be taken of discs, including appropriate protection during storage. The programs should be 'locked' and the disc 'write protected' if possible to discourage misappropriation and misuse. These barriers can easily be overcome by skilful users, but they do discourage the casual miscreant. Programs are copyright to the producer, but most expect and allow the user to create a working copy, enabling the original to be stored in a secure place. If such permission is not granted, then a second working copy is usually supplied. Some discs are designed to erase themselves if too many copies are made; some require the original to be inserted during any loading of a copy; some are copy protected, there being a number of different ways of doing this; and some have special numbers secreted deeply within their code identifying the original purchaser and thus providing the producer with the evidence to target the person who allowed the copyright to be flouted.

Plastic

This section covers equipment using three types of material: transparent plastic, i.e. the overhead projector; vinyl discs, i.e. the record player; and optical storage systems, i.e. laser discs.

The overhead projector

This is similar in principle to a film projector, lamp light passing through a lens, the transparent plastic film and a mirror system to reach the screen. The mirror system, which is positioned vertically above the centre of the film, has the sole function of turning the beam of light towards the screen behind the speaker. At the same time, it ensures that the picture has the correct orientation on the screen. The lens between the lamp and the transparent film is made to the Fresnel design. This is a system by which the curved convex lens is produced on as flat a plane as possible, and is made as a series of circles of the correct curvature set one inside the other. The lens so produced is not of as high a quality as the full convex lens and is liable to produce distorted colouration at the edges.

The user works at the side of the machine facing away from the screen, placing the film on the glass platform or stage in the correct orientation for reading. When the lamp is switched on, the light travels through the film into the mirror system and on to the screen, focusing being carried out by raising or lowering the mirror system with respect to the stage. The heat generated by the lamp is dispersed by a fan, which must be in operation during viewing. Almost all projectors now use low voltage lamps and a transformer must be present within the machine to adjust for this. A further control is responsible for varying the brightness of the lamp, and to lower costs it is advisable to use the reduced setting if that provides adequate lighting.

The record player

The recording on a disc is in the form of waves and troughs on the side of the groove. In a mono recording, the waves are usually on one side only, but in stereo the left-hand wall holds the curves for the left-hand channel and the right-hand wall holds those for the right-hand channel. The movements required by the needle or stylus in the stereo system are at right angles to each other and the distortion so produced in two directions is differentiated in the cartridge which carries the stylus. Because the movements require some flexibility in the stylus, it is essential that the correct type is fitted. A mono stylus and cartridge will not respond to both movements and will tend to damage the right-hand channel. Thus if a stereo record is to be played on a mono record player, a special cartridge should be used.

The stylus is triangular in shape with a rounded tip, usually made of a chip of sapphire or diamond. The latter is preferable as it lasts much longer. The radius of the tip is about 0.0007in. A more expensive stylus can be obtained with the tip in the shape of an ellipse; this fits the curves of the groove more exactly.

The vibrations of the stylus are turned into electrical signals by the cartridge. Two systems are commonly available for this, ceramic and magnetic. In the former, two piezo crystals are distorted by the vibrations of the stylus, producing small electrical pulses. This is a cheap and strong cartridge, but it does not follow the groove as well as the magnetic one and tends to introduce cross-talk between the two channels. If these problems are reduced, the cost then exceeds that of the magnetic cartridge. The magnetic cartridge is more delicate, working by the vibrations of the needle, which introduce fluctuating magnetic fields that produce a current. It is more expensive and frequently is manufactured in such a way that a worn stylus requires the change of the complete cartridge.

As the stylus follows the groove, the cartridge and the pick-up arm are pulled across the record. There is no drive across, and various forces act on the arm to create a satisfactory flow through the channel. Thus the stylus has to be kept in the groove by sufficient weight but there must not be so much weight as to damage the walls; a ceramic cartridge needs a larger weight than a magnetic one. There is also a distortion effect due to friction which pulls the arm towards the centre; this is compensated for by a bias. In good quality record players these forces are balanced out in the construction of the pick-up arm and the recommended adjustments.

The sounds produced by means of the pick-up arm and the cartridge are then transferred electrically to an amplifier and thence to loudspeakers or headphones. The quality of sound depends on the shape of the stylus, which deteriorates through use; the accuracy of the shape of the groove, which is gradually worn away; the weight of the stylus, so that it rides in the groove at an optimum pressure; and the speed at which the stylus travels. Wear of the stylus and the groove can be remedied only by replacement, the average life of a diamond stylus being the replay of 1,000 sides. Some record players have weight adjustment controls on the counterbalance end of the arm, but corrections should be undertaken only with reference to scales. Any variations in the speed of the turntable are the result of mechanical faults and require adjustment by an engineer.

For improved care of records and use of the equipment, additional facilities are useful. A lever to lift and lower the stylus on to the record obviates potential damage caused by the stylus hitting the record too hard or at an angle – the latter causes scratching, which destroys the edges of the groove. A reject control causes immediate raising of the arm, the turntable stopping as it returns to its resting position. When the stylus reaches a certain point, about 54mm (2.75in) from the centre of the record, automatic raising of the arm and return to rest, with the turntable stopping afterwards, is a common facility.

On some equipment, it is possible to play a stack of records one after the other. This can introduce two potential defects and thus should be discouraged. When the groove on one record lies against that of another, the friction between them induces wear and damage to their edges. There is also a drag effect which will introduce variations in speed and consequent distortion of sound.

Optical storage systems

These systems are characterized by carrying substantial amounts of densely packed data on discs which are considered practically indestructible. The discs are accessed and stored by means of low-powered lasers. In order to ensure accurate and rapid reading, more than one laser beam may be focused on the same point from different angles, but this does not occur in every device. Recording protocols differ from one format of these systems to another, although there is an increasing trend to encourage compatibility between them, as in the CD series. All, however, are able to compensate for short pieces of information that are not correctly read by the laser – for example, when surface dirt or cracks distort the beam. The recording protocols are so designed that the microprocessor can 'fill in' missing bits and provide an apparently faultless readout.

The ability of microprocessors to control the laser and manipulate the data being read at high speed has made this technology possible and provided it with the speed of access and accuracy that are characteristic. Where the data are digital, facilities may be provided that can transfer them to the CPU of a computer for further manipulation by the user, but this option is not present in all the devices. It is also worth noting that present technology and storage organization is such that magnetic hard discs provide much faster access times than optical storage systems. Nevertheless, such is the volume of data that can be stored optically that they are extremely useful devices and the longer access time rarely causes inconvenience.

The lasers used in these systems are low powered and will not cause any physical damage to a human being. They are also focused over a very short distance, which further reduces the possibility of their causing potential problems. Precautions are also taken to ensure that contact is very unlikely. In early equipment, a lid was lifted and the disc was placed on the carrier in the machine. Switches prevented the laser operating until the lid was closed. Such systems are now available only in those devices that are designed to be portable. Instead, in present equipment a disc is loaded by placing it in a drawer, which is then closed. Only then is it possible to start the laser, which normally operates from the inside and works its way outwards.

All these optical storage discs offer an immense amount of space for data. Each type of system currently available will be described below, but these are examples of the newest technology and are therefore open to a great deal of further development. It should be borne in mind that they are likely to be subject to many changes in the future.

CD audio

The combination of the accuracy of the digital recording and the absence of any replay of mechanical noise has led to CD audio discs being widely welcomed by users and to their gradually replacing the analogue vinyl recordings. In addition, the microprocessor control of the replay has introduced a range of extra facilities that users find particularly welcome in helping to manage their audio listening. The discs have to be held firmly in order to ensure that the laser can read the data accurately, but many of the early difficulties in doing this have now been overcome. Thus it is now possible to have CD audio in car sound systems and as the recording medium for light personal stereo systems that can be carried around the neck. For prerecorded sound, these will therefore provide strong competition for the ubiquitous stereo cassette tape players.

Basic controls like on/off, eject (to open the tray or drawer), volume, tone (sometimes enhanced as a graphic equalizer), pause and balance are present on all equipment. Many of the extra facilities are designed to provide greater control of the access and management of listening to sound. Most equipment provides a light-emitting diode (LED) display of the information and frequently this can be channelled to the machine from an infra-red hand control. Advances in these devices are such that sometimes the information is also displayed on an inbuilt liquid crystal display (LCD) screen.

The access and control information includes a display of the track number being played, the time elapsed from the beginning of a sequence, the time left to play on that track or sequence, and the user-programmed sequence of tracks that will be played (usually up to 20, but this can be programmed to repeat continually). The user can also use a fast search procedure to find a particular passage of sound; in some machines, this plays a short sequence of the beginning of each track. Alternatively, the user can identify a particular point in the middle of a sound sequence and programme the machine to locate it and play from there. In some machines also, more than one disc can be loaded at a time, so that after one has been completed the next starts. There is more likelihood of damaging discs if this is done, but the facility has become available so recently that there is no evidence of this.

Juke box arrangements are now available in which discs can be stacked and selected so that different tracks can be played in a user-programmed sequence. Access and control is fast and very accurate, and the quantity of sound that can be stored in this way is immense, each track or programmed sequence being identifiable and very quickly findable.

Early CD audio players were merely decks that had to be fed through separate amplifiers and speakers. However, the equipment is now available as combined units, although speakers are almost invariably detachable. The quality of sound on the recordings is normally of such a standard that the quality the user hears is dictated by the amplifier and speakers rather than by that on the disc. Output from the disc is digital, but the sound the user hears is analogue. Better equipment has a minimum of two digital to analogue converters to perform this translation. Currently, recordings are on only one side of the disc, but in the future it is probable that they will be made on both sides.

Laservision

Within this relatively new format, there are already some established incompatibilities. Three types of disc are available: those (sometimes known as CLV — Constant Linear Velocity) carrying feature films and their equivalent which can be run continually, although individual frames can be stopped and held rather unsteadily; those (sometimes known as CAV — Constant Angular Velocity) designed for interactive work, particularly training, in which each section and frame on the disc can be called up as a still or moving picture; and those (called AIV, LV or laser ROMs) which include digital computer data on the disc. The first two play on the same kind of player, although the user has much more control of the CAV disc than of the CLV disc. AIV discs play with all their facilities only on AIV players, for on standard laservision players the digital material cannot be accessed. The other discs will play on AIV players, usually without problems. CD video discs will not play on any of this equipment.

In training activities, the information from the laser disc may be controlled by a separate computer, which through its own magnetic discs can add further text and graphics to the presentation. Some users prefer this to be replayed on separate monitors (television sets), but for others having the display on one monitor is preferable. This also provides the opportunity for overlaying drawings of an object over its filmed picture. To do this superimposition, the equipment has to include a genlock facility which locks the television pictures from the laser disc and the computer together. This facility is normally built into the computer itself.

The laserdisc can be controlled by buttons on the machine, by a remote control handset or by instructions from a computer program. The controls normally include: power on/off, eject (when the disc is held in a drawer), play (single frame or continuous), rewind, slow speed (often the rate is selectable and usable in forward or reverse modes), still picture, scan (which supports searching at speed), and go to (either a 'chapter' number or a 'page' number may be inserted). There is no need to indicate the type of disc being used as the player recognizes this automatically. Teletext controls are also usually available so that extra textual data can be revealed from a suitably prepared disc.

By appropriate programming, all these controls can form part of the instructions sent to the player from the computer. At the same time, the computer can add material from its own storage systems, usually the magnetic disc but also any other store such as a CD-ROM (see below). Through this facility various frames or sequences can be recalled from the laserdisc in any order to produce a guided pathway through the visual and textual material, as determined by the producer. Such computer programs can also be designed to include the possibility of users producing their own organized sequences for their own purposes and adding any textual and graphical material, which can be stored on a magnetic disc. The laserdisc is unaffected by this process, so it will return to stock in the same state as it started. Only the user's magnetic disc carries the information.

As with all video products, the laserdisc is prepared for replay with a particular transmission standard. Thus a disc recorded for an NTSC standard will play back only with the appropriate player and television set. A laserdisc recorded for PAL will not replay intelligible pictures or sound with this kit but requires its own arrangement of PAL player and PAL television set. No discs are yet recorded for D-MAC, although PAL discs are likely to be acceptable on sets made for this standard, playing, of course, at PAL quality. Sound is available through two channels, which are individually selectable. They can be used for stereo output as a pair or carry different elements on each; for example, narration on one and natural sound on the other, or different languages on each. If stereo sound is being reproduced and high quality is required, it is better to feed this through a hi-fi music amplifier and speakers than to rely on the current technological state of stereo television speakers.

The laserdisc player can be connected to the television set through the aerial (RF) socket, but better pictures are reproduced if the transfer is effected through video and audio sockets or through a SCART or Euroconnector, where these are present. The computer output to control the laserdisc player should be the RS232 socket. During use, no attempt should be made to open the part containing the disc. It can be revolving as fast as 1,500 revolutions per minute (CD audio revolves between 200 and 500).

CD video

Only a few models of players are currently available. All use the drawer system to load the discs, and are able to replay all four different CD video sizes and both CD audio sizes. They are also able to replay the laserdiscs, both sound and vision, in the NTSC version but only the pictures in the PAL one. The difference is because the laserdisc uses two analogue sound channels and the bandwidth space they occupy has been taken up by the digital audio channel favoured by the CD video system. In the NTSC system, the picture information requires less space and it has been possible to squeeze the digital channel into the gap so that the analogue audio channels are unaffected.

The different sizes of disc offer different facilities, the smaller ones with short lengths of video only, the larger with a similar capacity to the laserdisc. All can be controlled by the user directly, but communication with a computer needs the addition of an extra circuit and socket. However, the facilities are not as extensive as those for the laserdisc.

The basic controls include: stand-by, stop/close, forward and rewind (the speed of each may be adjusted and still and step are available for frame-by-frame movement), previous and next (for jumping to adjacent chapters or audio tracks), sound track (selection between the two available on the larger discs), section repeat, and index selection (track, chapter, time and frame). The functions selected are shown on the television screen as numbers or bars although, if the remote control is being used, it should be pointed at the player, not the set. The sound is naturally stereo and as with laserdiscs is best played through a hi-fi amplifier, although there usually needs to be a digital to analogue decoder in the system.

The CD video players can be played through the aerial (RF) socket, but better vision results from using the SCART or Euroconnector into a suitably fitted television set. A videorecorder can be linked to the television set simultaneously, either by passing links through the aerial connectors (the CD video player receives aerial input and outputs it to the videorecorder, which then outputs it to the television set), or, more sensibly, by plugging the videorecorder into a second SCART socket or an unused aerial one. Although this sounds complicated — and if a hi-fi system is also involved, results in a mass of connecting cables — in practice the connections are fairly obvious. The presence of SCART plugs in the system is invaluable.

CD graphics and interactive
At the time of writing, players for these systems are not available though technical specifications have been produced. Both will reproduce digital pictures and sound including video covering the full screen, and will also be totally programmable through a computer. However, the range of facilities that will be provided will not be known until the equipment is produced.

CD-ROM
Based on the same technology, the CD-ROM is usable only with a

computer. Originally designed to provide an immense store for textual material, discs are now produced carrying digital recordings of photographs, graphics and sound. Appropriate computer programs can be used to retrieve these and then manipulate them in any way the user wishes.

CD-ROM players may be built into the computer box in place of a disc drive or may be a separate box linked through the RS232 socket. The separate box usually requires its own power supply. Mechanical controls are simple, one to open a drawer or raise a lid to load the disc, and one to switch on the power on the separate box. All other controlling functions are provided by the program the user is operating in the computer. If the CD-ROM is bought as a separate item, the user also requires an extra circuit within the computer to control it. This is usually a card which can be inserted very easily.

The standards for laying down the information on the disc and for linking the computer and its programs to this are emerging *de facto* from those used by the manufacturers and are now the basis of a proposed ISO agreement. They are based on standards agreed at a hotel called the High Sierra and have been given its name. The letters XA have been added to those of CD-ROM to indicate extended architecture to incorporate CD interactive-type graphics and sound.

Some CD-ROMs carry the program required to search them on the disc, and this is loaded into the computer when the CD-ROM is called by the user. Others provide only a program to call the data, the search program being any one the user chooses. As more experience develops, the trend will be towards the latter arrangement. The material may be viewed in sequence, but is more usually sampled in an order that meets the needs of the user. If the user wishes, any part of the stored information can be downloaded and incorporated in a database, wordprocessing activity or similar computer program.

Just as CD audio discs can be arranged in a juke box so that any part of any individual disc can be selected as required, so can CD-ROMs. Noting the high storage capacity of an individual disc as being equivalent to 250,000 pages of text, a juke box of 20 would be equal to five million pages, any part of one of these being accessible, theoretically, in a few seconds.

The CD-ROM is a fixed recording that cannot be altered by the user. Nothing can be added to or erased from the ROM itself. For some users, this is an inconvenient arrangement, and so there are two versions of similar technology – WORMS and erasable optical discs – available.

These two require their own equipment and are not interchangeable with CD-ROMs, but all operate on the same principles of lasers reading optically stored information.

WORM stands for Write Once, Read Many times. One version is a 12cm (5¼ in.) disc which is optically etched under the control of the user to store the relevant data. As more data are acquired, so extra sections can be etched into the disc. Thus the user can produce a continuing personal store of information. The capacity varies with the sophistication of the system being used, but 750Mb using two sides of a single disc is not unusual. On the 12in. disc, 2.6 gigabytes may be stored. Just like the CD-ROM, the WORM box for the smaller disc can be built into the computer or be external to it. The discs cannot be duplicated directly, although it is perfectly possible to load the data into a different store and then etch another disc or pass them on to be turned into a CD-ROM.

The uses are therefore more restricted, but valuable. WORM is particularly useful as a means of developing an archive of information, adding to the stock as the material becomes available. It can hold records of technical drawings, image stores, personnel records, audit trails and records of treatment of individual patients – all items that benefit from permanent records being kept and added to over time.

Erasable optical discs are, as the name implies, temporary stores of information that can be removed and new material written in its place. Capacities of 200 to 400Mb are available. Not as flexible as magnetic discs in their use, they nevertheless offer a magneto-optical storage system that is less subject to damage from external factors that can upset the magnetism or physically destroy all or part of the disc. The recording is made by the laser heating the surface and 'freezing' the polarity of reflected light created by a magnetic field. They usually need special equipment to interface with the computer, but some can often use a standard interface.

INFORMATION FROM REMOTE SOURCES

Up to this point, all the equipment discussed has been concerned with helping to retrieve information from material that is locally held in stores that the user can handle personally. In this section, the discussion turns to the retrieval of information that is contained in stores that are remote from the user, sometimes even in other countries. This does not, of course, include purchasing the material and receiving it through the post or via a delivery van. Instead the information comes in the form of sounds, still and moving pictures, texts and data directly into the user's own equipment for manipulation and study.

Facsimile (fax) transmissions are now becoming more common from such agencies as the British Lending Library, but these still arrive as pieces of printed paper as far as the user is concerned, and are treated as all other examples of that format. The use of fax is growing rapidly, libraries and other bodies now being able to answer requests from clients by transmitting documents and extracts directly by this means as well as to receive them. As will be mentioned again below, fax facilities are becoming an integral part of a computer, so that, for example, wordprocessed documents can be sent directly to other people's fax machines without the sender ever having to print them out. Equally a user can receive a fax in his or her computer, view it and even edit sections before deciding whether to print it on paper.

However, the main concern of this section is with the growing number of information sources that can be received by broadcasts or accessed through interactive systems, primarily through lines and cable. Many of these sources are commercial services providing specialist information on various technical subjects which interest only a limited clientele. Others are more general in their application, providing access to journals and newspapers. Yet others are designed as support services or provide notice boards of immediate information. The range is considerable and the number available is increasing constantly.

There are two distinctly different approaches. One, the broadcast services, offer a 'receive only' information provision. If the user wishes to comment to the information provider, other methods of communication are necessary. All the user can do is receive the information as the provider despatches it. This is particularly valuable for large volumes of information, immediate items for all users, and updating that has to be done frequently and with considerable quantities of change such as meteorological data.

The other approach is interactive systems. The user is connected directly to the provider, usually by line or cable, and a dialogue takes place between them. For example, the user may ask for certain information, analyse the possible quantity and then refine the request until exactly what is needed is actually sent. Thus in this system, both the provider and the user are sending messages to each other. They are directly connected.

Each of these two methods of accessing remote sources of information will be discussed below.

Broadcast services

Anything that is broadcast by radio or television or via a satellite is, in a sense, information. Receiving and storing television programmes on videocassette recorders have been described earlier. Other data are also broadcast and it is the retrieval of those which is described here. It is important to note that the compatibility of equipment with the particular broadcast standards, NTSC, PAL, SECAM and MAC, has to be maintained.

From some satellites, data may be received that draw coded pictures of the weather, the land and its uses and similar information. These are often referred to as 'remote sensing' satellites, and their output is similar to data from astronomic adventures such as those undertaken by NASA. An aerial, continually moving to pick up the transmissions, is connected through a decoder to a computer. The data are a series of numbers, so a program is needed to translate these into pictures that can be viewed and analysed. Various controlling instructions with the program can be used to enhance the quality of the pictures in various ways so as to clarify them or magnify various areas.

Other satellites are used as transmitters of information that is sent to them by earth stations. Not only are television programmes sent in this way, but computer data can also be transmitted. For most satellites used in this way, there are a limited number of 'uplinking' stations which have permission to send information to particular transponders on them. While theoretically anyone could do that, in practice if they did the result would be like the result of free, simultaneous use of the same telephone − that is, an unintelligible babble. Thus satellites remain systems which offer only 'receive only' broadcasts of information.

When considering broadcast information services, most users think only of teletext systems. These are commonly available to the general public, examples being Ceefax from the BBC and Oracle from the IBA. However, there are further transmissions of digital data that are accessible only to those paying for the service and equipped with appropriate receivers. The BBC refers to these as Datacast. They carry such information as betting prices for horse racing, press agency releases, financial prices and meteorological data; all large volumes of constantly changing information. The transmissions are sent in a similar way to teletext.

The signals are currently transmitted in the intervening lines between pictures. Nominally, each picture broadcast in Britain is 625 lines, but in practice only 585 are used to build the picture that is viewed. Most of the 40 lines between the pictures, which appear black when they are occasionally seen through a fault on the horizontal hold, are used for engineering instructions to ensure that the set responds accurately to the transmissions. However, there is unused space. Four of the lines on each channel are used to carry the teletext data. Each service is specific to the channel on which it is sent as it is linked to the pictures within the gaps of which it is transmitted. The information can be downloaded as a constant stream into a computer store and reformatted by a program there; but as a general public service, it is transmitted as separate pages, each with a maximum depth of 24 lines and length of 40 characters. Normally, the pages are transmitted sequentially, but frequently accessed pages such as indexes are sent more often by interspersing them at different points. One bonus of the services is the 24-hour clock in the top right-hand corner of each page, which is probably the most accurate free timepiece available.

The service cannot be recorded on videocassettes, but it can be accepted into a computer and pages can be stored there. Indeed, for many years, programs have been regularly sent out on Ceefax for users who require them, and a more extensive service could be provided if required, including transmission through a satellite to other nations within its footprint. Special decoders are needed; these are connected to an efficient aerial and tuned to the selected channel. The data are usually stored temporarily in the decoder before passing to the computer on command from the appropriate program. The program then organizes the information as the user requests, maybe using it to link to or capture other pages of teletext transmission.

This is a free service, but charging systems are possible. The receiver can be programmed by the broadcast to receive information only when a fee has been paid, and this may be decremented over time and then recharged. Many of the private broadcast services have to be paid for by the user and systems similar to this are in use.

The quantity of data that can be transmitted is considerable. On the present PAL service, 18Kb per second can be sent per line, but if a full frame of television were to be used − for example, in the night hours when no pictures are being sent − the despatch could be 5.6Mb per second. Using D-MAC, such a full frame of data could be as large as 20Mb per second, and this would need a receiving system with a very large memory to absorb it.

Radio too could be used to broadcast data as an information service. The capacity is not as high, somewhere between 300 bits and 5Kb per second being the figures generally given. Early experiments with this medium proved useful but have not been widely exploited. A decoder and program would be needed to receive the information. General broadcasts of information − for example, for selective areas of roads concerning traffic conditions − could be made to interrupt other radio receptions on cars, and the versatility and local relevance of radio is a facility for information dissemination that will be further exploited in the future.

Teletext systems were originally devised to provide sub-titling to enable the deaf to enjoy television programmes, but they have developed much further than these functions. Much use is now made of teletext to convey data and programs to support and develop the information provided on general television programmes. Additional software is offered for free distribution to users concerned with a wide range of topics from music to design, and much use is made of the system for distributing information. The public pages of Ceefax and Oracle information are now provided with attached links to speed up access for users and make them easier to interconnect into a continuing 'story'. Only sets provided with appropriate controls can make use of this facility.

Interactive systems
The main systems for interactive connections make use of the telephone lines or cables provided by companies specializing in the distribution of television programmes. The latter are limited in the extent of their network and are difficult to interconnect internationally, so currently the predominant method is through the telephone circuit.

The computer is the access point for the user, either built into a television set or, as is now more usual, a separate stand-alone system. It may be totally dedicated to accessing remote information stores, but more usually this is merely one of the functions for which it is used. For linking the computer to the telephone lines there must be a modem. This is a device that turns the digital signals produced by the computer into frequencies that can be sent down the telephone line attached to a carrier wave. Signals received from the remote system require this wave to be stripped off by the modem so that the original digital one can be used by the computer. The wiring of the connections between the computer and the modem has to be accurately completed, the RS423 socket being normally used.

The modem is a circuit board that can be in a separate box or plugged as a card inside the computer. External boxes usually need a separate mains source to provide the power, but internal cards are powered from that provided to the computer. Portable computers can make use of acoustic couplers, devices into which the handset of a telephone may be inserted, but these suffer from interference from external noise. Increasingly, such computers are provided with inbuilt modems and a cable for insertion into the telephone socket.

Most modems are increasingly standardized in their design to meet the Hayes protocols for linking to the telephone line and conversing between two computers, devised by a commercial company but now widely accepted as universal standards. 'Smart' modems identify and operate directly from the computer, offering automatic dialling of the numbers selected and undertaking the appropriate signals to the remote computer without involving the user, also invariably providing an automatic answering facility. Some are able to adjust the baud rate (the speed at which data are transferred between the interconnected computers) as needed. 'Dumb' modems, on the other hand, require the user to dial the number, press the buttons to link the computers, and send the initializing signals to commence the conversation between them. These can form part of a program, but the user has to control it.

The standards for the different baud rates have been determined and agreed by the CCITT (International Telegraph and Telephone Consultative Committee). Modems are divided by the baud rates they offer: V21 means 300 baud in each direction; V22 means 1,200 baud in each direction; V22bis means 2,400 baud in each direction; V23 means receiving at 1,200 baud but sending at 75 baud. V42 offers variable baud rate standards, error correction and data compression, but it is subject to enhancements and products that do not support every facility. The ISO adopts the CCITT standards, although the different committees may be working on the same topic at the same time. The baud rate speed has a significant effect on the time of the connection and also the appearance of the rate of response to the user's questions. Trends are naturally towards increasing the speed as much as possible.

Another important factor in increasing speed is the compression of the data. The more this is done, the less that is sent between the computers and the quicker the response is. Much work has taken place in France on this, and a telephone (Numeris) capable of transmitting 500Kb in a minute, a page of A4 in 5 seconds or scanning 200 pictures in 3 minutes, is now available. Such speeds reduce the time of interconnection and therefore significantly affect the costs.

Communicating with the remote computer with its information store can be done directly by calling the distant number and then ensuring that the modems link and the computers converse. Over long distances or in another country, this can be an expensive process. An alternative is to have a direct line laid between the two computers; again, this is very expensive in itself but it may be relatively cheap if there is a great deal of traffic between them. In this case the modems are linked directly to the outlet to the line, the so-called pad. More inexpensive to use is the Package Switched Service (PSS), or the international one (IPSS) if the remote computer is in another country. The user does not notice the change between the two systems. The basic charge is the cost of the call to the PSS system, which in most parts of industrialized countries is only a local telephone call away.

To use the PSS systems, the users have to provide an identification number (NUI — Network User Identification) relating to themselves. Many remote systems supply these to regular users as part of their service, but if not they can be purchased. The PSS service also needs to know the address of the remote computer being contacted (NUA — Network User Address) so that it can ensure the data go to the right place. Naturally, this is supplied by the remote computer service. If the link crosses national boundaries, the IPSS network is automatically used. It should be noted that the NUI is a national number, and therefore cannot be used when linking directly into another country's PSS system. This problem can be overcome by ringing directly into the PSS of the home country by an overseas call. Alternatively, a temporary NUI can be obtained during visits to individual countries overseas.

Dialogue between the user's computer and the remote information store depends on the form of the software that the user is operating to maintain the connection. Most programs available for communications offer facilities ranging from a simple conversation of questions and answers to the more complex exchange of files, also usually undertaken with simplicity from the user's point of view. Any connection usually requires the use of passwords of some sort to validate the user's right to access the system and also perhaps to locate personal areas of the remote computer.

Detailed descriptions of the way in which various communications packages are used are outside the scope of this book, in particular because they are dependent on the software being used. Various protocols are commonly available to provide facilities that extend beyond a simple conversation, probably using the ASCII code. X modem, Y modem and Kermit are file interchange systems that require similar facilities on the other computer to effect an exchange, and the details of their operation should be in the guide with the software. The range of options can include turning the user's computer into a form that behaves like (emulates) other terminals − that is, providing the keyboard with a range of codes for various keys that enhance the interaction that is possible − but if the user is in any doubt, the teletype emulation is usually applicable to all systems.

When the dialogue commences, the messages from the other computer may arrive as a series of separate pages − like the Prestel system − or as a continuous scroll of information, usually temporarily held at a screenful but at a single keypress moving on to the next, like BLAISE. Both may be downloaded into the user's local store or disc, and then scrutinized later after the telephone connection has been terminated. This is advisable, where possible, as it reduces the costs. Such collections of information should be carefully filed and labelled on the disc in order that they can be found again.

There are increasing numbers of these databases available for access. One useful connection is to electronic mail (email), which is a mechanism for swiftly exchanging messages with other users of the same system. The one most widely used internationally is Dialcom, which has users in an increasing number of countries. Gateways are available through the system to databases that provide air timetables, financial news, economic information etc.; Dialcom is not just an email operation. The standard X400 protocol that is being implemented will provide users with the facility of being able to send and receive fax and telex through the mailbox, so the different communication systems are gradually converging. Access to electronic mail requires the use of a password that is under the user's selection and control. It is advisable to choose an unusual code and change it regularly to ensure the security of the mailbox.

This trend in email to bring together the various communications options through one system is mirrored in the access to major databases. Various agencies have attempted to provide a 'one-stop shop', so that users can enter their system with a need and be guided to the major database where the answers may be held. For many users, such a service is of no added value as they are content with a particular database for most of their needs, but for others the increasing range available makes it possible to obtain information for a wide variety of requirements. Using good agencies that can sort and funnel needs to the right selection of databases can be a significant asset.

For most users, interaction with a remote database includes a dialogue which helps to narrow the problem to a particular group of pieces of information, and then these are downloaded into the local computer. Eliminating or at least reducing the expensive first part of this operation is an important goal.

Information exchange software is just such a tool. With this system, the user enters the areas of interest on the system, prepared before a connection is made, and the 'headlines' of the relevant material are downloaded. These are examined off-line, and the most interesting are highlighted. Returning on-line, the remote computer reads the list of highlighted items and sends them to the user's machine *en masse*. Off-line again, the user has plenty of time to peruse and edit to find the relevant areas.

Much of these developments are concerned with limiting the time during which the user is connected to the computer with the information store. Costs are levied on the user in a number of ways. For all, there is the telephone line charge, the PSS or IPSS charge if that system is used, and any telephone facility charge that might be levied. Other charges vary with the system being used. Some rely on an annual subscription only; some charge per minute of access time; some charge for computer contact time; some charge for the quantity of data moved; some charge for combinations of these.

Further developments are the full digitization of the telephone network, perhaps supported by a cable network. The arrival of such facilities will take some years, although limited interconnections for specific organizations may be available earlier. Digital networks will increase the speed of data transfer and provide further options and facilities to users.

EQUIPMENT CARE AND MAINTENANCE

If equipment is to give maximum performance for as long a time as possible, a system of regular maintenance is essential. The frequency of this will naturally depend on use, but as a rule of thumb, there should be weekly checks, monthly cleans and yearly inspections. The last operation should be done by qualified engineers. The comments that follow refer to the first two operations only.

In all aspects of care and maintenance, attention should be paid to the manufacturer's instructions, and the operating manual is an important reference point. For instance, the exact replacement type for lamps must be identified. Differences between the connectors of the lamp to carriers reduce the potential for mistakes, but it is possible to make errors by putting low voltage lamps into high voltage machines. The method of access to lamps varies between models; the operating manual should describe how this is done. On no account should lamps be changed or the inside of equipment investigated without the mains power being switched off and the equipment being unplugged.

Care of plugs
Plugs carrying mains electricity to equipment can be a major safety hazard. Physical damage is commonly caused by careless use, and they should be regularly checked for cracks, chips or breaks. It is also necessary to ensure that the cable emerging from the plug is correctly held by the gripper device, as this can become loosened if users pull plugs from sockets by tugging on the cable.

Care of lenses
All lenses and other glass surfaces in equipment are carefully and accurately positioned, so dismantling for cleaning purposes should be done only if there is no other means of access.

The biggest problems are dust and grease from fingers. Scratches cannot be eliminated, and if they interfere with effective viewing the lens or glass will have to be replaced. Many modern lenses are made of plastic and if they are rubbed with a cloth there is a chance that electrostatic currents will be created which appear to 'glue' the dust to the surface. Basic cleaning should consist of wiping surfaces with lint-free tissues or an anti-static cloth, which can be obtained from opticians.

If grease is present, breathing on the surface and wiping with a tissue or cloth may be sufficient to remove it. Should this not work, a small amount of spirit may be wiped over the area, but it is important to be careful not to allow this to touch glued joints as it may act as a solvent. On no account should dirt be scraped off a lens or glass as this can cause the surface to become scratched.

If access to the lens is so limited that a tissue or cloth cannot be used to reach it, a soft brush may be used, particularly if it is linked with a puffer to blow the dust off the surface.

Care of apertures

When film is being projected, the edges of the frame are defined by the edge of the aperture as well as by the boundaries around the picture. These are found particularly in cine projectors but also occur in some filmstrip and slide projectors. As many cinema goers will have noticed, bits of hair and apparently even cobwebs sometimes seem to hang from the top of the picture. These are attached to the bottom of the aperture in the gate (remember the aperture, like the picture, is inverted on the screen), and they move in the convection currents caused by the heat of the lamp.

Access to the apertures is gained by moving the projection lens out or swinging it to one side. A stiff brush should be used to clean around the edges.

Oiling

Most modern equipment has its mechanical parts permanently lubricated in sealed joints so that there is little need for oiling. However, some operating manuals indicate points where light oil is required. Depending on the amount of use, it is unlikely that lubrication need be done more frequently than every six months. Oil and any other lubricant must be kept away from all glass or film surfaces.

Care of heads

These delicate pieces of ferrite collect dust and deposits from the magnetic coating of the tape. They accumulate and prevent close contact, so regular cleaning is essential. At the same time, the capstan spindle and pinch wheel should be cleaned.

Abrasive tape cassettes can be purchased for use with audio and videocassette recorders and can be quite effective, particularly for heads. A weekly playthrough with these tapes can keep the quality of replay high. The use of videocassettes by themselves is an effective cleaner and may well be all that is needed.

General cleaning of videocassette recorders is better left to engineers, an annual maintenance operation usually being sufficient.

Care of styli
The stylus on a record player wears away and therefore needs replacement from time to time. In the case of magnetic cartridges, it is usual for the whole cartridge to be changed, but in ceramic cartridges only the stylus itself needs to be replaced.

In its travels along the grooves of the disc, the stylus picks up dust and also pieces of plastic which should be removed. Dust can be prevented by keeping the vinyl discs themselves clean with an anti-static cloth or a dust brush.

Liquids are available for cleaning the stylus. A small amount is placed on a brush, which is carefully drawn over the stylus tip. The liquid helps to loosen the material attached to the stylus and the brush clears it away. This is a delicate part of the equipment and the treatment should be gentle. Do not finger the stylus as grease will then be deposited and that will pick up more dust.

Care of headphones, microphones etc.
These require no special treatment to maintain mechanical and electrical quality, but they can transfer disease-causing organisms between users. Careful use of disinfectant over those parts of headphones which touch the ears and other handled parts will help to prevent cross-infections occurring. Microphone surfaces may be carefully wiped with cloths impregnated with disinfectant, but aerosol sprays are not recommended.

Care of optical storage discs
In general, these are strong materials that need little attention. However, accumulations of grease and dust on the surface can interfere with the laser beams and it is wise to remove them occasionally. Liquids are available for wiping over the surface to do this, many being incorporated into special devices. The important point is to wipe them from the centre towards the edge (radially) and not in a circular direction as the latter just moves the dirt to another section.

Care of television screens
The electrostatic attraction of dust to screens can be very powerful, and

screens should be regularly cleaned. Dusty surfaces prevent clear vision and intensify eye strain. Aerosol sprays and impregnated cloths are available to wipe over the viewing surfaces.

Care of computers

These machines are rugged and any maintenance usually has to be undertaken by a qualified engineer. As with all electrical equipment, care should be taken to keep liquids away from the circuit boards. If accidents do occur, they should be dealt with by engineers. Users can assist by keeping the outside surfaces dusted and keyboards lightly brushed, making sure that they are covered when not in use.

Fuses

Equipment sometimes carries an internal fuse, and all mains equipment should also be fused at the plug or socket. The fuses used should be correct for the power supply for the equipment; the correct rating is normally indicated by the manufacturer. As a rough guide, the following ratings may be used if no other instructions are given. They apply only to 220−50 voltage mains:

- 3 amp fuse: radio, audio and videotape recorders, record players, computers, all projectors with a lamp rating less than 500 watts.
- 5 amp fuse: television sets, all projectors with a lamp rating between 500 and 1,000 watts.
- 13 amp fuse: all other equipment.

Fuses which are built into equipment are of two types, replaceable and reinsertable. The replaceable variety can be removed and changed, and are usually similar in design to those used in mains plugs. Reinsertable fuses disengage from the circuit when they 'blow', and may be pushed back in when the fault has been rectified.

Major electrical faults and damage which cause fuses to blow will require the intervention of an engineer. However, a lamp failing in normal use is quite likely to break the fuse; therefore after a new lamp has been inserted it may be necessary to change the fuse as well.

MANUAL OF PRACTICE

In this section, each type of format and equipment is introduced to explain the operations required for viewing and/or listening. Because models vary, the detail of the instructions can only be limited, but the principles are the same in all cases. The operating manual that is supplied with the equipment should give further details. A list of sockets and controls that are commonly found is given with a simple explanation of their use.

Filmstrip projectors

1 Identify the format of the filmstrip. Is it single or double frame (pages 74−5)?

2 Check whether the projector is suitable for that format (pages 105−6).

3 Check that the lens is appropriate for the screen and distance. If there is only one lens, check if there is a mains source for the projector within the distance from which it will have to project. An extension lead may be necessary.

4 Detach the filmstrip carrier from the projector.

5 Place it on the table so that the side which is to be towards the screen faces downwards.

6 Locate the end of the trailer of the filmstrip and find the last two frames.

7 Look at the frames and orient the strip until they are arranged as you wish to see them on the screen.

8 Now turn the strip until the bottom left-hand corner of that picture is in the top right-hand viewing position (see figure 18).

9 Keeping the filmstrip in that position: in the case of the single-frame filmstrip, move the carrier so that it is vertical and attach the end to the upper spool; in the case of the double-frame filmstrip, move the carrier so that it is horizontal and attach the end to the left-hand spool.

10 Turning the spool holder clockwise, wind the strip on to it until the beginning is located.

11 Open the frame holder and pull the strip through until the first picture is at the centre.

12 Attach the beginning of the leader on to the front spool or spools.

13 If the spools carry cogs to locate in the sprocket holes, ensure that they do.

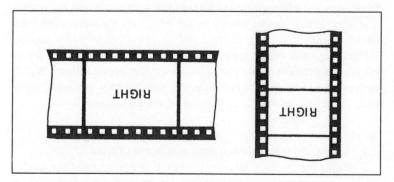

Figure 18. Double- and single-frame filmstrips oriented for projection

14 Close the frame holder.

15 Check that the aperture is correct for the filmstrip. A cover or gates may have to be inserted, removed, opened or closed.

16 Reattach the carrier to the projector, ensuring orientation as in 9 is maintained.

17 Attach the mains lead to the power source, point the projector at the screen, switch on and if necessary switch on the power on the projector.

18 Focus, usually by turning the outside of the lens.

19 To wind on frame by frame, turn the lower (single-frame) or right (double-frame) spool anti-clockwise.

20 On completion of viewing, rewind. Then detach the filmstrip from the spools and return it to the container.

The foregoing applies to a projector used with a front projection screen or with a rear projection screen with a mirror in between. If it is projected directly on to a rear projection screen, the following changes in the procedure apply:

5 Place the carrier on the table, the screen side uppermost.

9 Keeping the filmstrip in that position; in the case of the single-frame filmstrip, move the carrier so that it is vertical and insert the end of the filmstrip to the upper spool; in the case of the double-frame filmstrip, attach the end of strip to the left-hand spool.

19 To turn the double strip, wind on to the left-hand spool as you face the screen.

Slide projectors
For convenience of loading, slides should be 'spotted'. To do this, place

the slide on the table oriented in the way you wish to see it on the screen. The spot should now be placed on the mount on the bottom left-hand corner (figure 19).

In all projectors using front projection screens or rear projection screens via mirror, the slide is inserted in such a way that it enters the light path between the lamp and the lens oriented with the spot in the top right-hand corner as viewed from the rear of the projector.

To set up the projector

1   Locate the mains power point which is to be used.

2   From the distance between projector and screen and the size of the screen, select the appropriate lens (if necessary, see figure 12 on page 102–3).

3   If there is only one lens, check whether it is possible to locate the projector at an appropriate distance, with an extension lead if necessary.

4   Place the projector on a stand and adjust the screen to correct distortions. To check this accurately, insert a test slide and focus. The horizontal level of the projector is also normally adjustable by turning or lowering the feet.

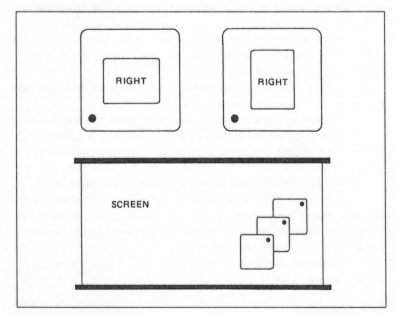

Figure 19. Slides with spots

To insert slides

  1 The slide carrier is usually one of three types:

  (a) A side-to-side carrier (see figure 20.1) used with manual projectors.

  (b) A straight tray (see figure 20.2) used with semi- and fully-automatic projectors. These vary in the degree to which they are enclosed, and usually take up to 36 slides. A circular tray which is held in the vertical is a possible substitute as it carries up to 80 slides.

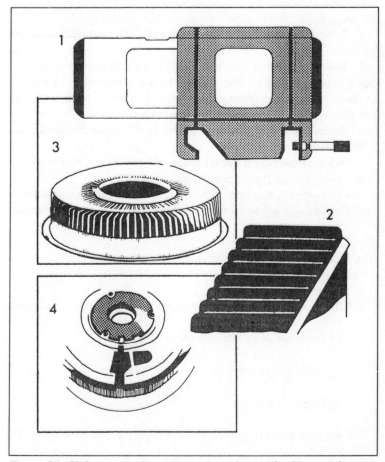

Figure 20. Slide carriers/magazines: 1 = side to side; 2 = straight tray; 3 = circular magazine for gravity feed; 4 = bottom plate of above magazine in correct place for loading

(c) A circular tray is used horizontally (see figure 20.3) with fully automatic projectors. Before loading, check that the rotating plate underneath is locked in the right position (see figure 20.4).

2   Slides should be inserted with the spot on the top right-hand corner.

(a) Attach carrier to projector and insert slide.

(b) Load the tray and push it into position.

(c) Load the tray and place it firmly on the projector, aligning the slot on the tray with the red spot on the projector.

To project

1   Switch on mains supply and if necessary the power switch on the projector.

2   Introduce the first slide into the light path. In manual projectors, this is done by sliding it across, in semi-automatic projectors, by pushing in the lever; in automatic projectors, press the forward button either on the projector or on the remote control device.

3   Focus by rotating the lens holder in its carrier or turning the appropriate control.

4   When removing the carrier at the end of viewing, ensure that all slides are removed from the light path.

In a rear projection system without a mirror, the slide is inserted with the spot top right as you face the projector and away from the screen.

Controls

The following controls are sometimes found on projectors:

(a) On/off for mains power.

(b) Focus control.

(c) Brightness high or low. Always use low-level lighting if acceptable as this increases the lamp life. This control may be a switch or an exchange of an external attachment.

   -◯- sign means low.

   ⌖◯⌖ sign means high.

(d) Reverse in order to return automatically to the previous slide.

   ⬇ is the usual sign.

(e) Forward in order to move automatically on to the next slide.

⬆ is the sign.

Ⓤ is seen also, the outside arrow indicating that not only is this the forward control, but it also releases the change action so that the tray can be moved freely either to a new position or off the projector.

Microform readers
1 Before viewing, check that the magnification from the lenses available is appropriate to the reduction ratio of the microfilm.
2 Check that the reader is plugged into the mains supply, which is switched on. If there is a mains power switch on the reader, this should be switched on after the microfilm has been fixed to the equipment.

Roll-film readers
3 (a) Open reel readers. The spool of film is normally attached to the left-hand holder, the loose end is pulled through the gate and attached to the right-hand spool. Because of the extensive variations between different readers in the arrangement of prisms and mirrors, the orientation of the film spool cannot be generally stated. If there is no indication on the reader, then trial and error is the only technique.
  (b) Cartridge. The cartridge is normally attached as shown on the reader to the left-hand side, and the film is either hand led or wound through the gate in the light path to be attached to the open spool on the right side.
  (c) Cassette. The cassette must be suitable for the reader. Placing the cassette on the reader is usually an obvious procedure, two spindles sticking up to receive the container. The film channel is on the side farthest from the user. The upper surface is usually either marked with arrows, a label or an impressed word in the case, or it is clear because the cassette can be placed on the reader only one way round.
4 Turn on the mains power.
5 Focus by turning the lens or adjusting the control marked accordingly.
6 To move frames:
(a) A crank may be attached temporarily or permanently to each reel for hand turning.

(b) A single crank in the front or at the side of the reader through gears turns both reels simultaneously.

(c) A motorized drive turns the reels mechanically at a varying speed.

Microfiche readers

3   If there is a tray, open it — usually by pulling it towards you. In some models, the tray has to be opened by winding it out or using a lever.

4   Insert the fiche. Place the fiche on the bottom of the open tray; the eye-legible heading is commonly on the user's side, but it may face upwards or downwards depending on the mirror system. If there is no tray, the fiche may be inserted with or without a plastic carrier in a slot. It is almost invariably inserted with the eye-legible heading downwards.

5   Identify the frame to be viewed, perhaps using the contents list on the first or last frame.

6   Guide the fiche into position by using the grid system or, in its absence, by trial and error.

7   Adjust the focus by turning the lens or the external control.

Controls

The following controls are sometimes found on readers:

(a) Image rotation to change the orientation of the frame.

(b) Lens change, which may be a lever.

(c) Roll film scan to raise or lower the frame.

(d) Tilt adjustment, which may adjust the front legs of the reader to tilt it for a more acceptable viewing angle. This may only change the angle of the screen.

(e) The working of the print operation on a reader-printer should be determined from the manual or instructions on the equipment.

Cine projectors

Open spool projectors

1   Select the position for the projector with relation to the mains power supply, the size of the screen and the lens available.

2   Attach to the mains power supply.

3   Fix the spool to the front reel holder, the loose length of film hanging from the front (screen-side) edge of the spool. The sprocket holes on a sound film should be on the right when looking towards the screen.

4   To lace the projector:

(a) Manual lacing: Open the covers to the sprocket drive wheels, and move aside the lens. Follow the path indicated on the projector, ensuring that there are loops above and below the channel behind the lens. Attach to the take-up reel and close the covers to the drive wheels and lens.

(b) Channel lacing: Open the channel, usually by a lever. Thread the film through the channel, attaching the end to the take-up reel. Close the channel.

(c) Self or automatic threading: Trim the end of the film using the attached clipper. Turn on the power to the motor drive and feed into the first sprocket drive channel. When sufficient leader emerges from the end of threading channel, stop the motor and attach to the take-up reel.

5   Check that claws are engaging the sprocket holes at the gate by turning 'inching' or 'animation' control. The film should move up and down the channel.

6   Plug in the external loudspeaker, if required, to the socket marked. Place the speaker in a suitable position.

7   Turn on the motor and lamp into forward movement. As the film is projected, adjust the focus by turning the lens holder or an external control. Adjust the height by raising or lowering the legs at the front of the projector.

8   Turn on the amplifier and adjust the sound volume to a suitable level.

9   Rewind the film by switching to stop and then rewinding or reversing. Stop when no. 3 appears projected. Switch off the amplifier, lamp and motor in that order.

10   To project for viewers, switch on the amplifier first, then the motor, then the lamp.

11   At the end of viewing, rewind the film back on to the original delivery reel. To do this, the film should have been completely driven through the projector. Turn off the amplifier, lamp and motor. Attach the loose end of the film directly to the front reel, passing on the projector side of it. Engage the rewind gear by the marked control and switch on reverse.

Controls

The following controls and sockets may be present on the projector:

(a) Forward (with motor) causes the film to pass through the projection path without light. Forward with lamp causes the lamp to illuminate the projector.

(b) Reverse (with motor) causes the film to pass backwards through the projection path without light. Reverse with lamp causes the lamp to illuminate the backward projection.

(c) Rewind causes a gear to be engaged to increase the motor speed. This should be used only when the film is out of the projection path, and should be disengaged when rewinding is complete.

(d) Still frame causes projection to stop with a single picture illuminated. It may be necessary to turn the inching (animation) control to move the shutter to let light pass. Refocusing may be needed.

(e) Framing control moves the position of the aperture to cover black frame lines which may be visible.

(f) Inching (animation) causes the film to be wound manually through the projection path for the inspection of individual frames.

(g) External speaker (◁) is the socket to which an extension speaker may be attached.

(h) Microphone (◯) is the socket into which a microphone may be inserted for voice-over commentary. Before doing this, the impedances should be checked.

(i) Bright/low adjusts the light output from the projector lamp.

(j) Opt/mag control selects the appropriate sound reproduction method.

(k) Volume, treble and bass control the amplifier and the quality of sound.

Soundtape recorders/players

Recorders/players may be battery or mains operated. Recorders/players may contain their own amplifier and speaker or require equipment to be added to provide these. Appropriate parts should be attached if necessary. Turn on the mains supply and the power switch on the recorder/player. Set the odometer to zero if it is to be used.

Cassette equipment

1   Open the cassette compartment. Various methods may be used. A lid may be lifted, a control pressed (possible markings: 'cassette', 'eject') to reveal a slot, or a slot may be apparent.

2   Insert the cassette into the compartment. Usually the side to be played is uppermost. The tape should be towards the heads. If inserted into a slot, the cassette usually clicks into position. A cassette carrier

may have to be pressed down into position.

3   Turn the volume control to the estimated level.

4   Switch on 'play'.

5   Modify volume, treble and bass controls as necessary. There may be separate controls for different tracks if stereo is being played.

6   At the end of playing, switch 'stop'. This may be the first pressure of the control marked 'eject'.

7   The cassette may be removed at this point or rewound by pressing the appropriate control. Removal may be a reverse of the operations in 1, although an 'eject' control is likely to be present to release the cassette partially.

Controls

The following controls or sockets may be present on the recorder/player:

(a) Play (▶).

(b) Fast forward (▶▶) causes the tape to move at speed in a forward direction.

(c) Rewind (◀◀) causes the tape to move at speed in a reverse direction. The odometer should operate accurately with both this and fast forward.

(d) Pause (▮) causes the tape to stop and hold the position. If it is used during recording, there should be no audible sound made.

(e) Record (a red mark or colour is standard) changes the mode of the recorder.

(f) Channel means track, both for selection of one being played and volume.

(g) Microphone (◯) refers both to a socket for plugging in and to the controls for the level of recording.

(h) External speaker (◁) is the socket(s) for the connection of this equipment.

(i) Headphones, headset (◯) is the socket for the connection of this equipment.

(j) Aux, gram or other equivalent words indicate sockets into which other equipment is plugged for recording on tape.

(k) CrO_2 (chromium dioxide) is the control which must be operated when this type of tape is being used in cassette recorders. Increasingly, this is recognized automatically by the equipment.

(l) Restart is used particularly if the tape pause cue tone has caused the cassette to stop. This will also restart the machine after it has been stopped by the assigned control.

Tape-slide equipment

Some of this equipment is supplied with the tape recorder, synchronizing device and the slide projector already connected; in that case, start at stage 4.

1   Check the mains supply is in an appropriate place, and insert the plug. In the case of multiple equipment, two or three power sources may be required or a multiaccess socket may be used.

2   Link the synchronizing device to the tape recorder and slide projector. Access to the tape recorder will be indicated as it must be a specially made machine, while the plug to the projector is to the remote control socket.

3   Load the slides and insert the tape.

4   Check that the synchronizing device is in the playback mode. As 'red' almost always refers to record, this colour should not be indicated.

5   Turn on the mains power on each part of the system.

6   Insert the first slide into the projector and focus. According to the recommended standard, the first cue tone on the tape should change first to the second slide. However, in some programmes the producers have used it to introduce the first slide; users should be aware of this.

7   Adjust the volume on the tape recorder to an estimate of the appropriate volume. In most programmes, the first slide is accompanied by introductory information or music so that final adjustment can be made then.

8   Play the tape. If the programme is to be used by one or two users only, headphones should be inserted first.

Controls

The controls found on this equipment are the same as those on separate tape recorders and slide projectors, listed earlier. Synchronizing devices have a control to select record or playback but rarely any other. On a few machines, it is possible to select the appropriate relays to recognize the different standards of cue tones (see page 123) and therefore to choose the one used with a particular programme.

Videocassette recorders/players

1   Place the television set and videocassette recorder in a suitable position so that there is no danger of their being knocked over. The mains supply should be at an appropriate distance, usually two separate sockets or a multiaccess junction box being necessary.

2   Link the player and the set together. This may be direct to the aerial input on the set, a video out to the video in socket, or a SCART connector

to a SCART connector. Note that a separate audio connection may be necessary if video sockets are being used.

3 If live viewing of a broadcast is to be available as well, the videocassette recorder has to be attached to a good aerial. The recorder then has to be tuned to the required channel(s).

4 Switch on the power on the recorder and the set. Select the video or audiovisual channel on the television set.

5 Load the cassette into the recorder. Check that there is no tape left in by pressing 'eject' or observing the visual indicator. Press the cassette into the loading slot, with the tape cover at the front and the label uppermost, and it will be automatically pulled into the machine.

6 If the tape is to be used from the beginning, if index points are to be employed or the position of starting identified using the odometer, press 'rewind'. If the tape will not rewind any further, set the odometer to zero. Now press 'fast forward' until the tape halts at the required index point or press 'stop' at the correct odometer reading.

7 Adjust the volume level on the set to an estimated level, and similarly adjust any tone (base/treble) controls.

8 Press 'play'. There will be a pause while the tape is partially withdrawn from the cassette and wound round the heads.

9 Further searching for particular sections may be undertaken by pressing 'search', 'fast forward' or 'rewind'. The picture will be seen passing at speed while the control is held until the user reaches the required point.

10 When viewing has been completed, press 'stop' on the recorder. The set may be switched off. There will be a pause while the tape is withdrawn from the heads and placed back in the cassette container. The cassette may be withdrawn with the tape positioned at the point when viewing ceased or rewound to the beginning. For the latter, press 'rewind', and do this after each stoppage until the odometer does not go down any more. This is because the tape will stop at the beginning of each recording, which may not be the same point as the beginning of the tape. Now press 'eject' and the tape will appear from the slot for replacement in its box.

Controls

Most controls are also present on remote hand-sets which signal the machine, usually by infra-red. These are repeated on the videocassette machine itself, together with additional items. The commonest are the following:

(a) Play is the control for forward (▶).

(b) Fast forward causes the tape to move forward at speed (▶▶).

(c) Rewind causes the tape to be rewound on the delivery spool (◀◀).

(d) Stop causes the programme and the tape to stop.

(e) Eject causes the tape to be slid through the door.

(f) Still causes the tape to stop with a still picture shown (■). In so-called digital machines, this is done electronically and therefore the tape is not being rubbed against the heads at the time. In non-digital machines, rubbing against the heads occurs and the tape may be damaged if the position is held for longer than about ten minutes.

(g) Record causes a programme on the assigned channel to be recorded. Usually this has to be applied at the same time as the play control. An instant record control is often present, and this causes the machine to record for a preset period of time.

(h) Timer switches the machine to record according to the user-determined time points. Details of assigning these are specific to machines, but usually include the need to indicate tape speed (standard or long play), day, time of start, time of end, channel and number of recording.

(i) Index switches the machine to recognize index points that have been marked on separate recordings.

(j) Edit and audio dub relate to altering recordings and are outside the scope of this book.

Record players

1   Place in an appropriate position for the mains power. If the equipment is a turntable deck only, it requires an amplifier and speakers, which must be attached.

2   Inspect the disc to identify the speed, and select that on the player.

3   Place the disc on the turntable and switch on the power supply.

4   Adjust the volume and tone controls to appropriate levels. If the amplifier and disc offer stereo reproduction, also adjust the balance control to obtain the best levels between the speakers. These may be adjusted during replay.

5   Lift the arm, either manually or by a control.

6   Move the arm over the disc to the point immediately above the place where the user wishes the replay to start. The turntable should now be turning.

7   Lower the arm either manually or by a control.

8   At the end of play, the arm returns to its rest, which causes the turntable to stop. Alternatively, the user may interrupt the continuous replay by lifting the arm off, either manually or by a control.

Controls
  (a) Reject is used to stop a replay at any time. The stylus is lifted and returned to its rest.
  (b) The speed selector, usually giving an alternative between 33⅓ and 45 rpm, should be operated only when the turntable is stationary.
  (c) Arm lift (▼) and arm lower (▼).
  (d) Graded control for the arm weight, which is located at the rear end of the arm, should be adjusted to the manufacturer's recommendations, usually with a measuring device under the cartridge.
  (e) Balance for stereo channels alters the relative volumes between the left and right speakers.

Microcomputers

A basic computer set consists of a keyboard and processing unit, a backing store such as a disc drive and a television screen. Other items are peripherals. Because of the rapid technical development over the last few years, users will meet basic sets that are separated in different combinations, some requiring mains power for each item, some for just one from which it is passed to the others. The instructions below set out to describe a general position, but there will be variations that users will meet.

Note that, with the exception of some 5-pin DIN (round) plugs, all connectors associated with computers can be inserted in only one way. Provided they have been properly wired by the manufacturers, there is no possibility of causing damage. Usually, too, plugs can be inserted into only one socket and therefore mistakes at this level are unlikely. Where they are present, screws should be used to hold plugs firmly in sockets.

1   Connect the keyboard to the processing unit and disc drive. Attach this unit to the video display unit (television set), preferably using SCART plugs and sockets (if provided). Connect the audio outputs to the amplifier through auxiliary or external sockets, if required.

2   Connect any additional peripheral devices to the processing unit. These may include a printer (to the serial or parallel printer socket, as appropriate), modem (to the RS232 or 423 socket), CD-ROM drive (to the RS232 socket, if external) and external hard disc system (to its own socket).

3 Connect all items that have mains leads to the power supply and switch on. Normally there are also switches for power on the processing unit, the visual display unit, the CD-ROM drive and the printer. They may also be present on the disc drive and modem. All these items usually have a light that glows when power is being provided, so this is a further check to show that the supply has been switched on.

4 If a program from a disc is required, insert it into a drive and shut the door. If a CD-ROM is to be used, press the load control and a lid will lift or a drawer will slide open so that the disc can be inserted and the system closed.

5 The method of starting a program is dependent on the operating system of the computer and the functions within the software. No general statements can be made.

6 On completing use of the computer, ascertain the policy for the machine. Some institutions arrange for computers to be permanently on, but others require them to be switched off at the machine and also at the mains power supply. Remember to switch off all items which you switched on. Before doing this, however, remove any floppy discs by opening the door on the drive, and 'park' by program control any hard disc that has been in use.

Controls

In general, the keyboard or other input device such as a mouse or tracker ball provides all the controls to operate the equipment and the software. Instructions should be obtained from manuals accompanying the software or from any information provided on the screen as the program is used. These arrangements are specific to the operating system and the program, so generalizations cannot be made.

Controls are provided on printers and on some modems and other peripheral equipment, and users should refer to their instruction manuals to understand their uses.

CD audio

1 Connect the CD audio player to an amplifier, if this is not part of the system, using the audio out leads to external line socket. This is sometimes marked as CD.

2 Connect to the mains power and switch on. Switch on the power on the CD player. At this point, on most machines, a light will glow.

3 Press the open or close or eject control to open the drawer. Insert the disc in the circular depression, the label side uppermost – the laser

beam comes from below. Close the drawer, usually by using the control but sometimes by just pushing it shut.

4   Adjust the volume and tone controls to a suitable level. These may be on the amplifier or on the player.

5   A display will normally indicate the number of tracks on the disc and the time length. Either press the play control or select the track by the appropriate system. This varies between machines, sometimes offering a number or time pad, sometimes a track select which moves the number along singly or in jumps (skip control). When the appropriate point is reached, press the play control and the machine will play.

6   The machine will stop playing at the end of the disc or at a preprogrammed point. It will also stop when the stop control is pressed.

7   Remove the disc by opening the drawer as in stage 3 above.

8   Turn off the power on the player and at the mains.

Controls
On many players, remote control hand-sets operating through infra-red signals are now available and most controls are repeated on them. Those most frequently found on the player itself are listed below, but additional ones are frequently introduced.

(a) Open/close/eject opens and closes the drawer for inserting the disc.
(b) Play causes the laser beam to read the chosen area of the disc.
(c) Stop stops the playing of the disc at that point.
(d) Pause pauses play at that point. Pressing play restarts at the same position.
(e) Fast forward moves the display rapidly forward to a later track or time. The skip control accelerates this, for example moving forward five tracks at a time.
(f) Rewind moves the display rapidly back to an earlier track or time. The skip control operates in this direction as well.
(g) Search (given various names) causes sampling of a few seconds of each track, or plays track at speed to help identify a point. May be used independently or linked with another control, such as fast forward or rewind.
(h) Programme allows the user to select a sequence of tracks from one disc in personal order. Several programmes may be prepared. It may make use of a store (or memory) control to hold the sequence in memory.

(i) Repeat causes a single track or a programme to be repeated individually or as a whole.

(j) Index (or several other types of control) causes the display to reveal information about the track being played, the time elapsed, the time left on a track and the programme sequence.

Laserdiscs

1   Connect the laserdisc player to the mains supply. Use the video out socket to a video in on the television set, or aerial (RF) out to the aerial socket on the set, or the SCART plug interconnection between the player and set. If computer control is required, the connection is either between the computer input socket on the player to RS232 on the computer or a socket on the genlock board, or a SCART plug interconnection directly between the computer and player or indirectly through a special link box. Audio output sockets can be connected separately to the set or to an external hi-fi system.

2   Switch on the mains power supply to all devices and also the power controls on each one. The indicator lamps should light.

3   Insert the disc, the label on the side to be used uppermost. The data it refers to are actually recorded on the other side, as the laser operates from below. Use the open/close or eject control to open the drawer or unlock the liftable cover.

4   Press the play control and the disc will replay. If computer control is required, control of the player's facilities will be through the computer keyboard.

5   Use various call and index controls to move the display faster, select a time point or a frame or a sequence; use rewind or reverse controls to move backwards through the information.

6   Press stop to cease play.

7   Press open/close or eject to retrieve the disc and return it to storage.

8   Switch off the power controls on all devices used and also the mains power supply.

Controls

Most players are supplied with remote hand-sets that use infra-red beams to control the use of the disc. Alternatively, the control may be through the computer keyboard. The following are the principal controls which may be found on both the player and the hand-set, or on one of them only.

(a) Power switches on the mains power.

(b) Open/close or eject opens and closes the drawer or releases the lid to permit loading of the disc.

(c) Play replays the disc.

(d) Pause holds the picture and sound at a certain point.

(e) Stop stops the replay.

(f) Fast forward shows pictures at between three and eight times the normal pace.

(g) Rewind or reverse shows pictures at between three and eight times the normal pace in a backwards direction.

(h) Scan is similar to fast forward and rewind, depending on the direction chosen, but at a slower speed.

(i) Still/step moves the replay one picture at a time in either direction.

(j) Channel selects one of the two or both channels of sound to be on or off.

(k) Index places the frame number on the screen display.

(l) Search, in conjunction with a number pad, selects an individual frame or chapter. Sometimes a mode control is used to identify whether the number selected is for a page or a chapter.

Part 4

THE USER AND THE MATERIALS

INTRODUCTION

So far, our consideration of the user of NBM and the materials themselves has focused on them as separate entities, identifying needs and characteristics. Bringing them together within the library raises a number of issues, which are the subject of this part.

First, the librarian has to acquire the materials. This involves, amongst other problems, identifying various sources of supply. Having acquired them, consideration has to be given to cataloguing, classification and indexing so that the user can find what he or she needs from the collection. A manual of practice is introduced after this section to give clear guidance on procedure. Making materials available also means that the librarian has to store them, and this is dealt with later in this part. Finally, the issue of copyright is discussed because some users may wish to obtain duplicates. The legal constraints on copying NBM are not the same as those for books.

ACQUISITION OF MATERIAL

A library is often judged on the quality and quantity of its stock. Indeed, librarians often complain that their collections are assessed by what they do not have, rather than by what is on the shelves. A professional librarian should have the expertise to be able to create a collection of materials that will satisfy the diverse requirements of most clients. Part of this expertise lies in the knowledge of the current bibliographic organization of NBM. (No attempt is made here to establish methods of assessing the needs of library clients.)

The pattern to be adopted is as follows; each step is described in detail in this chapter:

1 Identify what exists.
2 Decide by means of evaluative tools what to preview.
3 Obtain the documents.
4 Preview.
5 Decide what to purchase or hire.
6 Consider the need to let clients know the reasons for selection or rejection of documents.
7 If the materials to match the need do not exist, consider producing the material within the library.

Before following this pattern, it will be necessary to consider the problems hampering acquisitions. These may be traced to those deriving from publishers or those from distributors, or they may be problems resulting from a lack of bibliographic control.

Publishers

In Part 2 the complexity of the production of NBM was mentioned and publishers of them were considered in their national, local, institutional and individual aspects. It is extremely difficult to obtain statistics about the number of companies producing NBM for sale or hire. Some indication of the complexity may be gained from the brief survey that follows.

Film production can be divided into two main parts: the 'theatrical' cinema, which shows mainly 35mm film; and the 'non-theatrical' area of 16mm and videorecordings. The 'non-theatrical' is the major interest here. It includes feature films, cartoons, documentaries and training and

183

educational films. These are usually distributed for hire or sale through film and video libraries. These films may be produced by film giants such as Disney, industrial companies such as British Petroleum, broadcasting institutions such as the BBC and organizations such as embassies and professional associations. There may be limitations on who can use them and where they may be shown; some of these are a result of local booking conditions, copyright, company policies and medical restrictions. A similar pattern may be perceived in relation to videorecordings. However, the distribution pattern for videorecordings also involves many smaller outlets, for example garages and local bookshops as well as high street video shops.

Similarly, the production of sound recordings can be divided into two main parts: the commercial record and cassette industry, and semi-commercial institutions. The former is extremely well organized by large companies such as EMI and CBS. Current output is controlled in a similar pattern to that for book publishing by trade publications such as the *Music master* catalogue. The semi-commercial side is not so well organized. It includes institutions such as the Institution of Civil Engineers, industrial companies such as Tarmac PLC, and commercial concerns like the Bradford and Bingley Building Society.

The publishing of microcomputer software is very diverse. Commercial provision includes book publishers such as Longman and Thomas Nelson, traditional computer companies such as Microsoft and Logica and specialist companies such as Eyetech. Colleges and schools have produced software that has gained national recognition; examples are Lancaster University, Teesside Polytechnic and Jordanhill College of Education.

This software may be bought direct or through local specialist distributors. Retail outlets include high street computer shops and bookshops. However, materials are also distributed through telecommunications, for example MICRONET 800. Public domain software can be accessed via bulletin board systems such as Compulink.

The publishing pattern of other NBM is more diverse. It is impossible to impose a coherent structure in this area. There are a number of commercial companies which produce NBM and some, such as the Slide Centre, have established large lists. Industrial companies have also produced materials; examples are British Gas, the National Coal Board and ICI. There has often been close cooperation between the commercial companies and other bodies to produce an item. Thus the Engineering Industry Training Board produced open-learning packages on engineering design by employing the varied skills of the BBC, the Universities of

Cambridge and Southampton, the Open University and Cranfield Institute of Technology and by using case studies provided by leading engineering companies. Professional associations have also contributed in this area, for example the Institute of Supervisory Management and PIRA. Book publishers have also become involved, among them the Longman Group, Macmillan and Routledge.

On a local scale, the picture becomes even more complicated. Local producers of NBM are perhaps most prolific within the education sector. The largest producer in the UK is probably the Open University. NBM devised originally for its students has roused such interest from other institutions that its sound tapes and films have now been made available to any purchaser. Open University Educational Enterprises has been established as a publishing firm to market Open University publications and also other educational materials.

However, it is productions made within individual institutions that perhaps best illustrate the difficulties. All sectors of education from primary schools to polytechnics have produced materials designed initially for their own internal students. A notable example is Newcastle upon Tyne Polytechnic Products Ltd, which includes books, periodicals, videorecordings and microcomputer software among its output. There is always the possibility that these may be valuable in other institutions, and there is no single method of publicizing such material. Some areas have established area resource organizations which have produced locally inspired material and sold it to local schools. A few of these, such as AUCBE (Advisory Unit for Computer Based Education), are now selling to the national market.

Art galleries and museums are also major producers, specifically of slides, postcards and posters of their exhibits. Again, some of these have realized the potential value of a wider market and have arranged national distribution. The National Portrait Gallery's London slide sets, for example, are distributed through the Slide Centre.

There are also commercial producers who have concentrated on their local market, producing, for example, slides of local views; and some public libraries have produced a great many valuable publications in the local history field.

Distributors

Many of these producers also distribute their own materials, and this can cause problems for the librarian who is used to dealing with one or two library book suppliers. There is no equivalent in this field to the bookshops, although some NBM such as portfolios and other items published by book firms may be obtained from them. The major supplier of a comprehensive service is T. C. Farries and Co. Ltd of Dumfries. There are well-established library suppliers for sound recordings, such as the Long Playing Record Library which will provide discs, CDs and cassettes. The Slide Centre has established its position as a distributor of filmstrips and slides produced by a number of other companies as well as of its own productions.

Chivers, the library book suppliers, also provide videorecordings to libraries. Videorecordings and motion pictures can be obtained from film libraries. There are over 150 film libraries and each has its own catalogue and distribution system. The Video Gallery offers a comprehensive collection of educational, sporting and entertainment videos for libraries. There is a catalogue of 1,200 videos, a facility for tracing videos and an update service. Book publishers such as Andre Deutsch also distribute video story tapes.

The librarian used to obtaining books on approval will find more difficulty with NBM. The fragility of some materials has caused a few publishers to insist on the library paying for any material which is damaged during preview. The dishonesty of some librarians, who have copied the material and returned the original, has resulted in some distributors refusing to supply material on approval. Indeed, some small publishers will supply material only after payment and not in response to an order alone. As one remarked privately, 'Why should we give you an interest-free loan?' The problems associated with piracy of computer programs have resulted in many commercial providers refusing to supply these on approval. They will, however, often allow the library to make one copy for security purposes.

Bibliographic control
The diversity of production and distribution agencies creates problems for the librarian in identifying materials available, and this is further aggravated by the absence of any one bibliographic tool to cater for all the current output. It is as well to remember that there are many more book publishers and book publications than publishers and publications in the field of NBM, but books enjoy an established and comprehensive distribution network. A single work, *Whitaker's British books in print*, enables the librarian in the UK to identify a majority of the book publishers' output. This work currently lists 448,814 titles from more than 13,137 publishers, and copes with 600,000 amendments each year;

the microfiche and CD-ROM editions update this information monthly. The *British national bibliography* enables the librarian to establish the existence of the great majority of books published since 1950 via an author, title, series and subject approach, and is also available via online computer access and CD-ROM.

However, the equivalent of these works does not exist for NBM, and information about these materials is usually dependent upon the publishers' own publicity systems. As has already been pointed out, there is no legal requirement for the deposit of NBM at the British Library or anywhere else, and so it is difficult to establish a British national NBM bibliography. Of NBM, film is perhaps the best organized, with the *British national film and video catalogue*, although even this does not include the complete film output of the UK.

At a national level, the most exciting development has been the *British catalogue of audiovisual materials*. This resulted from the British Library/Inner London Education Authority Learning Materials Recording Study and was published in 1979 with a supplement in 1980. It included the more common types of audiovisual materials, but excluded 16mm films, videorecordings and musical sound recordings. Approximately 60 records arise from direct reporting by publishers of information on their products. This, unfortunately, is now a closed file although the data are still available on BLAISE-LINE, its AVMARC database. For school materials, NERIS (National Educational Resources Information Service) is currently providing a partial service, particularly in the field of computer software.

In summary, while there is an excellent bibliographic system for published books and a well-tried distribution network, there is no system for NBM, merely hundreds of separate publishers' catalogues and lists. The librarian faced with this requires perseverance, luck and an occasional prayer!

The steps in acquiring materials, which were identified at the beginning of this section, will now be followed. The first three are: identifying available material, evaluating from printed sources and obtaining documents. These will be considered together under the heading of bibliographic organizations. Although bibliographic organizations and tools are listed separately below, there is a considerable overlap between them. The following outline does not attempt to list all the sources of help available but it points out a general pattern and some of the major examples.

BIBLIOGRAPHIC ORGANIZATIONS

This section describes a range of organizations that a librarian may look to for help and advice. It is not a complete listing. For further details, a useful source of information is the *International yearbook of educational and instructional technology 1989*, London, Kogan Page, 1989.

British Library
Any librarian in the United Kingdom would almost certainly first turn to the British Library for information concerning bibliographic organization. The British Library is empowered to take a central role in NBM organization. It funded fundamental research in this area, but its achievements have been patchy. Unlike its USA counterpart, the Library of Congress, its prime mission of 'library of last resort' has not embraced convincingly the wide range of NBM. Certainly there are no complete national collections of photographs, films, posters etc. However it has been an important catalyst for a number of developments: its services are pioneering the use of the newer formats; it has the largest sound recording collection in the UK in the National Sound Archive; and it supports databases of audiovisual materials in AVMARC and HELPIS, which are available through BLAISELINE.

British Library Research and Development Department
The main purpose of the department is 'to provide financial support for research and development projects relating to information problems (including library-related problems)'. It is giving priority in the period 1989—94 to a number of programme areas, including 'Research into the applications and implications of information technology, including electronic publishing and library automation' and 'Educational research concerned with the whole process of finding, using and communicating information, especially work in the further education sector and work relating to the new curriculum such as the GCSE'.[1]

As a result of the encouragement given and funds supplied by this department, there is a much sounder intellectual grasp of the role of NBM in libraries. Thus it has supported research into young people's reading habits and their use of audiovisual and computer materials, particularly in public libraries; funded a conference on the electronic campus; provided grants for studies of desk-top publishing trends and CD-ROMs in school libraries; and published Graham P. Cornish's work, *Archival collections of non-book material: a listing and brief description of major national collections* (1986).

Document Supply Centre

The Document Supply Centre does not supply NBM other than microfilm. However, it has been active in using the new technologies, for example compact discs for storage and retrieval. It has also been conscious of its duty in supporting the exploration of the issue of the interlending of audiovisual materials. A member of its staff, Graham Cornish, acts as secretary to the working party on audiovisual materials and has been active in promoting the compilation of regional directories of audiovisual collections. He notes that 'the working party are at last having some success in creating a better awareness of AV materials and improving the general attitude to interlending and AV'.[2]

National Sound Archive

In 1983 the British Institute of Recorded Sound became part of the British Library. At last a major collection of audiovisual material was the responsibility of the British Library.

The main objective of the department is to preserve sound recordings of all kinds: music of all countries and periods, literature and drama, language and dialect, speeches and historical events, and wildlife sounds. The National Sound Archive, located at 29 Exhibition Road, London SW7 2AS, provides a free listening service by appointment. Total holdings are around 750,000 discs and 50,000 tapes, numerous documents, vintage gramophones, a unique collection of non-commercial cylinders and a video collection. The member record companies of the British Phonographic Industry ensure that it receives two copies of about 75% of all issues, including CD audio, as they are published.

The National Sound Archive is researching the life expectancy of various optical disc forms and offers a listening and viewing service free of charge, except to commercial users. This facility is also available at the Document Supply Centre, Boston Spa.

Of particular value is its *Directory of recorded sound resources in the United Kingdom* (British Library, 1989), which lists 480 holdings including libraries, museums, archives, county record offices, local radio stations, learned societies, recording groups and private individuals. It has a regional and subject approach.

National Discography Ltd
The British Library has actively encouraged the development of the
National Sound Archive and, in particular, the creation of a database
of its acquisitions. In partnership with the Mechanical Copyright
Protection Society it has established National Discography Ltd with the
brief to 'create a database of very detailed information on all recordings
that are or have been commercially available in the UK, theoretically
going back to the very beginning of recorded sound'.[3] It should be
available as an external service in 1990.

Council for Educational Technology (CET)
This has had a chequered history since it was founded in 1967 (as the
National Council for Educational Technology) with a policy to advance
the practice and theory of educational technology. While its concern
necessarily lies with the educational sector, in undertaking the task of
gathering and disseminating information on all aspects of NBM it has
funded research into their bibliographic organization. Notable early
publications in this area included: L. A. Gilbert and J. Wright's *Non-
book materials cataloguing rules* (NCET with the LA 1973; also known
as the LA/NCET rules); and O. Fairfax, J. Durham and W. Wilson's
*Audio-visual materials: development of a national cataloguing and
information network* (CET, 1976; working paper no. 12).

The *British catalogue of audiovisual materials* was produced in
collaboration with the British Library. The organization has funded
considerable work on the use of online information and also on
microcomputers in libraries. This includes J. A. Gilman's *Information
technology and the school library resource centre* (CET, 1983). The
council's involvement with 'user specification', copyright and a variety
of bibliographies is mentioned elsewhere. Further information about it
can be obtained from the journal *CET news*.

Its counterpart, the Scottish Council for Educational Technology
(Dowanhill, 74 Victoria Crescent Road, Glasgow G12 9JN) – which
incorporates the Scottish Central Film and Video Library – should also
be noted; its services include a software preview service. It has an
excellent information and bibliographic service on NBM and their
equipment, and produces open-learning packages.

Microelectronics Education Support Unit (MESU)
This is now part of the CET. Its role is to encourage curriculum work
in schools and promote and spread good use of microelectronics and

computers in education. It is based at Unit 6, Sir William Lyons Road, Science Park, University of Warwick, Coventry CV4 7EZ. It provides a central information service which includes a library of books, periodicals, teaching materials, audiovisual materials and software.

National Interactive Video Centre

This centre (24 Stephenson Way, London NW1 2HD) is supported by the Department of Trade and Industry and two manufacturers, Philips and Thorn EMI. It is an active information centre providing a collection of journals, books and topic files, and also manufacturers' brochures. It publishes *Interactive update*, a bimonthly journal covering all aspects of interactive technology in Britain and Europe. A register of research is also available for a contact and referral service. An important feature is a systems display area enabling clients of the Centre to see and use interactive video materials and equipment.

British Film Institute (BFI)

This is the major source of information concerning film in the UK. It was established in September 1933, 'to encourage the development of the art of the film, to promote its use as a record of contemporary life and manners, and to foster publication, appreciation and study of it from these points of view'. The development of television resulted in the Institute also deciding to 'foster study and appreciation of film for television generally, to encourage the best use of television'. However, while the majority of its services are still geared to demands for film, it is clear that television is a growing interest.

Anyone over the age of 16 may become a member or associate, and corporate membership is available to educational establishments and film societies. The National Film Theatre, on the South Bank, London, offers a wide range of programmes, has helped to establish a number of regional film theatres and runs the Museum of the Moving Image (MOMI).

The National Film Archive is the national collection of film, and tries to cover any film shown or programme transmitted in Great Britain. It has more than 102,000 titles, with some 14,000 viewing films, and three million still photographs; the latter can be duplicated for purchase. It adds some 1,500 recorded features each year. It also has a TV off-air recording scheme with ITV and Channel 4. Some 1,000 TV programmes are added each year, although its coverage of video materials is limited. The archive is developing a computer-based record-keeping system which will allow the production of computer-typeset catalogues. The first volume of the *National Film Archive catalogue, Non-fiction films*, was published in 1980. Its catalogue of stills, posters and designs was published in 1982, and its catalogue of viewing copies in 1985; those are also still available.

The Institute's Distribution and Non-Theatrical Programming Unit provides advisory and booking services for venues throughout the UK and coordinates films and TV drama on offer.

The Library Services provide an information and study centre for film and TV which is international in scope but has special relevance to the history and practice of British cinema and TV. The book collection, it is claimed, includes almost everything published in English on film and television. Other documents include scripts, current and extensive back runs of periodicals, press books, newspaper clippings and documentation relating to individuals. Its major publication is the *British national film and video catalogue* (BNFVC). This, published from 1963 onwards, is a quarterly record of British and foreign films available in Great Britain. Coverage of videorecordings began in the mid-1970s. There are two sequences, non-fiction titles and fiction. Features (covered by *Monthly film bulletin*) and newsreels have been excluded since 1969. It is classified by subject, with alphabetical indexes under subject and title, and a production index which includes distributors, actors, sponsors, technicians and production companies. In the 1987 edition, for the first time, a number of interactive video titles were included. It also publishes the *Guide to BFI Library Services resources*.

Subject catalogues include *Films and videograms for schools* and *Films and videograms for managers*.

The Stills, Posters and Designs Department has an extensive collection of stills, colour transparencies and sketches. The records have been computerized to produce a printout for the department's catalogue of stills, posters and designs. Other publications include *Sight and sound* (which is concerned with the aesthetic aspects of film) and *Monthly film bulletin* (which reviews all feature films and some shorts and gives basic information about the film: credits, plot synopsis and a critical assessment).

British Universities Film and Video Council
Founded in 1948, the Council exists to encourage the use, production and study of audiovisual media, materials and techniques for teaching and research in higher education. It aims to provide 'a forum for the exchange of information and opinion in this field'. The Council is based at 55 Greek Street, London W1V 5LR.

The Audio-Visual Reference Centre offers a unique preview and research facility for audiovisual materials produced in universities, polytechnics and other institutions of higher education. It runs an information service which consists of a small reference library, a file of appraisals on NBM for its members and an enquiry service. Its newsletter, *Viewfinder*, is published three times per year and gives details of new releases and information about conferences, publications etc. The Higher Education Film and Video Library makes available films and videorecordings on a non-profit-making basis.

The Slade Film History Register includes copies of all British newsreel issue sheets as well as information on collections of archive and television in the UK and overseas. A microfiche edition of the issue sheets is available for purchase.

Publications include *The BUFVC catalogue*, which is published annually in microfiche form. It lists 6,500 items, which include documentary and non-fiction films, videotapes, sound tapes, computer software, videodiscs and tape-slide programmes currently available in the UK. They have been appraised for use in degree-level teaching or research. The catalogue brings together two catalogues, *Audio-visual materials for higher education* and *HELPIS*. The database is also available through BLAISE-LINE. The *Researcher's guide to British film and television collections*, third edition (1989), is an invaluable directory to archival collections of film and television material.

Library of Congress

Compared with the British Library, this organization has produced a wealth of bibliographic tools, even though NBM do not have a very high priority in the overall objectives. However, the Library of Congress does have one of the largest collections of NBM in existence. It has some ten million prints and photographs, 250,000 reels of motion pictures, over one million sound recordings − from wax cylinders to CD audio − and over six million microform units and 80,000 posters. Its catalogues include *Motion pictures and filmstrips 1953−8, 1958−62* and *1968−72*. These exclude microfilm, and have been superseded by *Films and other materials for projection 1973−* (three quarterly issues per year, with annual and quinquennial cumulations), which now includes transparency and slide sets. This ceased in 1978 and has itself been superseded by *Audiovisual materials*. For earlier materials on film, information is supplied in K. R. Niver's *Early motion pictures: the paper print collection in the Library of Congress, 1897−1915* (1985). The Library of Congress has also produced *The George Kleine Collection of early motion pictures in the Library of Congress: a catalog* (1980). This lists approximately 3,000 films. The Library of Congress will supply prints of restored films.

Sound recordings are listed in *Music and phonorecords 1953–72*, which includes musical and non-musical sound recordings as well as libretti and books. It has been brought up to date by *Music: books on music and music recordings 1973–*, which includes Library of Congress printed cards and the cards of cooperating libraries. It has also published sound recordings of American poets and American music.

In 1977 the Library of Congress also established the Center for the Book to serve as a 'catalyst in focussing national attention on the importance of books, reading and the written word'. However, the Center does recognize the persuasive power of the media by cooperating with CBS Television in the programme 'Read more about it' and the ABC-TV cartoon character Capn O. G. Readmore!

Photographs of prints are catalogued by K. F. Beall in *American prints in the Library of Congress: a catalogue of the collection* (Library of Congress/Johns Hopkins Press, 1970), which contains entries for 12,000 prints from over 1,250 artists; and P. Vanderbilt in *Guide to the special collections of prints and photographs in the Library of Congress* (Library of Congress Reference Department, 1955).

National Information Center for Educational Media (NICEM)
As the result of research by the University of Southern California's Department of Cinema, this databank of computer records for a large range of NBM in the USA has been established at PO Box 40130, Albuquerque, New Mexico. It holds some 330,000 entries from 1964 to date and also has information on publishers and distributors. Indexes are supplied printed online as file 46 on DIALOG information service (AV-ONLINE) and on CD-ROM. The Center also publishes a number of source books; for example, *Science and computer literacy audiovisuals* (1986) and *Vocational and technical audiovisuals* (1986).

Library users can also use the databank as a cataloguing service by adding extra information to establish a personal catalogue of their holdings.

Educational Products Information Exchange (EPIE) Institute
A major source of information concerning NBM in education, the EPIE Institute (PO Box 839, Water Mill, New York) is an independent non-profit-making agency. Its services include an educational equipment

testing laboratory, information on the use of equipment, research into the selection and use of NBM in education, training programmes and a publications output. Its publications include *EPIEgram: materials*, which focuses on the needs of users of NBM materials; *EPIEgram: equipment*, which considers a wide variety of equipment; *MICROgram*, about educational software and computing; and *TESS* (The Educational Software Selector), a directory of software with 7,000 entries and 3,500 evaluation references.

Libraries
The pioneering work of librarians in NBM has resulted in the establishment of a number of collections that are excellent examples for those beginning in this field. A selection is given below. Case studies of libraries involved in NBM are regularly presented in the periodical *Audiovisual librarian.*

1 *Birmingham Public Libraries, Visual Aids Department* A loan service for illustrations, posters, wallcharts, slides and filmstrips. The Central Library also has a record and cassette library, art posters and art packs for schools, and special collections of Edwardian and Victorian photographs.

2 *Central London Polytechnic, Library Technology Centre* This was opened in 1982 with the principal aim of stimulating interest in the application of information technology among librarians and information professionals. It has been active in organizing seminars and demonstrations of library systems with particular emphasis on microcomputer applications.

3 *Centre for Information on Language Teaching and Research (CILTR)* (Regent's College, Inner Circle, Regent's Park, London NW1 4NS) Concerned with modern languages and their teaching. Has some 17,000 books and textbooks plus slides, videorecordings, software and recorded language teaching materials. Provides listening and viewing facilities. Its publications and library are of interest to all librarians, not just those concerned with modern languages.

4 *London Borough of Camden, Libraries and Art Departments* Have one of the largest audiovisual collections in a public library.

5 *Brighton Polytechnic* An integrated library and learning resources system. Library media services have a brief to purchase NBM; provide off-air recordings of radio and television programmes; provide information services on NBM; and analyse the effectiveness of NBM in teaching and learning.

6 *Newcastle City Libraries and Arts* Operate a picture loan service which is partly funded through Northern Arts. Around 250 prints are available, many by local artists.

7 *Wiltshire County Library, Children's Library Service* Supply 'information and inspiration in a variety of media: books, records, filmstrips, videorecordings, slides, wallcharts, tapes, models'. Also an exhibition stock, project collections and a circulation service of framed prints. Imaginative development of the potential of documents closely linked to their clients' needs.

8 *Gateshead Public Library* Leading exponent of the use of tele-communication for community information. Special scheme linked with local supermarket for the ordering of goods by old-age pensioners using library Prestel sets.

Vendors

Economic factors are important reasons for librarians to choose one or two reliable suppliers of library materials. Such suppliers are numerous for books — they readily supply material with library markings and stationery incorporated. There are a number of suppliers of sound recordings, for example Morley Audio Services (Elmfield Road, Morley, Leeds LS27 0NN), which offer specialist services for spoken word, language and music. In the field of slides and filmstrips, the Slide Centre are an invaluable source and their annual catalogue is an essential tool for the librarian. The firm of T. C. Farries & Co. Ltd (Irongray Road, Ochside, Dumfries) offer the major NBM service in the UK. They have produced the *AV catalogue*, which is arranged in Dewey classified order: Part 1 — Non-fiction — slides, filmstrips, audio and videocassettes, wall-charts and multimedia kits; Part 2 — Fiction — audio and videocassettes; and Part 3 — Educational computer software catalogue for Amstrad CPC 464, Amstrad disc, Archimedes, BBC, Commodore 64, Electron and Spectrum. Items are supplied in publisher's packaging, and library servicing is available. Vendors of this type are·more common in the USA with its larger market, and the annual publication *Audio video market place* (Bowker) gives many examples.

However, just as the library relies on bookshops as well as on library suppliers, so the librarian must be aware of the smaller firms supplying specialist services for the various forms of NBM. Some examples of these are: Mantra Publishing, which produces dual- and single-language multicultural picture books and cassettes for children and adults; Studio Two, for models of dinosaurs; Tavistock Videotapes, designed for a range of current approaches in counselling and effective communication and interaction; and CAA, for tape-slide programmes on architecture and building. Library videorecording suppliers include Chivers Ltd and Wynd-up Video. There are a number of general suppliers of computer materials who regularly advertise in computer periodicals such as *Personal computer world.*

Further details of suppliers are given in the printed sources section which follows, but the librarian involved in this area must be prepared to search through lists of distributors and advertisements in periodicals to obtain up-to-date details of the suppliers of specialist aspects of NBM.

Exhibitions
New developments in equipment, and the opportunity to see a wide range of NBM, make it essential to attend exhibitions. Local equipment suppliers regularly hold exhibitions, and at a national level there is a wide range: Visual and Audio International, the major exhibition for all types of audiovisual equipment and materials; the International BKSTS Conference and Exhibitions, organized by the British Kinematograph Sound and Television Society, which shows the latest developments in the full range of equipment and services; Photography at Work; BETT (British Education and Training Technology); and Personal Computer World Show, which is the major exhibition of microcomputers. Details of these exhibitions may be found in periodicals such as *Audiovisual librarian, Audio visual* and *Personal computer world.*

Personal contact
Close contact must be made with other librarians and specialists involved in this field, with experts from local radio and television stations and with local film and photographic societies. Area resource organizations enable libraries to share the problems of selection, and further details may be obtained through CET and their information officer. The information service of the Microelectronics Education Support Unit will also provide details of microcomputer experts within their region. In certain areas local self-help groups, such as NEMROC (North East Media Resources Organizing Committee), have produced directories which provide details of local experts and organizations in a variety of NBM. *Personal computer world* has a regular feature on computer clubs, such as the Church Computer User Group. However, it is to the professional associations that librarians will turn most readily for help and advice. In the UK, the Aslib Audiovisual Group, the Library Association

Audiovisual Group and the Library Association Information Technology Group have been most prominent in establishing workshops and conferences.

In the USA the American Library Association has established standards for resources through such bodies as the Audiovisual Committee of the Public Library Association.

PRINTED SOURCES

This section is divided into the following divisions: general, paper, still pictures, moving pictures, sound recordings, realia/specimens, micro-computing, optical storage systems, CD-ROM and videodiscs. There is some overlap between these, and reference should also be made to the sources available from the various bibliographic organizations which have been mentioned above. Both American and British printed sources are listed here, but it must be stressed that no attempt has been made to give a complete listing; these are only examples to explain a general pattern of searching.

General
A comprehensive listing of NBM via online computer databases is not available. AVMARC had the potential on BLAISELINE for such a listing but is no longer updated. AV-ONLINE on DIALOG is available for USA coverage. The National Educational Resources Information Service (NERIS), c/o Maryland College, Leighton Street, Woburn, Milton Keynes MK17 9JD is a database of teaching and learning resources as well as curriculum information and case studies. Its services are available to teachers and searches can be carried out on curriculum topics, including form and age level. The development of the OCLC service in the USA and UK offers the librarian, through the OCLC computer catalogue, access to over seven million records which include a high percentage of published NBM. However, the majority of these are of US origin. It is specialist online databases such as BUFVC and the National Discography which offer models for future development, but there still remains a particular deficiency in listing multimedia materials.

Particular reference should be made to the sources mentioned under the various organizations. The major guide to bibliographic sources is P. Liebscher's *Audiovisual librarianship: a select bibliography, 1965 – 1983 (Audiovisual librarian)*. It covers over 1,700 entries of books, pamphlets and periodical articles written in English since 1965, on all aspects of the librarianship of NBM. Supplements are carried in each number of *Audiovisual librarian* (1 – , 1973 –), a quarterly journal published jointly by the Library Association Audiovisual Group and the Aslib Audiovisual Group. It is an invaluable source of news of developments and reviews of books and NBM on the subject of audiovisual librarianship. It also contains news of microcomputer equipment and materials. Also note *Educational media catalogs on microfiche* (Olympic Media, 1986); and *Educational media and technology yearbook* (Libraries Unlimited), an annual publication which includes a 'mediagraphy' of print and non-print sources.

One of the pioneer works, by A. Croghan, is *A bibliographic system for non-book media: a description and list of works*, second edition (Coburgh, 1979). It is essential reading as an example of how to organize information sources in this field. The most useful general handbook is still J. Henderson and F. Humphreys's *Audiovisual and microcomputer handbook*, fourth edition (Kogan Page, 1984).

It is, of course, essential to use periodicals to keep up to date through the calendars of events they provide, and through their reviews of new NBM and equipment. *Audiovisual* (EMAP MacLaren, 1972–) is published monthly. It is a valuable source for new developments in equipment and NBM use in industry and commerce. Its annual supplement, known as the *Directory*, lists equipment manufacturers, production services and NBM publishers. Trade names are included. The *Times educational supplement* (Times Newspapers, 1910–) has a resources section, NBM and equipment reviews and articles relevant to current awareness.

Comprehensive printed listings do not really exist. The catalogues available listing all types of NBM do not have the complete coverage required. For material published after 1982 – i.e. after the final update of the *British catalogue of audiovisual materials* (British Library, 1979; plus the supplements of 1980 and 1983) – it is necessary to engage in tedious checking of published catalogues. Moreover, these sources are descriptive and the librarian must look elsewhere for evaluation. A useful source for this is *Media review digest* (Pierian Press, 1974–). It is an annual index to and a digest of reviews, evaluations and descriptions of NBM appearing in a variety of periodicals. Also note *Tech trends*, which has regular features on media and technology (Association for Educational Communications and Technology, 1956–). It contains reviews of bibliographic tools and describes new equipment.

Directories and yearbooks are invaluable sources for technical details and addresses of manufacturers, publishers and specialists, and for finding out about current work in the NBM field. The British librarian does not have access to a general NBM directory, and would benefit from the equivalent of *Audio video market place* (Bowker). This is annual and lists American and Canadian publishers of NBM, associations, equipment manufacturers, cataloguing services, library suppliers etc.

Publishers' catalogues are invaluable for a librarian who wants to have a complete coverage of NBM materials. Two of the most important are the ones from the following publishers.

1 The Drake Educational Associates Ltd (St Fagans Road, Fairwater, Cardiff CP5 3AE), who supply a wide variety of forms and their subjects. They are major producers whose output includes Educational Productions and Drake Educational Film; their catalogues are a necessity. Apart from their own material, they stock materials from a wide range of publishers.

2 Top Chart Educational, 23 Bath Street, Glasgow G2 1HU, who offer a wide range of NBM from publishers, including a number in North America. Particularly useful for audio language courses – their catalogue includes 82 languages in some 520 courses, such as those offered by Berlitz, Linguaphone and the BBC. They also provide educational audiovisual materials and computer software.

The Open University have developed an international reputation as a supplier of learning resources and their catalogues should be in most libraries. Open University Educational Enterprises, 12 Cofferidge Close, Stony Stratford, Milton Keynes MK11 1BY is the address for purchase of all Open University products.

Guides to publishers' catalogues do not provide complete coverage, and subject access is particularly difficult. A useful insight into the commercial audiovisual world is provided by J. M. Pemberton's *Policies of audiovisual producers and distributors: a handbook for acquisition personnel* (Scarecrow, 1984). There is also the *Educational media catalogs on microfiche* (Olympic Media, 1986), which is an American publication, and *Free stuff for kids*, seventh edition (Exley, 1988). An indispensable and dependable listing is *Distributors index* from the BUFVC, which lists 550 distributors of audiovisual materials within the UK. It is organized under subject headings, and each entry is annotated and includes addresses and telephone numbers.

Museums and art galleries are prolific publishers of NBM and there are two essential, but now dated, guides. The first is M. Roulstone's *The bibliography of museum and art gallery publications and audiovisual aids in Great Britain and Ireland* (Chadwyck-Healey, 1980), which contains more than 15,000 publications and audiovisual aids from over 1,000 museums and galleries. The majority of them are not listed in any other bibliography. NBM in this catalogue include posters, slides, films, discs, tapes, models and reproductions. Paul Wassermann has edited *Catalog of museum publications and media*, second edition (Gale, 1980), an index and directory of publications and audiovisuals available from US and Canadian museums and art galleries. Some updating is possible through *The newsletter of the Audiovisual Museums and Galleries Association*, which is an important listing of contacts in this field, and the *Museums and galleries in Great Britain and Ireland* (Reid, 1987).

There is no one comprehensive specialist subject source guide, though a wide range of tools is available, including the catalogues of specialist subject publishers and subject bibliographies. The British Universities Film and Video Council is perhaps the major supplier of such guides for higher education. An excellent example is O. Terris's *Twentieth century dramatists: A list of audiovisual materials available in the UK* (BUFVC, 1987). A further problem is the wealth of subject material that is unpublished, but available through exchange or special arrangements. General subject guides include the *Higher education learning programmes information service* (available from BUFVC). It lists multimedia produced by universities and polytechnics, to encourage the exchange of materials.

Specialist subject guides are numerous and include the following: O. Bates, *Food safety: an international source list of audiovisual material*, second edition (BLAT, 1987); I. Spring, *Media studies; materiography* (Jordan Hill College of Education, 1985); M. C. Jones, *Non-book teaching materials in the health sciences* (Gower, 1987). More esoteric audiovisual material is available from the International Bee Research Association (1985). Medical material is covered by the *Graves medical audiovisual library* (Holly House, 220 New London Road, Chelmsford, Essex CM2 9BJ). There is a catalogue for this postal service of medical and paramedical NBM. A regular newsletter is available for subscribers.

Specialist subject publishers include the following examples. The British Council, Design, Production and Publishing Department (65 Davies Street, London W1Y 2AA), promote cultural, educational and technical cooperation between Britain and other countries. As well as books they produce catalogues of exhibitions, for example the illustrated catalogue, *British Council collection 1983–84*, which contains more than 4,500 paintings, sculptures, drawings and graphics; tape-slide programmes, for example on British books and libraries, and microcomputers in schools; videorecordings, for example on the overhead projector; and sound cassettes, for example a series of interviews with leading British novelists and dramatists. The British Cement Association (Wexham Springs, Slough SL3 6PL) provide the *Catalogue of publications, slide sets and films*. This includes a wide range of material on construction, civil engineering and the built environment. The Royal Society of Chemistry Education Division (Burlington House, Piccadilly, London W1V 0BN) produce materials for chemistry education in schools, universities and polytechnics. Their chemistry cassettes present authoritative accounts of various aspects of chemistry, and are prepared and spoken by distinguished chemists.

The Historical Association (59a Kennington Park Road, London SE11 4JH) aim to stimulate public interest in all aspects of history. Their periodical, *Teaching history*, reviews NBM and has a regular evaluative guide to microcomputer software. The Welding Institute (Abington Hall, Abington, Cambridge CB1 6AL) produce books, computer software, slides, wallcharts, overhead projector transparencies, and film and video for students of welding technology. They also produce a news video, *The Welding Institute news video*.

Details of equipment may be obtained via the manufacturers' publicity material, the annual distribution lists and periodical advertisements. Directories and yearbooks will also give lists of equipment and their manufacturers' addresses. A general source is *Audiovisual and microcomputer handbook* (Kogan Page, 1984). It is designed to help both the expert and the beginner to find their way through the morass of conflicting information, advice and advertising which exists with regard to audiovisual equipment and services. It also lists software producers and distributors and training courses. In the USA the *Equipment directory of audio-visual, computer and video products* (International Communications Industries Association) is essential reading.

Criteria to judge equipment by may be obtained from standards and specification sources such as USPECS, from CET. Evaluation of equipment can be located in general periodicals such as *Audio visual* and in specialist periodicals for the various forms. Note also the services of the Educational Products Information Exchange in the USA.

The Consumers' Association also evaluates equipment in its periodical *Which?* (1952−). However, their reports should be treated with caution as they are judging for domestic rather than institutional usage. Whether a cassette tape recorder can survive a fall of 3ft on to a concrete floor is perhaps more important than the question of its control knobs being aesthetically pleasing!

Paper
Paper as a medium for NBM includes a wide range of forms − wallcharts, portfolios, posters, art reproductions, games, programmed

learning materials etc. There is no comprehensive source for the quest of this material. The series produced by M. C. Apple, *Illustrations index 1982—86* (Scarecrow Press, 1989), does not have an equivalent in the UK. Wallcharts, posters and art reproductions tend to overlap, and there are numerous shops selling these forms.

There are many publishers' catalogues, two examples being Lancaster Geography Poster (University of Lancaster, Lancaster LA1 4YB) which has a large display of material which reflects their name; and the Pictorial Charts Educational Trust, based at 27 Kirchen Road, London W13 0UD.

The general guides to art reproductions are somewhat out of date. An international listing of art reproductions comes from Unesco, *Catalogue of colour reproductions of paintings prior to 1860* (1980) and *Catalogue of reproductions of paintings, 1860—1979* (1981). These carry a small reproduction beside each entry, together with information on printer, publisher and price. There is also an index of artists, publishers and printers. A comprehensive source is *Art index* (H. W. Wilson, 1929—), which includes listings of reproductions in arts periodicals and museum publications. The National Gallery's *Postcard collection*, volume 2 (1989) and Stanley Gibbon's *Postcard catalogue* (1986) are useful for this particular format.

There are a number of suppliers of games. Cambridge Publishing Services Ltd (PO Box 62, Cambridge CB3 9NA) produce a wide range of geography games. The Society for the Advancement of Games and Simulation in Education and Training (Centre for Extension Studies, University of Technology, Loughborough, Leicestershire LE11 3TU) publishes a quarterly periodical, *Simulation/games for learning* (1971—), and members also receive *SAGSET news*, which includes current information and reviews of games, simulations and books.

Portfolios are numerous and the most famous publisher is Jonathan Cape with their Jackdaw Series (30 Bedford Square, London WC1B 3EL). Their form has been adopted by a number of producers.

Still pictures
These include photographs, slides, filmstrips, overhead projector transparencies and microforms. Many of the sources also include illustrations collections. There are a number of commercial picture libraries, the finest in the UK probably being the BBC Hulton Picture Library (35 Marylebone High Street, London W1M 4AA) which contains over six million photographs, drawings, prints etc. However, picture libraries charge for their services and anyone interested in using this form

is advised to look at H. P. Harrison's *Picture librarianship* (Library Association, 1981), and also to enquire into the service of the British Association of Picture Libraries and Agencies. D. N. Bradshaw and C. Hahn's *World photography sources* (Bowker, 1983) covers over 2,000 collections and indexes them alphabetically, geographically and via subject.

The major guide to British collections is J. Wall's *Directory of British photographic collections* (Royal Photographic Society, 1978), of which it is said, 'Every kind of photographic collection has been the subject of this enquiry . . . from the discovery of photography to the present day.' It is arranged by main subject, owner, location, title and photographer indexes. Also note R. Eakins, *Picture sources UK* (Macdonald, 1985), and, for the USA, E. H. Robl, *Picture sources 4* (Special Libraries Association, 1983).

One of the most useful publishers' catalogues for slides and filmstrips is that of the Slide Centre Ltd, 143 Chatham Road, London SW11 6SR.

The Francis Frith Photo Archive 1860 – 1970 is an unrivalled collection of photographs of cities, towns and villages in the British Isles. It is available in a 67-volume microfiche set of 300,000 photographs (from Charlton Road, Andover, Hampshire SP10 3LE).

Other publishers include JAS Educational Airphotos (26 Cross Street, Devon TQ13 8NZ), for stereo photographs of terrain and the urban environment; and Visual Publications, The Green, Northleach, Cheltenham GL54 3EX, who sell slides and integrated media kits. Two of Visual Publications' subject specialists are fine and applied arts and sciences, in particular earth sciences. The Women Artists Slide Library (Fulham Place, Bishops Avenue, London SW6 6EA) holds a reference library of slides, books, catalogues, theses, cuttings and posters of women in the visual arts.

Major slide library catalogues are those of the Design Council, whose *Slide library catalogue* (1973) is extremely dated; a new catalogue is still promised. The Council's aim is to encourage good design by photographing objects in its own collection which meet its criteria and also objects which it does not possess. The Crafts Council (12 Waterloo Place, Lower Regent Street, London SW1 4AU) runs a slide library and loan service with over 30,000 35mm colour slides featuring the work of leading craftspeople. Catalogues classified by craft are available. The Victoria and Albert Museum's National Art Slide Library has more than 500,000 slides listed in subject catalogues. The majority of catalogues are available on site only, but there are shorter listings available for borrowers.

Photographs are available from a number of firms, for example, the Photographers Gallery, 5 Great Newport Street, London WC2 7JA, where the stock includes the original work of photographers and postcards of Victorian photographs. Aerofilms Ltd, Gate Studios, Boreham Wood, Hertfordshire WD6 1EJ, publish the *Aerofilms book of aerial photographs*. It holds photographs from the Victorian age to date, but this firm specializes in aerial views from the 1920s to the present. Over 500,000 aerial photographs are for sale. Suppliers of overhead projector transparencies are listed in the *Audio visual and microcomputer handbook* and major publishers include Audiovisual Productions (Unit 3, School Hill Centre, Chepstow, Gwent), who cover a wide variety of subjects.

Cameras and projectors are reviewed in the general equipment sources. The specialist periodicals include the *British journal of photography* (Greenwood, 1860–). A specialist yearbook is the *British journal of photography annual* (Greenwood, 1964–), which includes a picture section, a feature section and a formulae section. *Visual resources* (Gordon and Breach) is also a valuable source of information on sources of slides, for example, sources for slides of medieval manuscripts.

Microform materials are covered by *Guide to microforms in print* (Meckler, 1989). Meckler is a major publisher of bibliographical tools for microform; its catalogue contains in excess of 125,000 titles. A companion volume is the *Subject guide to microforms in print* (1989). It includes 'monographs, journals, newspapers, government publications and different types of archival material'. The *Index to microform collections*, volume 2 (1988), is a time-saving guide to 50 collections.

Specialist periodicals include *Microform review*, January 1972–, a quarterly journal containing reviews and evaluations. There is also a *Cumulative index Vol. 1–10, 1972–1981* (Meckler). The National Centre for Information Media and Technology (CIMTECH) puts out *Information media and technology*, a journal of a national information service for the materials and equipment for micrography and reprography. It contains reviews and micrographic abstracts.

Specialist directories include *Microform market place* (Meckler, 1989), an international directory of micropublishing. It contains a full listing of organizations and their publishing programmes.

A current microfiche publishing programme of great value to media studies is that of Chadwyck-Healey Ltd, Cambridge Place, Cambridge CB2 1NR. This publishes the BBC Radio 9 o'clock news broadcasts, together with printed name and subject indexes, beginning from 1 January 1978. Subscription is annual. Other publications on microfiche from this firm include *BBC radio: author and title catalogues of transmitted drama, poetry and features 1923–1975* and *BBC television: author and title catalogues of transmitted drama and features 1936–1975*, together with a chronological list of plays transmitted. Its *New York theatre 1919–1961* contains over 26,000 photographs from the Vondaman Collection.

Equipment is evaluated in *Guide to microfilm production equipment* (G. G. Baker, 1984). This firm also produces a *Guide to microfilm readers and reader-printers*, fifth edition (G. G. Baker, 1986).

Moving pictures

The sources for this section have been divided into cinefilm and videorecording, although there is considerable overlap between the two and many cinefilms are also available as videorecordings. Bibliographic tools published by the British Film Institute, BUFC, Library of Congress and NICEM should also be consulted. One of the most important reference books is that produced by the American Film Institute, *Catalog of motion pictures; including feature films 1911–1930* (University of California Press, 1989). A guide to home videos in the USA is *Variety's complete home video directory* (Bowker, 1988), which lists 25,000 video titles in various subject areas.

Cinefilm

As far as cinefilm is concerned, there are numerous film hire libraries, but perhaps the major source for feature films is the British Film Institute's *Films on offer 1987/88*. This lists some 7,000 titles available from the BFI. It is complemented by the BFI *Film and video library* (1987), with which it alternates from year to year; and *Films and videograms for schools* (volume 1, 1983; volume 2, 1985), which lists over 1,500 films and videocassettes. Other major film libraries include CFL Vision (Wetherby, West Yorkshire LS23 7EX). This specializes in 16mm films and videocassettes produced or acquired by the Central Office of Information; these are distributed for non-profit showings. The catalogue includes general, educational and industrial material. CFL Vision also provide interactive videodisc courses and will hire out equipment outside a 50-mile radius of London. Concord Video and Film Council (201 Felixstowe Road, Ipswich, Suffolk IP3 9BJ), are specialists in films of controversy and concern, for example adoption, ecology, nuclear weapons and world poverty. Their catalogue lists over 2,500 titles, including videocassettes. Founded by members of the Society of Friends they also provide a distribution service for over 100 charities.

Glenbuck Films (Glenbuck Road, Surbiton, Surrey KT6 6BT) specialize in motion pictures and have a strong list of 4,000 titles. Guild Sound and Vision Ltd (6 Royce Road, Peterborough PE1 5YB), are probably the biggest commercial distributors of audiovisual educational programmes in the world outside the USA, and have a large film sale and hire business.

Companies which market their own films include BBC Enterprises (Room 503, Villiers House, The Broadway, Ealing, London W5 2PA). Their film and video output is available for purchase from that address. The hiring of BBC materials is through BBC Enterprises Limited Film Hire (6 Royce Road, Peterborough PE1 5YB). Video Arts (2nd Floor, Dumbarton House, 68 Oxford Street, London W1N 9LA) offer 16mm film and videocassettes); they distribute amusing but practical films on management problems. Free videos and films can often be obtained from embassies; for example, Canada House Film and Video Library (Trafalgar Square, London SW1Y 5BJ) lists some 900 titles covering all aspects of Canadian life. Educational institutions also produce videos, for example City of London Polytechnic Media Services Department (Calcutta House, 10 Old Castle Street, London E1 7NT). Esoteric subjects are readily available on videos; an example is *Masterstrokes*, on creating specialist paint finishes such as marbling, by Oakart Ltd (5 Frederick Mews, Kinnerton Street, London SW18 8EQ).

A number of industrial concerns also distribute films, for example Shell Film Library (Unit 2, Cornwell Works, Cornwell Avenue, Finchley, London N3 1LD). They make films available on loan to commercial and industrial firms, educational institutions, public libraries, film societies, scientific, technical and cultural societies, international institutions and, in fact, organizations of all kinds. The British Telecom Education Service (PO Box 10, Wetherby, West Yorkshire LS2 3EL) produce films on all aspects of communication, including satellite technology.

There are a number of subject guides, for example *Health films and videos* (BMA/BLITHE Film Library, 1988), which contains for each item a synopsis, details of intended audience, copyright holder and an independent review. *Circles catalogues* (Women's Film and Distributor's Ltd, 113 Roman Road, London E2 0HU) reviews more than 150 films and videos on women's film-making. The US *Educational film video locator* (Bowker, 1986) lists more than 48,000 films and provides a subject and audience level index. A number of periodicals on video are now available, for example *Newsbrief* (BBC, 1988–) and *Library video magazine* (American Library Association, 1986–).

Specialist periodicals include *Monthly film bulletin* (British Film Institute, 1934 –), which reviews feature films and shorts. It includes credits, a synopsis of the plot and an evaluation. *Screen digest* (Screen Digest Ltd, 1971 –) gives 'monthly news, summaries and intelligence' on cinefilm, television and videorecording. There are regular background supplements including videocassette systems, industrial films and cable television.

Equipment for cinefilm and videorecordings is evaluated in the general equipment sources and the specialist periodicals.

Videorecordings
Comprehensive guides to videorecordings are available. Many deal only with the entertainment aspect of the format. A more general source is The Video Gallery (1 Church Street, Douglas, Isle of Man), which lists new releases and back issues under detailed subject headings and includes fiction and non-fiction videos. *Which video* (Argus) evaluates equipment and software. Educational Media International (25 Boileau Road, London W5 3AL) produces detailed catalogues on a number of subjects, for example education and training, health and safety etc. The loose-leaf handbook *Video production techniques* (London, Longman, 1989), is an important updating service for the video producer. Berger and Tims (7 Bresenden Place, London SW1E 5DE) produce a catalogue of non-fiction videos available for purchase that have been cleared for home viewing rights.

It is important to remember that cinefilm and videorecordings are increasingly being listed in the same bibliographic tools and therefore references under cinefilms should also be considered.

Newsreel Access Systems (150 East 58th Street, 35th Floor, New York) has produced a CD-ROM database of details of 130,000 newsreels (made between 1894 and 1987) held in archives around the world.

Videodiscs are a newer source and bibliographic tools are starting to appear. Note Sears' *Video discs: a history and discography* (Greenwood Press, 1981). The first general guide is *Internationale Bildplatten Katalog* which lists some 1,000 titles; it is published by Schule Schone (Markgrafenstrasse 11, D1000 Berlin 61, Germany).

Sound recordings
The bibliographic sources for musical recordings are relatively well organized compared with other NBM, although there is no comprehensive retrospective discography for LP records. It is the non-musical recording

that presents perhaps the greatest problem. The reference tools published
by the Library of Congress, NICEM and BUFVC should be consulted.
The indispensable retrospective listing for recorded music, compiled by
F. F. Clough and G. J. Cuming is *The world's encyclopedia of recorded
music* (WERM) (Sidgwick and Jackson, 1952; second supplement, 1953;
third supplement, 1957). This work covers all electrically recorded music
up to 1953. There is no comprehensive listing for non-musical recordings
although a useful source is *Spoken word and miscellaneous catalogue*,
published annually by *The gramophone*. *The new Penguin guide to
compact discs and cassettes* (Penguin, 1988) is an indispensable source
for creating a new record collection. It evaluates over 3,500 classical
music recordings. Its counterpart for popular music sound recordings
is the *New rock record* (Blandford Press, 1981), which lists some 35,000
LPs. *Words on tape: an international guide to the audio cassette market*
(Meckler, 1989) identifies over 20,000 spoken word sound tapes. A wide
range of publishers' catalogues is available, some describing only tapes
or records or CD audio, while other firms are now publishing all these
forms. Popular music has a trade list: *Music master* (John Humphries,
1974 –). This is an all-industry master record catalogue of popular
records, tapes and CD audio.

  Subject specialist publications and publishers include the following.
Argo spoken word (Decca Classics, PO Box 2JH, 52 – 4 Maddox Street,
London W1A 2JH) offers a wide range of the spoken word, including
all the plays of Shakespeare (with the Marlowe Dramatic Society). Audio
Learning International (740 Holloway Road, London N19 3JF) have a
large range of subject cassettes. Seminar Cassettes (218 Sussex Gardens,
London W2 3UD) produce discussion tapes, for example on current
controversies. Sussex Tapes Ltd (Townsend, Poulshot, Devizes,
Wiltshire SN10 1SD) originally published recordings of debates between
notable academics, particularly for undergraduates, but have broadened
their range to include GCSE material, for example a course on the
appreciation of classical music. There has been a growth in audio books,
usually in an abridged version, but a number of publishers specialize
in whole-book versions, for example ISIS Audio Books (55 St Thomas
Street, Oxford OX1 1JG); and Serengeti Records (43A Old Woking
Road, West Byfleet, Surrey KT14 6LG) which specializes in African
and Asian music on CD audio.

  There are periodicals in sound cassette form, for example *Personnel
training bulletin* (Didasko, Didasko House, Wennington, Huntingdon,
Cambridgeshire PE17 2LX). Many local radio stations have been active

in establishing tape archives, for example BBC Radio Newcastle has a *Catalogue* (1982) of its tapes. Details of local radio archives can be found in *Directory of recorded sound resources* (British Library, 1989).

Reviews of recordings and equipment can be located in the specialist periodicals. *The gramophone* (General Gramophone Publications, 1923 –) is a monthly periodical which reviews new classical records, CD audio and cassette releases. Its *Classical catalogue* (1953 –) comes out quarterly, and lists LP records and tapes currently available in the UK. The *Spoken word catalogue* is annual, and indexes documentary, children's, foreign languages, instructional and sound effects publications. This and its CD audio catalogue are available on microfiche. *Schwan record and tape guide* is an American publication for currently available records and tapes and the same publishers have also introduced the *Schwan compact disc catalog* listing some 8,000 discs on 450 different labels. *Q* (EMAP Metro, 1986 –) reviews rock music and provides invaluable retrospectives.

Guidance on equipment can be obtained from specialist periodicals and yearbooks such as *Hi-fi news and record review* (Link House, 1970 –), which has articles on how to select equipment, and lists recordings of the year. There is also an information section on sound equipment, and a directory of brand names, makers and suppliers. A more specialist guide is *Dial electrical/electronics* (Dial Industry, 1988), which identifies products and services by product type, supplier type and company name.

Realia/specimens

Given tenacity, a scale model of almost anything can be located. Plastic model kits can be purchased from many manufacturers, notably, in the UK, from Airfix Ltd. There are no comprehensive reference sources for suppliers in the UK, but diligent attention to advertisements in periodicals can prove fruitful. The following publishers are given as examples. Educational and Scientific Plastics Ltd (Worthing Road, East Preston, Rustington, Sussex), specialize in models of the anatomy, skeleton etc. CL Rexroth Ltd (Cromwell Road, St Neots, Huntingdon, Cambridgeshire) produce sectional engineering models and other NBM. Griffin and George (Bishop Meadow Road, Loughborough, Leicestershire LE11 0RG) also produce moulded models and cut-out card models. Studio Two Educational (6 High Street, Barkway, Royston, Hertfordshire SG8 8EE) provide a wide range of NBM, but of particular interest are their plastic kits and cardboard replicas of prehistoric animals and Egyptian artefacts.

Some museums also supply models; for example, the British Museum produces (amongst many other items) a cut-out model of the king's helmet from the Sutton Hoo ship burial.

Microcomputing

The librarian who has to acquire microcomputer software does not have an easy task. The bibliographic control of this format has yet to be established and it is difficult to identify sources of information which are accurate and unbiased. The wide range of equipment and of computing languages exacerbates the problems of acquisition.

The increased demand for software has resulted in the rapid growth of suppliers and the wise librarian will exercise caution in the evaluation of software and choice of supplier. The decision of the library to standardize on a particular microcomputer or a limited range of microcomputers should be influenced by the software that is available or likely to be published. Software is the major cost in the use of microcomputers.

A number of institutional bodies have been established to offer advice in this area. These include the National Computing Centre (NCC) (Oxford Road, Manchester M1 7ED), which develops computing techniques and provides aids for the more effective use of computers. Members have access to a large database of information and the Centre publishes a number of guides, including a *Directory of hardware* and a *Directory of software*. The educational user should also contact the Micro-electronics Education Support Unit (now part of CET).

Another important source of information is CHEST, which is a Computer Board national initiative established to support computing in the higher education and research community. Its primary objective is to get the best possible value by negotiating reduced prices with software suppliers, arranging central funding for some software purchasers and negotiating suitable licence agreements for software purchases. Its directories list software utilities, application packages and suppliers. The CHEST is held online on the NISS bulletin board system and is accessible through each member institution's computer centre. It is also available in print form.

MICRONET 800 also offers a national service for its members. It issues guides to hardware, software, bench tests, buyers' guides, details of user clubs and a news magazines. Telesoftware services are also available.

The publishers of software are numerous and include the following. There are various local education authority consortia; for example, RESOURCE (Exeter Road, Off Coventry Grove, Doncaster DN2 4PY), a consortium of Barnsley, Doncaster, Humberside, Rotherham and Sheffield local authorities, which publish materials, both nationally and locally, relating to all aspects of computers in education. There are specialist suppliers such as Triptych Systems Ltd (Buckingham House, Station Road, Gerrards Cross, Buckinghamshire SL9 8EL), which supply software for the building industry; and traditional book suppliers such as Longman. Viewbook Information Education Ltd (Unit 33, The Enterprise Centre, Bedford Street, Stoke-on-Trent, Staffordshire ST1 4PZ) provide a preview disc catalogue as a sample of books and texts stored on computer disc. There are also computer manufacturers such as Apple Computers (UK) Ltd (6 Roundwood Avenue, Stockley Park, Uxbridge UB11 1BB).

There are a considerable number of subscription services which operate an 'exchange service'. For example, the Central Program Exchange (Wolverhampton Polytechnic, Wulfruna Street, Wolverhampton WV1 1LY) offers the subscriber a service which includes the copying of up to ten programs per year, extra programs requiring a small fee.

The major printed sources for software are in periodical form. These include general publications such as *Personal computer world* (Computing Publications Ltd, 1978−), which is a guide to software and equipment, and *Which PC?* (FOCUS, 1986−). Specialist subject periodicals include *Microdecision* (VNU Business Publications, 1981−), which provides a directory of retailers and software for business users; and *Educational computing* (BBC Enterprises, 1980−), which includes a directory of educational computing software. Finally, there are periodicals for particular makes of equipment, such as *Atari user* (Europress, 1985−). The latter type of periodical is essential once the library has decided on a particular make of microcomputer.

Specialist subject sources include the Economic and Social Research Council (ESRC) Data Archive, which publishes a software bulletin and a regular update of the computer dataset held in the archive. The journal *Teaching geography* has a regular computer page with updating news and reviews of computer software.

There is no UK general catalogue for microcomputing software. The standard source for computing is *The computer users' yearbook* (VNU Business Publications, 1969−) and the parallel *Software users' yearbook* (VNU, 1985−). The USA has *The software encyclopedia* (Bowker,

1988), which provides fully annotated listings for 28,500 microcomputer programs. The same company provides *Microcomputer software and hardware guide* online on DIALOG.

AVP (Schools Hill Centre, Chepstow, Gwent NP6 5PH) have produced a catalogue of software for the BBC, RM Nimbus and IBM PCs: *Computer programs: a comprehensive guide to the best educational software.*

Telesoftware is increasingly an important source for computer programs. This is the transmission of programs from one computer to another by broadcast radio or television or via telephone lines. Such public domain software is designed to be widely available without licensing agreements. Shareware carries with it an obligation to pay a small fee if the software is retained. Bulletin boards for software are an important source, as are computer user groups. An excellent guide is provided by I. Noble, 'Public domain software for librarians'.[4] A. R. Samuels *Shareware for library applications* (Meckler, 1988) is a detailed coverage of US material. Prestel facilities are listed in *Connexions* (Marathon Videotex).

Optical storage systems
The bibliographic tools for CD audio have been considered under the section relating to sound recordings.

CD-ROM
The rapid growth in CD-ROM materials has resulted in new bibliographic guides. It is worth noting that the major information reference companies, Whitaker, Bowker and H. W. Wilson, have put their databases — such as *Books in print, Whitaker's British books in print* and *Film literature index* — into the format. They also supply customized CD-ROM workstations. Chadwyck-Healey have produced the French and German national bibliographies on CD-ROM.

One of the first general guides is *CD-ROM directory*, third edition (TFPL, 1988), which has sections listing CD-ROM products, company information, CD-ROM drives, books, journals, and conferences and exhibitions. It is international in scope, giving information on 390 products and some 350 companies. A useful concise introduction is N. Akers, *CD ROM, interactive video and satellite TV in the school library* (LA School Librarians Group, 1989). This gives a brief introduction to the hardware and appropriate software. It is aimed at school libraries but it will repay scrutiny by any librarian entering this field. CHEST has listed CD-ROMs that academic librarians and computer centres have shown interest in purchasing.

However, there is still a lack of bibliographic tools and diligent searching through microcomputer periodicals and publishers' catalogues is required. The publishers include: Silver Platter (10 Barley Mow Passage, Chiswick, London W4 4PH; 37 Walnut Street, Wellesley Hills, MA 02181, USA) for such databases as LISA, Audiovisual online, Software − CD etc.; Multilingual Statte (Hartington Road, London W4 3PT) for Harrap multilingual dictionary database; and UMI (White Swan House, Godstone, Surrey RH9 8LW) for dissertation abstracts, newspaper abstracts etc.

CIMTECH (PO Box 109, College Lane, Hatfield, Hertfordshire AL10 9AB) are important providers of information on CD-ROMs and the allied equipment. *Library and information briefings*, from Central London Polytechnic, Library and Information Technology Centre (235 High Holborn, London WC1 7DW) includes updates on equipment.

Videodiscs

The bibliographic tools for videodiscs have been considered under film and video but it is important to note that particular tools are not available to trace discs for use in an interactive manner. No general guide has appeared for this form. Certain publishers have published a limited range. For example, BBC *Domesday*, *Ecodisc* and *Volcanoes*; Rank Training have produced management discs; Ferranti International have published for the IBM AT ten videodiscs covering basic mathematical concepts and real-life applications. A notable publisher of higher education training videodiscs is the Open University.

The major source of information is the National Interactive Video Centre (NIVC) (24−32 Stephenson Way, London NW1 2HD). This maintains a database of research and a listing of interactive videodiscs. The Centre's periodical, *Interactive update*, appears bimonthly. The most important UK guide to equipment and authoring is C. Bayard-White, *An introduction to interactive video*, third edition (NIVC, 1987). Information concerning equipment is available from many of the above services.

PREVIEWING AND PURCHASE

The bibliographic organizations and publications listed above can help the librarian to decide which NBM should be considered for further selection. A review may even give information to enable the librarian to purchase the document sight unseen. However, a review of a particular document may not exist, or may give insufficient detail for a decision to be made. The librarian will then have to consider previewing the item.

If a library supplier is used, it may be possible to obtain the items on approval; and some publishers will supply direct for a short approval period, against either an official requisition or a full cash deposit. Publishers of sound recordings used to be very unwilling to send any material on approval because of damage problems. However, the introduction of CD audio has resulted in a number of 'try before you buy systems', for example, Squire Gate Music Centre. In larger libraries, such as a public library system, the easiest course might be to buy one copy of everything that seems to be suitable, and then decide whether further copies are required. Film will normally be hired out for previewing, and with a number of suppliers the cost of hire may be offset against the purchase price paid later. However, certain firms for both videorecordings and computer software may refuse to supply libraries because they consider they reduce sales to private users of NBM. The time involved in previewing should not be underestimated; indeed, the cost in staff time may be much more than the purchase cost of the document. It has been argued that the librarian cannot in any case preview NBM for clients who have their own specific needs and that the librarian's view is subjective even when objective guidelines are available. Bearing in mind these points, the librarian still has to make a decision over which items to purchase from the wealth of materials available. Each institution will need to decide on its approach to previewing, but some general points can be made.

A selection panel or committee is usually more accurate, if initially costlier, than a single assessor. One writer states in this regard that the 'best judgements derive from discussion with a group of mixed expertise; the majority can depend on the specialist in their midst for guidance on factual accuracy (if relevant) but contribute their individual unprejudiced views on the success or effectiveness of presentation'.[5] Wherever possible, more than one person's opinion should be sought; or it should be made possible to refer a decision to a selection committee if doubt arises.

The skill of previewing cannot be gained from reading about techniques. The more experience the librarian has had in assessing NBM, the more likely that a valid critical judgement will be made. However, it is possible to consider some general criteria for evaluation. There are similar criteria for the selection of book materials and NBM. The major differences tend to be in the areas of technical organization and packaging. The following points are not a complete list.

Relevancy to the library and its clients
(a) Relevant to the objectives of the library?
(b) Relevant to the needs of the clients?
(c) Can factual material be found in material already in stock?
(d) Is there already adequate subject coverage in other materials?
(e) Can it be linked to other material in stock?
(f) Would it have to be for reference only?
(g) Is it designed for individual or group use?
(h) Is it in a suitable format for clients, for example slides rather than filmstrip?
(i) What physical environment is required, for example black-out facilities?
(j) Is suitable equipment available in the library or to clients externally?

Subject contents
(a) Factual accuracy?
(b) Currency of information?
(c) Lack of bias?
(d) Is it stimulating, produced with sensitivity and understanding of the needs of the proposed users?
(e) Is the organization of the subject logical?
(f) Vocabulary: correct level for the intended age range?
(g) Concepts: correct level for the intended audience?

Organization of material
(a) Contents list and index: are they accurate and do they represent the material?
(b) Titles and captions: relevant and accurate?
(c) Narration, dialogue, sound effects: relevant and accurate?

(d) Balanced approach; for example, are cinefilm sequences pertinent and of an appropriate length? Balanced use of narration, dialogue and sound effects?

(e) Has one medium been used where another would have been more appropriate, for example tape-slide instead of slide-notes?

Technical organization

(a) Artistic, stimulating and descriptive?

(b) Paper: clear, use of white space, correct type, size of paper, links to illustrations?

(c) Film: sharp image and of good quality? Effective use of colour and correct colour rendering?

(d) Sound: faithful reproduction, clear and intelligible? If used with visuals, good synchronization of sound and image?

(e) Suitable physical size and format?

(f) Symbols used readily understood?

(g) Typography and labelling: legible from correct viewing distance?

(h) Are there appropriate notes or guides?

(i) Is accompanying material necessary or merely a gimmick?

Packaging

(a) Attractive?

(b) Easy to handle and store?

(c) Durable and easy to repair?

(d) Self-explanatory contents list?

Cost

(a) Value for money?

(b) Cost to add it to stock in processing time?

(c) Will material soon be dated and have a limited shelf life?

It is stressed that librarians must establish personal criteria which reflect the needs of clients. For particular forms, such as sound recordings and microcomputer software, more precise criteria would have to be drawn up.

Once the criteria have been decided upon, it is helpful to formalize them into a policy statement or put them in an assessment form, as can be seen in figure 21. Such forms can ensure a more consistent approach by reviewers, and can also be filed for future reference to prevent the same document being inadvertently previewed twice.

Non-book Materials Assessment Form

Title	Format
Publisher	
Technical description	
Content summary	

Level: Primary / Secondary / Further / Higher / Adult education / General

	POOR → GOOD				
	1	2	3	4	5
Accurate information					
Unbiased					
Current					
Authority of publisher					
Vocabulary					
Appropriate format for subject					
Interesting					
Logical arrangement					
Suitable pace					
Suitable length					
Colour					
Clarity					
Synchronisation					
Durability					
Value for money					

Extra features: notes, guides, accompanying material

Is storage difficult? Yes / No	Compatible with own machinery? Yes / No
Similar material in stock? Details:	Purchase advice: Yes / No / Discuss
Assessor	Date

Figure 21. Assessment form

REASONS FOR SELECTION OR REJECTION

It is, of course, not sufficient merely to collect NBM; the client must be encouraged to use such materials. This can be achieved by offering accessions lists and exhibitions, and participation may also be helped by publicizing the selection criteria and procedures. A few libraries have also published the criteria they use in selecting NBM, while others have published the reviews of their assessment panels.

There are obvious problems in this policy of open dissemination of decisions concerning purchase. Criticism from staff and clients is one, and explaining the reasons for rejecting a certain document almost invites someone to ask for it. The heavy commitment in staff time and expense should not be underestimated. However, in considering the importance of selection of materials it would appear to be vital to inform clients of the reasons for the selection and rejection of NBM, either formally or informally.

The traditional means of publicizing new purchases are, of course, also applicable for NBM. Indeed, their very nature lends itself to exhibitions and displays. Non-clients may well be encouraged to use the library as a result of such activities. Special film weeks have been mounted by some libraries, during which films are shown non-stop. Displays of new posters and wallcharts can brighten a library's entrance hall as well as draw attention to new purchases. A number of public libraries have organized microcomputer clubs on branch premises and have also provided access to online databases such as TAPS.

PRODUCTION OF MATERIAL

A librarian who has exhausted all bibliographic avenues and still not found the material to satisfy the client's requirements has one further possibility: to produce the material in-house. This has been a common practice for off-air recording from radio and television. In the UK a licence may be purchased to record all Open University broadcasts, and school broadcasts may be freely copied provided they are kept for only a certain period (three years for radio and television). A number of libraries have been quick to realize the potential of NBM as learning devices. They have used them for in-service training of staff and also for user education. Examples of such programmes have included sound cassettes illustrating reference work, 'trigger' videos showing excerpts of users' behaviour in a library, and tape-slide presentations illustrating the work of a librarian for careers conventions.

It is in the local history area that libraries have been most prolific as producers, with postcards and posters of local views and of historical personalities the top sellers.

In summary, the process of acquiring NBM involves the librarian in the following: searching printed sources; contacting institutions and individuals for specialist advice and services; creating criteria for evaluation; deciding which documents to purchase, which to hire and which to preview; and, finally, establishing a previewing system. If suitable documents cannot be traced, librarians may be in a position to produce them for their clients, although it is more likely that this activity will be linked to their own needs for training of staff and user education.

CATALOGUING, CLASSIFICATION AND INDEXING

The challenge faced by librarians has been succinctly stated by Foskett to be one of 'ensuring that individuals who need information can obtain it with the minimum of cost (both in time and money), and without being overwhelmed by large amounts of irrelevant matter.'[6] The process of obtaining this 'relevant' information from the library collection is known as information retrieval. Any document may be sought by a client under a number of headings — form, subject, author, title, publisher, etc. However, the librarian adopts a physical storage system which usually organizes the documents under only one, or perhaps two, of these headings — for example, non-fiction documents by subject. To meet the needs of the clients, therefore, librarians have traditionally dealt with the other possible approaches through a substitute record, the catalogue. This is a familiar sight in most libraries, though its value has been questioned.

Ignoring this problem of use, two questions need to be asked. Do all NBM need to be catalogued and classified in the same way and to the same extent? Is the experience that librarians have gained in cataloguing books applicable to non-book documents or do they have to devise new methods and a new theory? The stress here is on a general collection of book and non-book documents. The requirements of libraries with specialized collections serving clients with special interests are beyond the scope of this work. For example, the Visnews Film Archive has devised its own systems, which are of interest but not generally applicable.

Management decisions
1   Are substitute records to be made for all the documents in the library? This is a decision that has to be reached before a library begins to catalogue or classify a single document. For example, a primary school may decide that its curriculum and likely use of documents does not require a catalogue. All work in the school may be project-based around set topics with a certain number of documents on each one. Each topic will have a colour code for its documents, for example those on animals could have a blue colour flash on the spine. The teacher will then be able to say, 'I want you to look at all the documents with the blue spine code.' Or a public library with an illustrations collection may decide

that this material is self-indexing, that is, arranged by subject headings. A client requiring an illustration of the 1988 Wimbledon Football Association Cup-winning team will look under the major grouping of sport and then under the subject heading of football. This system works more than adequately for very large collections such as the Hulton Film Library, which has over ten million items arranged basically by A – Z subject headings within five major groupings. Similarly, faced with a slide set, do the librarians catalogue each slide or just the whole item?[7] Their decision will be based on their knowledge of their clients' requirements.

2   Accessibility to NBM must be considered. Are the documents to be freely available for access by browsers, or are they to be stored on closed access? If a closed-access system is chosen, then there is additional pressure to have very detailed catalogue descriptions of each document in order to prevent the client asking for material which may be of little benefit.

In addition, storage by an accession number system relieves the cataloguer of the need to consider helpful classification by browsing. Deciding on an open-access system requires less descriptive information from the catalogue as the clients have the opportunity to search through the documents themselves to aid in selection.

3   An integrated catalogue should be considered. Ideally, the storage of the library materials should be completely integrated to allow the client to browse amongst the whole stock for a subject rather than have to search through separate form divisions. Standardized packaging may achieve this with sound recordings, slide sets and films; but it is likely that charts, specimens and models will need to be arranged in parallel. Also, any integrated arrangement of material will always be bound by administrative factors related to buildings, staffing and security. A solution to these problems is to set up an integrated catalogue, which will consist of entries for both NBM and books in the collection.

Some librarians have discovered problems in constructing an integrated catalogue: 'There is a risk of items being lost or overlooked in the plethora of information; the catalogue quickly becomes unwieldy; it is difficult to file the entries successively; constant signalling has to be involved to indicate clearly the media or form being described on any item.'[8] These are technical problems which can be overcome to some extent by the use of material designations, and by clear guidance on the use of the catalogue. At issue is the librarians' willingness to overcome these technical problems for the requirements of clients rather than just to construct a catalogue for the librarians' own needs. The client benefits from a catalogue that gives a complete record of all the documents in the library collection; there is no problem in looking up a subject such as insects and finding everything, whatever its form, recorded in the one catalogue. When there is more than one catalogue, if a collection of poems by T. S. Eliot is required, for example, the client could remain unaware that the library not only has these in a printed form but also has a sound recording of Eliot reading his poems — the client may have no reason to consult the sound recording catalogue. Finally, the practice of publishing books and non-books together is growing; for example, a book on the EXCEL spread sheet may well have a computer disc of templates bound into it.

4   The value of the computer is undeniable. It is difficult to understand now why there were some concerns expressed about the practicality and indeed usefulness of computerizing audiovisual data on a large scale. The publication of the *British catalogue of audiovisual materials* illustrated that it was possible to establish 'a single computerised system that gives access to a combined catalogue of the nation's output of documents in all physical forms, whether printed or audio-visual'.[9] There are now large integrated computerized catalogues, such as OCLC, which demonstrate the ease of use and are provided throughout academic and public libraries. The number of records is irrelevant; equipment and software is now available that will cope with the small school library and the regional library systems.

As usual, the needs of the client are paramount and the computer enables the librarian to tailor the provision in a more cost-effective way. Once the database is established, form catalogues — for example videorecordings — can be easily printed off if that is what is required; specific subject searches involving a variety of formats require only a key stroke.

The development of microcomputers has brought the concept of a computerized catalogue within the reach of smaller libraries, and has also facilitated user programmes. Thus the Hypercard software for the Apple Macintosh can be used so that each card/screen gives an approximation of a slide from the collection.

At Teesside Polytechnic the client group has been identified as requiring multiple access to the variety of material. NBM are included because clients require that information, but the management decision was that the computerization would enable the provision of a separate videorecording catalogue which lecturers could use in their own rooms for ordering the playing of specific video programmes.

Thus management decisions are, as usual, dependent upon the library and its clients. NBM do not impose a particular approach which would drastically alter the cataloguing and classification system already in use, even when that system involves a computer.

Cataloguing NBM

The publication of the revised second edition of the *Anglo-American cataloguing rules* (AACR2) confirmed that all formats could be catalogued to the same standard. It simply stated that 'The rules cover the description of, and provision of access points for, all library materials commonly collected at the present time. The integrated structure of the text makes the general rules usable as a basis for cataloguing uncommonly collected materials of all kinds and library materials yet unknown.'[10] The librarian's bible had recognized that librarianship is concerned with information first, and secondly with the form in which the information is encapsulated. The revised edition notes that technological developments such as videodisc and microcomputer files have necessitated rule revision, particularly in chapter 9, Computer files. Nevertheless, these new information carriers can be catalogued by the librarian and they do not differ in substance from other non-books. The principles that underlie AACR2 are a sound guide for the cataloguing of all NBM.

Perhaps the clearest exposition of what a client may demand from a catalogue was written by C. A. Cutter in 1876:

(1) To enable a person to find a book of which either (a) the author is known, (b) the title is known, (c) the subject is known; (2) To show what the library has (d) by a given author, (e) on a given subject, (f) in a given kind of literature; (3) To assist in the choice of a book (g) as to its edition (bibliographically), (h) as to its character.[11]

Although Cutter was referring to the need to help a client in the choice of 'a book', the passage of over 100 years and the introduction of a number of new information carriers does not invalidate his statement.

The attack made upon the catalogue functions and uses; the arguments concerning the principle of authorship; and the developments of ISBD, chain indexing, PRECIS and computerization are not fundamentally altered by the introduction of NBM into the library. The weaknesses and strengths of the library catalogue may be shown up by the introduction of NBM, but the catalogue functions still centre around those expressed by Cutter.

The information given in a catalogue entry for a document may be divided into three areas, which may be seen in the following example from the *British national bibliography*:

Heading	PRESTEL and education: a report of a one year trial
Description	Vincent Thompson. — London: CET, 1981. — 29p;30cm
	ISBN 0-8614-055-0(pbk): Unpriced
Subject description	371.335

The areas are: the descriptive cataloguing of the document (the body of the entry); the establishment of headings for the document, by which the entries are arranged in the catalogue; and a subject description of the document.

The descriptive cataloguing of a document

It must be stressed that this description is applicable not only to the library catalogue but also to the entry of documents in other bibliographic tools. The only difference is that the former must relate to one particular library (or group of libraries) and its clients, while the latter normally takes no account of any particular library or its needs. Further, it is suggested that every part of the physical description is necessary for every library. In order to know what elements to leave out to satisfy a particular library's clients, all these elements must be known to start with! In using AACR2's chapter 1, General rules for description, as a basis to discuss the physical description of NBM, it is important to stress the following points:

1   The physical description of any item 'should be based in the first instance on the chapter dealing with the class of materials to which that item belongs'. Thus computer discs should be catalogued according to the rules in chapter 9, Computer files, and not solely on chapter 1.

2   It is likely that only a national bibliographic agency (e.g. the British Library) will record all the elements described in the areas, i.e. 'third level of description'. Other bodies will choose either the first or second level of description.

3   The description established will not normally be used by itself, but will usually form part of a complete entry in a catalogue or other bibliographic list. The organizational factors (headings, classification numbers etc.) used in arranging entries in a catalogue do not form any part of the standard description for an item.

The framework of chapter 1 will give the physical description as outlined in figures 22 and 23. The numbering of the framework refers to the specific AACR2 rules. As can be seen from the former, this: (1) gives all the elements that are required to describe NBM; (2) assigns an order to these elements; (3) prescribes punctuation for the elements.

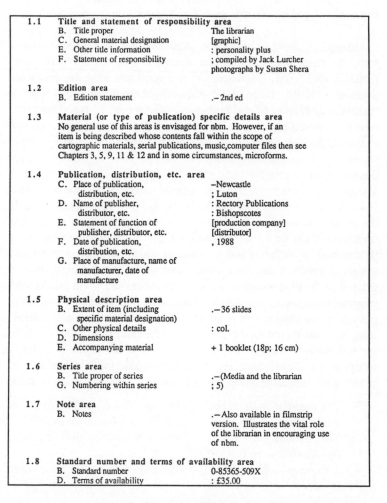

1.1	**Title and statement of responsibility area**	
	B. Title proper	The librarian
	C. General material designation	[graphic]
	E. Other title information	: personality plus
	F. Statement of responsibility	; compiled by Jack Lurcher photographs by Susan Shera
1.2	**Edition area**	
	B. Edition statement	.– 2nd ed
1.3	**Material (or type of publication) specific details area**	
	No general use of this areas is envisaged for nbm. However, if an item is being described whose contents fall within the scope of cartographic materials, serial publications, music,computer files then see Chapters 3, 5, 9, 11 & 12 and in some circumstances, microforms.	
1.4	**Publication, distribution, etc. area**	
	C. Place of publication, distribution, etc.	–Newcastle ; Luton
	D. Name of publisher, distributor, etc.	: Rectory Publications : Bishopscotes
	E. Statement of function of publisher, distributor, etc.	[production company] [distributor]
	F. Date of publication, distribution, etc.	, 1988
	G. Place of manufacture, name of manufacturer, date of manufacture	
1.5	**Physical description area**	
	B. Extent of item (including specific material designation)	.– 36 slides
	C. Other physical details	: col.
	D. Dimensions	
	E. Accompanying material	+ 1 booklet (18p; 16 cm)
1.6	**Series area**	
	B. Title proper of series	.– (Media and the librarian
	G. Numbering within series	; 5)
1.7	**Note area**	
	B. Notes	.– Also available in filmstrip version. Illustrates the vital role of the librarian in encouraging use of nbm.
1.8	**Standard number and terms of availability area**	
	B. Standard number	0-85365-509X
	D. Terms of availability	: £35.00

Figure 22. AACR2: general rules for the description of all library materials, together with a worked example

> The librarian [graphic] : personality plus/compiled by Jack Lurcher;
> photographs by Susan Shera. — 2nd ed. — Newcastle: Rectory Publications
> [production company] ; Luton: Bishopscotes [distributor], 1988. — 36
> slides: col. + 1 booklet (18p.; 16 cm.). — (Media and the librarian; 5). —
> Also available in filmstrip version. Illustrates the vital role of the librarian
> in encouraging use of nbm. — 0-85365-509X: £35.00

Figure 23. Worked example as it could appear on a catalogue card

Although it is suggested in the example that it is possible to construct from the basic principles similar descriptive entries for both book materials and NBM, it is important to realize that these are problems peculiar to NBM. Using the framework, these peculiarities will be discussed and some of the problems will be pointed out. However, reference should be made to individual cataloguing rules, such as, for example, the Computer Files Cataloguing Group standards.

Source of the description
The chief source of information for printed monographs is the title page; few modern books lack one. Information in this form is unusual for NBM; the traditional method of giving details is to scatter them around the document. Thus on a slide set the information required may be found in a number of different places, none of which carry the 'traditional' weight of the title page. Such sources may be the title slide, information printed on the slide mounts, a set of notes for the slides and information printed on the packaging. AACR2 recognizes this problem by using the concept of 'the chief source of information' in relation to a specific NBM; thus, for videorecording the film itself is the chief source (for example the title frames). However, the individuality of each type of NBM is recognized and guidelines are offered to considering which source of information should be given first preference. The categories include:

(a) The material itself, including the container where this forms an integral part of the item, for example a cassette or cartridge.
(b) The container, where this is completely separate from the item, for example a box.
(c) Accompanying data, that is guides and other leaflets issued with the item.
(d) Other sources, for example reference works.

The order of preference for each of these categories is given by the specific material chapter. Thus for motion pictures, preference is given to textual material before the separate container, while for slides, preference is given to the container.

A further problem may arise when the item being catalogued consists of more than one form. For example, *An Alaskan adventure* (British Petroleum Educational Service, 1977) is a study kit which contains four filmstrips, a sound cassette, teacher's guide, sheets of stickers, a painting book, six charts, five cut-out sheets of model making, four pamphlets, four copies of pupil's books and 16 copies of commentary notes. All of these forms have different information on them, and none is identifiable as being the major constituent of the kit. The chief source of information for such items is usually the container itself. Alternatively, the cataloguer must create a description that satisfactorily identifies the item.

Finally, in contrast to the above example in which there is an overabundance of 'chief sources of information', consider one with no apparent sources at all. This is a model of an oil rig. It has no information on it other than its name, 'Sea quest'. The cataloguer has to use his judgement and create an entry to describe the item; for example: Sea Quest: [oil rig].

Cataloguing rules cannot always give precise help. Rule 6.0B1 states that the 'chief source of information' for a tape cassette is the cassette and label. However, it is the inlay card that usually gives the most pertinent and easily observable information. Wise cataloguers will exercise their professional skills in choosing the information that gives the clearest description for their clients.

Descriptive cataloguing and the AACR2 framework
In order to discuss the problems arising as part of the descriptive cataloguing of NBM, a focus can be provided by making use of the framework of chapter 1 of AACR2.

1   *Title and statement of responsibility area*   This contains title statement (1.1B), general material designation (1.2C) and statement of responsibility (1.3F).

1.1B   *Title statement*   The title usually poses few questions that are not answered by the rules stated in AACR2. However, there are perhaps three points that need to be mentioned:

(a) The use of uniform titles: A uniform title is the particular title by which a work that has appeared under varying titles is to be identified for cataloguing purposes. The choice may be between alternative titles, as in these examples from films: *The fearless vampire killers*, also known as *Dance of the vampires*; *Pope Joan*, also known as *The devil's impostor*; *The Barratts of Wimpole Street*, also known as *Forbidden alliance*. In these cases, the title would be that on the copy in the library, with the original title in the notes area.

(b) Supplied titles: Often NBM have no title and one must be supplied. Such a situation is very common with illustrations, specimens and models. Thus a Japanese doll has no title page or similar source, unless it comes with a descriptive card, so the cataloguer must supply a title, '[Japanese doll]'. A particular set of slides with no title may be described as [Beatrix Potter: scenes from her books]'. Essentially, the supplied title must be an appropriate description of the intellectual contents.

(c) Collective titles: An individual item may contain several works and there may be two or more titles associated with its description. Sound recordings, in particular, often have two or more titles associated with a single item; for example, the Open University sound cassette which has *The development of the social sciences* paired with *The social scientist at work*. If there is no collective title associated with the work, then it will be necessary to record the titles in the order in which they appear in the chief source of information.

1C   *General material designation*   Material designation may be defined as the physical form of the document being catalogued, as a slide or a model. This may be further divided into two elements; a general material designation − for example videorecording − and a specific material designation − for example videodisc. Material designation is used to give an 'early warning' to the catalogue user. Using the general material designation from the British List, a slide illustrating a robin would be written as: 'The robin [graphic]'; while a sound cassette would be given as: 'The robin [sound recording]'.

There has been considerable debate concerning the merits of general material designation. AACR2 states that it is an 'optional addition' and there was no agreement concerning the descriptive terms for British and American libraries other than to agree to go in separate ways; hence the taciturn British chose the term 'graphic'; the expressive Americans chose 'art original', 'chart', 'filmstrip', 'flash card', 'picture', 'slide', 'technical drawing' and 'transparency'!

The British Library has decided to leave out the general material designation. The following examples illustrate the possibilities:

AACR2 British List:

general material designation

```
Energetics [graphic]/by R.S. Lowrie — Oxford: Pergamon,
1969. — 6 transparencies: col.
```

specific material designation

AACR2 North American:

general material designation

```
Energetics [transparency]/by R.S. Lowrie. — Oxford: Pergamon,
1969. — 6 transparencies: col.
```

specific material designation

AACR2 British Library:

```
Energetics/by R.S. Lowrie. — Oxford: Pergamon, 1969. — 6
transparencies: col.
```

specific material designation

There is an obvious appeal in the idea of such an 'early warning system' for the catalogue user who wants to know quickly the form of the document. However, there is a lack of evidence concerning client preference and whether a statement such as 'graphic' is sufficient description for the user. The ability of the client to scan a catalogue card and note the designation quickly has also not been researched. The advent of shortened catalogue entries — for example, as in online catalogues and indexes to the COM catalogue — will mean that the format may not be listed.

There are other methods of 'early warning'. One such is the colour coding of catalogue cards; in this system all slides would be on blue cards, all sound discs on green cards etc. However, Weih's objections should be noted:

Colour-coding is not recommended for the following reasons:

1 Photo reproduction of catalogue data is impractical because the use of colour film raises costs.
2 Colour-coding is also impractical for computer produced books, microform, or online catalogues.
3 To make colour-coding economically feasible in centralised cataloguing, an internationally accepted standardised colour code would have to be established. At present there is no such standardisation. Individual resource centres using such services would have to colour code by hand, a time-consuming task.
4 As new types of media are acquired, the media centre would soon run out of distinctive colours. Shadings of colours could lead to confusion if the quality of the colour were not maintained.
5 Colour coding erodes the all media approach to resource centre materials.[12]

In addition, catalogues reproduced on microfilm would be able to reproduce such colour differentiation only at great expense. However, it may help in an integrated catalogue to have the NBM listed on different coloured cards where the vast majority of stock is of books. The client searching for an NBM item would have a quick visual guide in these circumstances.

Another possibility is a media code in the top right-hand corner of the catalogue card, as in this example from Furlong and Platt:

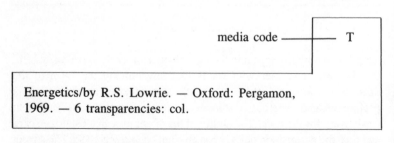

The usefulness of a media code is open to question, particularly as the client has to remember a further set of letters. Furlong and Platt list 16 such codes:[13]

F	Film	P	Picture
FL	Film loop	R	Record
FS	Filmstrip	S	Slide
K	Kit	SP	Specimen
MA	Map	TC	Tape: cassette
MO	Model	TR	Tape: reel
MF	Microform	W	Word card
MS	Microscope slide	WA	Wallchart

It is strongly recommended that a media code is not used. Clients do not remember such codes and often require the help of library staff to determine their meaning. To remember codes plus the classification number may be asking too much of the average catalogue user.

The problem of material designation is further complicated by the number of terms used to describe the physical forms. It is crucial for library clients that they are helped to identify easily the particular format that they are interested in using. The librarian is faced with a proliferation of terms and often different definitions of terms. For example, the term 'chart' can mean a flipchart, wallchart, star map or navigational chart. AACR2 has not completely 'tidied up' this area and indeed a number of terms – such as flipchart, photograph, postcard, poster, stereograph, study print and wallchart – are not defined in the glossary.

However, AACR2 has established a common vocabulary and, perhaps more importantly, a forum within which librarians can work toward a revised glossary for NBM terminology. For the librarian wishing to identify the books in the library collection, the term 'text' can be used as a general material designation. This is used 'to designate printed material accessible to the naked eye' (for example, a book, pamphlet or brochure). However, if it has been decided not to use a general material designation there is no specific material designation and it is deemed sufficient to identify a text in the physical description area by a statement of number of pages etc.

To summarize, there needs to be a material designation so that the client can identify the form of the document. Librarians must decide whether or not their clients and the format of the catalogue require that there should be a general and a specific material designation. Similarly, it should be determined whether or not the term 'text' or an equivalent should be featured as a specific material designation.

The next problem is a document which includes more than one format: for example, a sound cassette with a filmstrip; or a slightly more complex one with a microcomputer cassette, transparencies, slides and sound cassette. If it has been determined that the library's clients require a general material designation, then the term used in the United Kingdom is [multimedia] and in the USA it is [kit]. However, this applies only if no one format is the predominant constituent of the document. Rules 1.9 and 1.10 give clear guidance.

No dominant component

> Coffee [multimedia] . — Wakefield Educational Productions, 1972. — 4 pamphlets, 3 samples of coffee, 12 slides, 6 study prints.

Here no one format predominates, so the general material designation [multimedia] is used. Each format is arranged in alphabetical order in the physical description.

A predominant component

> Churches. — Newton Abbot: Student Recordings, [197–?] — 41 slides: col. + 1 sound cassette.

Slides are the predominant format and it has been decided to record the accompanying format, the sound cassette, at the end of the physical description.

It is often difficult to decide which is the predominant component, and fine professional judgement is required. The problem of 'accompanying material' will be further discussed (see page 239).

Similarly, it is often difficult to decide which is the dominant medium, and again fine professional judgement is required.

1F *Statement of responsibility* This has been variously defined. ISBD(G) states that it is 'A statement transcribed from the item being described, relating to persons or corporate bodies responsible for the creation of intellectual or artistic content of a work, or for the performance of the content of a work.'[14]

AACR2 uses the term 'statement of responsibility' and defines it as 'A statement, transcribed from the item being described, relating to persons responsible for the intellectual or artistic content of the item, to corporate bodies from which the content emanates, or to persons or corporate bodies responsible for the performance of the content of the item.'[15] For a book, this is usually easily determined and this name will become the main heading as, it is argued, a client will remember a document by that feature. Thus *Hamlet* was written by Shakespeare and this is an identifying feature which can readily be established and would be used by catalogue users.

Is this also true for NBM? How do users of the catalogue decide who is the creative force behind a document such as a videotape of Laurence Olivier's *Hamlet*? Here there is the problem of the performer and his interpretation. Would clients think of the main entry as Shakespeare or Olivier? Do they think of it as Shakespeare's or Olivier's *Hamlet* when they search for it? The question of the performer is an added element in the definition of an author. It broadens our interpretation beyond the writer. ISBD(G) has determined a wide range of persons and bodies who may be deemed responsible for a work − writers, composers, graphic artists and choreographers; adaptors of an already existing work; collectors of anthropological and other field recordings; persons responsible for the direction of a performed work; organizations or individuals sponsoring the work of any of the above; and performers.

The range of people associated with a non-book material may be seen in the following examples:

Sound recording of the novel *The hobbit*
  author: J.R.R. Tolkien
  performer: Nicol Williamson
  adapter and producer: Harley Usill
Sound cassette *Improve your golf*
  narrator: Harry Carpenter
  discussion between Dai Rees and Harry Doust
  executive producer: Ivan Berg
Cinefilm *O lucky man*
  producers: Michael Medwin and Lindsay Anderson
  screenplay writer: David Sherwin
  director: Lindsay Anderson
  performers: Malcolm McDowell, Helen Mirren, Arthur Lowe
  music and songs: Alan Price

It is difficult to establish who has the intellectual credit for these works and with whom lies the 'prime intellectual responsibility'. The more cynical may remember Danny Kaye's comment:

Screenplay by Glock,
from a story by Blip,
from a chapter by Ronk,
from a comma by Stokes,
from an idea by Gropes,
based on Joe Miller's jokes.[16]

It is little wonder that AACR2 Rule 7.1F1 states 'Transcribe statements
of responsibility relating to those persons or bodies credited in the chief
source of information with participation in the production of a film (e.g.
as producer, director, animator) that are considered to be of major
importance.'

A further problem is that the functions of the authors of NBM are not
always clear. This can be seen in the credit list for *The American West:
myth and legend* (EAV, 1976) (filmstrip/sound cassette), which reads:

supervising editor: Robert Gindick
scripts and picture research, part 1: James H. Handelman
scripts and picture research, parts 2 and 3: Verna Tomasson and
Robert Gindick
editor in chief: Gladys Carter
music arranged and performed by: Lorre Wyatt
sound engineer: Stephen M. Aronson

What is a 'supervising editor'? Is he the same as a compiler or does he
receive the scripts and alter them to suit his intellectual or artistic mind?
What control does he have over the pictures so carefully researched and
the music so creatively arranged and performed? Even if Robert Gindick
has the primary intellectual responsibility, is it certain that the next time
the term 'supervising editor' is used it will have the same meaning?

The earlier cataloguing rule LA/NCET has perhaps most aptly summed
up the situation as one where 'the creative responsibility for intellectual
or artistic content is characteristically shared among several persons and
bodies, performing between them a variety of functions, the relative
importance of which to the work is difficult to determine and which often
permits no analogy with the authorship of books and texts'.[17] Thus it
is important to establish first a standard description for a document and
then to add headings and/or uniform titles. If an author can be clearly
established, then enter under author. However, if no author can usefully
be given as a heading, then a title is used instead.

2 *Edition area*   There are no problems arising here that previous experience in book materials will not make clear. The use of terms such as '2nd ed.' or 'revised version' is familiar.

3 *Material (or type of publication) specific details area*   This area is used for the description of cartographic materials (chapter 3), music (chapter 5), computer files (chapter 9), and serial publications (chapter 12 and, in some circumstances, chapter 11). This area enables the cataloguing of documents which contain more than one form, for example a map on a microcomputer cassette or a serial issued as a videorecording. The solution is to draw upon information given in the appropriate part of AACR2 for cartographic materials (chapter 3) and computer files (chapter 9). Thus in the first example, chapter 3 would be used to determine the scale designation etc. It enables the cataloguers to describe the file characteristics of computer software, for example the data and/or the program.

4 *Publication, distribution etc. areas*   This includes publisher and place of publication, distributor and place of distribution, statement of function of publisher and distributor, date of publication and distribution, and manufacturer. It is not a section that poses any serious problems, and experience gained in cataloguing book imprints is relevant. Decisions between two publishers, various places of publication, and the problems of a lack of date are relatively easily resolved. There are, however, some problems which need to be discussed further.

The company or person responsible for issuing a book is known as the publisher, but for NBM they may be described as the publisher, manufacturer or production company or have some other identifying tag. Whichever is used, the important fact is that they are responsible for the issue of the intellectual content. If they have not manufactured the item, they are still responsible for having chosen the firm which does so, and will have similarly selected the firm distributing it. It is important to distinguish between the publisher and the manufacturer of the physical item. A firm such as Educational Productions takes other companies' master copies and duplicates them for the mass market as well as being publishers in their own right.

Trade names pose a problem, particularly for commercially issued sound recordings. For example, the sound cassette *Brothers in arms* by Dire Straits has the information on its inlay card: Phonogram (Publisher) and Vertigo is the trademark of Phonogram. Thus the publisher, following AACR2 Rule 6.4D2, is the trademark, Vertigo.

AACR2 describes a distributor as an agent or agency having 'exclusive or shared marketing rights for the item'. While it may be helpful to list a sole distributor or even a company with a major distribution right, it is doubtful if it is worthwhile to list an item freely available from a number of distributors. Thus Disney items are distributed solely in the UK by the Slide Centre and that should be recorded. However, Longman/Common Ground items are widely available and the distributor should not be listed.

The date cannot be found on many documents, particularly on illustrations, posters and photographs. Following AACR2 Rule 1.4F7 gives an approximate date, for example [198?]. Where there is a choice of dates — for example, in a multimedia item — give the earliest and latest dates, for example 1979−82. Another problem with dates arises when the intellectual content recorded in one form is transcribed to another format without any alteration. For example, Dylan Thomas's *Under Milk Wood* was released as a sound disc in 1954 and the sound cassette version was released in 1969. This would be written as 1954 [i.e. 1969] with a note explaining the dates.

5 *Physical description area*   This includes the extent of the item (including specific material designation), other physical details, dimensions and accompanying material. Reference should also be made to the points discussed under area 1C. General material designation (see pages 230−4). It may also be necessary to add some physical descriptions in the notes area.

The aims of this area are: to enable the user to distinguish between the various physical forms of a work (for example, *Michelangelo* by A. Bertram is available as a filmstrip or a slide set); to assist the user to identify the work; and to describe all elements present (for example a slide set with 16 slides plus notes, or a kit including five or six formats).

The description of the physical details should not be a complicated task, provided that the cataloguer is aware of terminology such as double frame, overlays, tactile, panavision, digital and computer laser optical card, and provided that he or she helps clients to understand these by providing descriptive notices near the catalogue. More onerous is the timing of recordings, for example sound discs and videocassettes. How much effort needs to be put into precise timing depends upon client needs, but certainly within education such timing is usually very important. AACR2 Rule 8.5D1 states that all graphic materials except filmstrips, filmslips and stereographs should have their height and width described. However, the measuring of graphics, such as posters and wallcharts, is perhaps not so important except when they are stored by size.

A final problem in this area concerns 'accompanying material', and the comment on pages 233–4 on the cataloguing of documents which contain more than one form should also be noted. In AACR2 this term is used to describe material which is secondary to the predominant component. Rule 1.5E1 gives four ways of recording information about accompanying material:

(a) In a separate entry.
(b) In a multilevel description (see Chapter 13).
(c) In a note (see Rule 1.7B11).
(d) At the end of the physical description.

A policy decision must be made by the cataloguing agency in this area. The most appropriate course in many libraries would possibly be to record the details at the end of the physical description. Thus 'The Honey bee/by J.F. Free. — Wakefield: Filmstrip Productions for Educational Productions, 1966' would have a physical description which would read '1 filmstrip (41 fr.): col. + teacher's notes'. If, however, no one component is predominant, then Rule 1.10C2 applies and this gives three methods to consider, depending on the item being described.

(a) List the extent of each distinct class of material without further physical description. End the element with 'in container', if there is one, and dimensions of the container; thus:

> 10 study cards, 100 student sheets, teacher's handbook,
> 40 spirit masters: 18 × 25 × 19 cm.

This method is particularly useful for study kits where a full physical description is unnecessary for the client.

(b) Give separate physical description for each class of material. Place them in separate lines; thus:

> Living in space; — New York: Doubleday Multimedia, 1972.
> 1 filmstrip (61 fr.): col.
> 1 sound cassette (12 min.): 3¾ ips, mono.

This approach is particularly important where the client requires a detailed description of the format in order to obtain the appropriate equipment.

(c) If an item has a large number of heterogeneous items, give a general term in the extent, such as:

> Newcastle Metro. — Newcastle: Rectory Press, 1983
> 74 pieces: ill., facsims., maps.

The Jackdaw portfolios are a typical example of this type of document, and it is to be regretted that AACR2 was unable to give a suitable specific material designation. Some libraries use a term such as 'portfolio' or even 'kit'.

The cataloguer must accept, as AACR2 does, that all the potential specific material designations cannot be listed. If specific material designations, such as work card or friezes, have to be introduced then a checklist of these should be marked in the working copies of AACR2.

The cataloguer's main problems are that he or she may have to play the material to get the full physical details, and may require a larger time allowance than for cataloguing a book. This is not true for all forms or even all examples within a form, but from personal experience using a pro forma system the times seem comparable.

To summarize, the collation of NBM will fit, for the most part, into the existing framework, but the cataloguer has to understand the requisite terminology and technical specifications, and also what detail is required for the users of the library's catalogue.

6 *Series area*   No special problems arise in this area with regard to NBM. It is sometimes difficult to determine whether a phrase on a slide set is a series statement or merely the publisher's added information. Thus the statement 'economic history' on a slide set may be referring to its subject rather than being part of a series on economic history. The cataloguer will have to base a decision on experience and by checking the publisher's catalogues. If there is still a doubt, then it should go in the notes area.

7 *Notes area*   AACR2 states that the reason for notes in the catalogue entry is to give 'useful descriptive information that cannot be fitted into other areas of the description'. This area is important for some NBM because it allows the client to establish a clearer picture of the possible value of the document before having to handle it. A computer disc is not easily browsed through, and a clear description of its contents on the catalogue card will save some wear and tear through unnecessary previewing.

Because many of these documents are aimed at a particular type of client – for example the nurse in training or the primary school child – it may be important to state this in the notes area so that the user has an idea of the intended audience. This may be difficult for the cataloguer to determine, especially for graphic material such as slides, illustrations and posters. Client level is often found assessed in the publishers' catalogues or the library document assessment forms, if such a system is used in the library (see also the section on acquisition of materials, pages 218 – 19).

It may also be necessary to describe the equipment required – for example a U-matic videocassette will be useless to a client who has access only to a VHS machine – or to describe the peripherals required for a computer program (for example, a mouse).

The packaging of the document may also have to be noted, as, for instance, in the case of a boxed kit which may have to be kept out of place in the normal shelf sequence. A document may be kept in closed access for security reasons. Finally, it should be noted whether the document is available in another format, perhaps a videorecording available in two formats, or a computer program available in cassette and floppy disc.

8   *Standard number and terms of availability area*   An increasing number of NBM have International Standard Book Numbers (ISBN) and some libraries may find it useful to have a record of this on their catalogue cards in case of future reordering; tracing details of this material can be difficult if the publisher's catalogue is not available. Some publishers use 'item numbers' which can prove useful when reordering, and these should be provided in the note area (see Rule 1.7B19).

The terms of availability area is perhaps more applicable for current bibliographies than for the library catalogue. It is rarely useful to have the price of an item on a library catalogue entry, for inflation will soon outstrip it. However, lacking the equivalent of Whitaker's *British books in print* to give an up-to-date price, this may offer some guidance if a client has to be charged for losing the document. Details such as whether the item is for hire belong to the bibliography and not to the library catalogue.

AACR2 as a framework can be used for all NBM, including computer materials. The detailed guidance given in the code for monographs is the result of many years of careful and exacting work by book cataloguers. It is hardly surprising that the chapters on NBM are not as detailed and that the non-book cataloguer must rely more on professional experience. However, the revised second edition has provided more examples and the new chapter 9, Computer files, has considerably strengthened the general nature of AACR2.

The headings for a document
Once the document has been physically described, the next step is to create suitable headings for it. The heading is the element by which the

entry is filed in the catalogue. Thus a document can be filed by author, title, form or its subject.

Author/title
The arguments concerning authorship have been looked at closely in the discussion concerning the statement of responsibility. Once the statement has been established, the cataloguer has to decide if one or more of those elements should become headings. In many cases there will be no statement of responsibility and then entry should be under title. To some extent the various forms differ as to whether or not they have an author heading; sound recordings usually have an author heading; filmstrips, slides, wallcharts and posters sometimes have an author heading; and models and motion pictures rarely have one.

The need for entry under author is perhaps open to scrutiny for NBM and will have to be decided from experience of how the clients of the library ask for this material. Many librarians have suggested that the usual approach is by subject and that clients rarely search for NBM under a specific author. This view has to be treated with some caution, for it is often that of librarians working in school library resource centres dealing with the requests of teachers and pupils.

Form
This has to be considered as a heading which might be sought for; a client might ask for all the filmstrips in stock on librarianship, for example. In an integrated catalogue this will involve checking each card individually for its material designation. However, this type of enquiry is perhaps so infrequent that it can be dealt with by the librarian as it arises rather than by a deliberate policy of providing a form entry for each document. Preparation of select form lists is another possibility, if this is a regularly recurring type of enquiry.

Subject description of a document
Generally speaking, clients use subject headings most often to search the catalogue for NBM. As with books, there are two elements to consider: the analysis of the subject content of the document and its subsequent classification; and the establishment of an index which will help clients to retrieve documents about named subjects successfully.

The analysis of the subject content of a document, and the expression of it for the benefit of clients, does not have to differ between books and NBM. A book on home beer brewing, a videotape on methods of brewing beer, a sound cassette giving instructions on how to brew beer and a specimen of home brewing apparatus − these do not differ in subject, despite the variety of forms. All subject indexing systems have strengths and weaknesses and the introduction of NBM may highlight these; it does not cause fundamental changes.

However, for the librarian who has not previously been involved in the subject analysis of NBM it is perhaps as well to point out the main problems. When analysing a book a librarian can usually establish its subject fairly quickly by looking at the title page and the contents list. From experience, the librarian presumes that the sub-themes of the book do not usually have to be classified as there are likely to be other books in the collection which have these as their main themes. A main subject heading will be given for the book, with perhaps one or two added headings for particularly important sub-themes. Consider the following example. The librarian is asked to catalogue *The American West: myths and legends* (EAV, 1976) (sound cassette/filmstrip set) and analyses it in this way. There is a teacher's guide which contains the dialogue of the sound recording, but no description of the 278 frames of the filmstrips. The librarian has to look at them through a viewer. The illustrations, which can be quickly glanced at in book form, now pose problems as he or she laboriously uses the machine. A conscientious librarian, worried about clients who may not realize from a single classification number the wealth of visual information in the filmstrip, notes that it contains material on cowboys and Red Indians and that it is also about the falsification of the history of the American West. It also shows how the media in general (through novelists such as James Fenimore Cooper), films (through stars such as Gene Autry and John Wayne, and directors such as John Ford), and television (through series such as 'The Lone Ranger') falsified the true picture. The real American West is then portrayed through folk songs, illustrations of the Mexican War, the Californian Gold Rush and Oklahoma Territory, and through further illustrations by the artist Charles Russell. The idea of manifest destiny is used to explain the myth making, as are Buffalo Bill, the Mormons, the Battle of Little Big Horn, Davy Crockett, Billy the Kid and pioneer women such as the real Calamity Jane. The librarian knows that all of this information could be used by the clients. But they cannot easily browse through the format, and the librarian knows there is not a great amount of visual information in the library on this subject. The problem is, how far should the document's subject content be analysed?

In other words, how exhaustive should subject indexing be? Is the right policy one of 'summarization', that is, a statement of the overall theme of the document; or one of 'depth indexing', statements of all the concepts within the document that might be helpful to clients? If one picture speaks a thousand words, then how many subject entries are required to make certain that all possible subject enquiries are catered for?

Bearing in mind such factors, plus the cost of making an entry and the difficulties of using a bulky catalogue, the answer must be to rely on encouraging clients to phrase subject enquiries in such a way that these difficulties can be overcome. Thus the client searching for an illustration of Buffalo Bill and failing to find a precise subject reference should be encouraged to think of less specific headings such as 'cowboys' and look at the material found under that heading. A client wanting a picture of John Ford may well find a source in printed guides to film material or the librarian may advise him or her to look in an encyclopedia. The library collection is a living collection with many possible entries to its material. It is important to remember this in deciding on a policy on the exhaustivity of subject indexing. NBM may require as a norm more subject entries than books, but the number should be kept within limits that take note of cost, the client's ability and the librarian's own searching skills.

'Specificity' is a problem that should be noted in connection with the analysis of NBM. How far does the system allow precision when specifying the subject of the document? To the newcomer, some NBM are perhaps surprisingly more specific in their subject content than books; for example: *Minienvironments, part 4: river bends*; *Ammonia: the Haber process*; *Why overtime?*; and *Heavy industry in Great Britain*.

This is not a new problem. Any cataloguer will know of books that are as specific as these and gather dust on the classification shelves until he or she plucks up courage to deal with them. Yet NBM do seem to have more than their fair share of these very specific subjects.

A further problem is that such specific subjects often require a long classification number. *Why overtime?* could be classified at 658.3222 and *Heavy industry in Great Britain* at 338.0942. These are not particularly extensive numbers but they are rather too long to put on a filmstrip container if the classification number is acting as a location device. It may well be necessary to consider giving the full number in the catalogue to act as a guide to the content of the document but only use part of the number — say four digits — to act as a physical location device. In this case, the catalogue card would read 658.3(222) with the digits within parentheses not being given on the actual document.

Conclusion

It is not necessary to introduce new cataloguing, classification and indexing systems solely in order to deal with NBM. It seems pointless to confront clients who have conquered their fears of the classified catalogue — or those, indeed, who may have had long years of practice in using it — with the need to learn a new method for part of the collection. Future shock is a problem for both librarian and clients and it should not be increased by introducing new retrieval tools unless they are absolutely necessary. If the present system used in the library for the retrieval of books has been successful for the users of the catalogue, then there is no reason why it should not be used for NBM. Extra guidance in finding NBM in the catalogue should suffice.

There has been no attempt in this section to praise or damn any one system of information retrieval. All have their strengths and weaknesses and, as has been said, NBM merely highlight these rather than posing any fundamental questions.

MANUAL OF PRACTICE

Cataloguing NBM

This section does not attempt to give all the details concerning the cataloguing necessary for NBM. Instead it highlights the variations from the cataloguing of books. For a fuller picture the reader is referred to the standard works. As mentioned at the beginning of part 4, policy decisions have to be made concerning the links between NBM and books and the provision of an integrated catalogue. Also NBM can generate more entries than a book, and a decision must be made on the maximum number of entries. However, such a decision should not be inflexible, for it must be recognized that special provision should be made for some documents. A policy on which forms to consider as self-indexing should also be settled at an early stage. Illustrations collections are perhaps the most obvious example; slides may also be treated in this way, depending upon the extent of the collection. A decision must also be made concerning simplified cataloguing. The following example illustrates the necessity for the cataloguer to be concerned with the amount of information he or she needs to supply when describing a document. It is based on the AACR2 third level of description.

Airports [multi-media]/devised and produced with Gerald Lloyd. — London: British Airports Authority: BP Educational Service, 1978.

1 airport timetable.
1 construction sheet.
1 currency exchange card.
1 cut-out model (6 sheets): card + instruction sheet.
1 filmstrip (36fr., 4 title fr.): col.;35mm + commentary notes.
174 miniature flags of the world: col.
1 painting book.
1 slide kit and slide viewer.
1 sound cassette (ca 30 mins.): 1⅞ ips, mono.
5 teacher's guides.
4 wallcharts: col.; 71 × 101 cm folded to 36 × 25 cm.
  In box 38 × 29 × 8 cm.
Investigates the world of airports.
For children aged 8−14.

Technical assistance received from Air Education and Recreation
   Organization.
Construction sheet for a cardboard glider.
Cut out model of a typical airport building and vehicles.
15 copies of filmstrip commentary.
Painting book tells story of two girls travelling to Spain.
Wallcharts concern themes of location, people, aircraft and travelling.

ISBN 0-901918-91-1; £27.99 (Education: £14.95)

387.7

1 LLOYD, Gerald
2 BP Educational Service
3 BRITISH AIRPORTS AUTHORITY
4 BRITISH PETROLEUM
      see
      BP

First level of description:

Airports/devised and produced with Gerald Lloyd. — British Airports Authority, 1978.

1 airport timetable; 1 construction sheet; 1 currency exchange card;
1 cut-out model; 1 filmstrip; flags of the world; 1 painting book;
1 slide kit and slide viewer; 1 sound cassette; 5 teacher's guides;
4 wallcharts.

Investigating the world of airports.
Intended for 8 – 14-year-olds.

ISBN 0-091918-91-1

387.7

All that is required?

Airports kit. — British Airports Authority, 1978.

387.7

The cataloguer will have to take considerable care in choosing the level
of description appropriate for the clients. The first level of description
may be appropriate for the majority of NBM. However, the physical
description area for this level (1.5B) is limited to 'extent of the items'
and it may be important to add on 'other physical details' (1.5C) and
'dimensions' (1.5D) such as the speed of a sound disc or the size of a
wallchart.

As has previously been mentioned, it may be necessary to shorten a classification number to accommodate it on some packaging – for example, a filmstrip tub.

A decision must also be reached regarding guiding within the library and the catalogue. The printed guides will have to include details concerning the location of NBM, instructions on how NBM are arranged within the catalogue and lists of material designations.

The librarian has to make these policy decisions on the basis of the needs of the library's clients, the forms of documents acquired, the organization of the stock and, last but not least, the staff available for cataloguing. Once these initial policy decisions have been made, the various tools and equipment required can be considered. First, an appropriate cataloguing code must be selected. It is strongly recommended that AACR2 is used for the cataloguing of NBM. It will need to be annotated by the practising cataloguer, in particular to:

(a) Define any terms that are unclear or required by clients.
(b) Annotate Chapter 21 to make it absolutely clear which rules can be used for all materials and which only for texts, sound recordings etc.
(c) Decide where extra elements will be required for particular forms if descriptive level 1 or 2 is used.

Examples illustrating AACR2 by Eric Hunter and the sample cards in *Non-book materials: the organisation of integrated collections*, third edition, by Jean Weihs, are also essential for the cataloguing room.

Equipment such as tape recorders may also have to be provided within the cataloguing room, as well as timing devices and table rulers.

The organization of the cataloguing process depends upon individual library requirements but some general points can be made. Individual media should be processed in batches, for example a number of slide sets together. This will ensure that problems peculiar to a particular medium can be treated at the same time, any equipment required being on hand. It is recommended that a document is catalogued first and then subject analysed. The item will have to be thoroughly searched for descriptive information and this search can be utilized for the subject analysis. If an assessment form system is used then this can prove useful for subject analysis. Only as a last resort should a document be played or projected as this is time consuming.

A pro forma is very helpful in speeding up the cataloguing process. These can be designed to meet the individual library's needs. The pro forma in figure 24 (overleaf) was designed for practical exercises in cataloguing of NBM by librarianship students, but there is no reason why it shold not be used elsewhere. The terminology and pattern are based on AACR2. The pro forma should be completed in the following order: description of the document; physical description; series; notes; and item number. This will create a standard item description. Then the main heading and tracings for added entries and references can be given. Finally, the classification and subject indexing can be entered.

Figure 25 (on pages 252–3) illustrates a completed pro forma for a single media document. This would then be handed to a typist or keyboard operator who would produce the catalogue card shown in figure 28 (on page 258), plus any other entries required from the tracings section on the pro forma. Figure 26 (on pages 254–5) illustrates the method for a mixed media document. The only major difference is the use of the column 'entry order' on the right-hand side of the physical form designator section. This indicates in which order the physical forms should be typed on the catalogue card. Figure 29 shows the resulting catalogue card. Figure 27 shows a pro forma for a computer file based on chapter 9, AACR2. Figure 30 shows the resulting catalogue card.

In summary, the practical cataloguing, classification and indexing of NBM should not cause any major problems. Once policy decisions are made and the cataloguers are familiar with NBM and cataloguing tools, a steady output can be expected.

Cataloguer: initials	Classifier: initials	Location	Acc. no.
Classification	Additional classification		
Subject headings + references or Subject index entries			
Main heading			
Description of the document			
Uniform title Title (or supplied title) General material designation Statements of responsibility			
Edition	Material specific		
Place Publisher, Sponsor Place of distribution Distributor Date of publication			

Figure 24. Blank pro forma for cataloguing and classification of NBM

No.of items	Physical description				Entry order
	Sound cassette (min.): analog, digital ips, mps, mono stereo				
	Sound disc (min.): analog, digital, 33⅓ rpm, 45 rpm, mono stereo				
	Slide : sd. col. b.&w.				
	Videocassette disc ( ) sd., si., col., b.&w., in.				
	Computer cassette : sd., col.; × in.				
	Computer laser optical disk : sd., col.; in. chip cartridge				
	Poster : col. b.&w. × cm.				
	Wallchart : col. b.&w.; × cm folded to × cm.				
	Other specific material designation	Extent	Other physical details	Dimensions	

Series
Notes

Standard number		Terms of availability
Tracings		

Figure 24. Continuation

Cataloguer: initials	Classifier: initials	Location	Acc. no.
I CB	RF	Yarm Branch	85920

Classification	Additional classification
658. 054	

Subject headings + references or Subject index entries

   I. BUSINESS FIRMS : Applications of Computers 658.054

Main heading
     COMPUTERS in business

Description of the document

Uniform title

Title (or supplied title)   Computers in business : Spread sheets

General material designation   [Videorecording]

Statements of responsibility   / Sunday Times; presented by Andrew Neil and John Humphrys

Edition	Material specific

Place   [Liverpool]

Publisher, Sponsor   : Taylor Made Films

Place of distribution

Distributor

Date of publication   / 1988

Figure 25. Completed pro forma for cataloguing and classification of NBM (videorecording)

No.of items	Physical description	Entry order
	Sound cassette (min.) : analog, digital ips, mps, mono stereo	
	Sound disc (min.) : analog, digital, 33⅓ rpm, 45 rpm, mono stereo	
	Slide : sd. col. b.&w.	
I	(Videocassette disc) *(20 min.)* (sd.) si., (col.) b.&w. in.	
	Computer cassette : sd., col.; × in.	
	Computer laser optical disc : sd., col.; in. chip cartridge	
	Poster : col. b.&w.; × cm.	
	Wallchart: col. b.&w.; × cm folded to × cm.	

	Other specific material designation	Extent	Other physical details	Dimensions	

Series
— (Sunday Times business video series)

Notes
— VHS. — TMF/ST-2.

Standard number		Terms of availability

Tracings
1. NEIL, Andrew   *2. HUMPHRYS, John*   *3. 658.054*

Figure 25. Continuation

Cataloguer: initials ICB	Classifier: initials RF	Location Yarm Branch	Acc. no 85917

Classification 382.9142	Additional classification

Subject headings + references or Subject index entries
    1. COMMON MARKET 382.9142
    2. EUROPEAN ECONOMIC COMMUNITY 382.9142
    3. E.E.C. (EUROPEAN ECONOMIC COMMUNITY)
                                   382.9142

Main heading
        HAYWARD, O.G.

Description of the document

Uniform title

Title (or supplied title)   The Common Market

General material designation   [multimedia]

Statements of responsibility   / by O.G. Hayward.

Edition	Material specific

Place   — London
Publisher, Sponsor   : C.I. Audio Visual
Place of distribution
Distributor
Date of publication   , 1971.

Figure 26. Completed pro forma for cataloguing and classification of NBM (multimedia)

No.of items	Physical description				Entry order
1	(Sound cassette) (4o min.): analog, digital 1⅞ ips, mps, (mono) quad				1
	Sound disc (min.): analog, digital, 33⅓ rpm, 45 rpm, mono stereo quad				
16	Slide : sd. (col.) b.&w.				2
	Videocassette disc ( ) sd., si., col., b.&w., in.				
	Computer cassette: sd., col.; × in.				
	Computer laser optical disc : sd., col.; in. chip cartridge				
	Poster : col. b.&w. cm.				
	Wallchart : col. b.&w.; × cm folded to × cm.				
	Other specific material designation	Extent	Other physical details	Dimensions	

Series
—(Incernational studies; ISI)

Notes
— Historical background to the EEC; organisation and prospects Teacher's notes

Standard number		Terms of availability

Tracings	1. THE COMMON MARKET 2. INTERNATIONAL STUDIES 3. 382.9142

Figure 26. Continuation

Cataloguer: initials	Classifier: initials	Location	Acc. no.
ICB	RF	Yarm Branch	85921

Classification	Additional classification
005.369	

Subject headings + references or Subject index entries

   I. SPREAD SHEET PACKAGES   005.369

Main heading   As easy as

Description of the document

Uniform title

Title (or supplied title)   As easy as

General material designation   [computer file]

Statements of responsibility   / Trius.

Edition
    - Version 301. - Programs (8 files).

Place	- [USA ?]
Publisher, Sponsor	: Trius
Place of distribution	; Beer, Devon
Distributor	: Shareware Marketing
Date of publication	, 1989.

Figure 27. Completed pro forma for cataloguing and classification of NBM (computer file)

No.of items	Physical description				Entry order
	Sound cassette (min.) : analog, digital ips, mps, mono quad				
	Sound disc (min.) : analog, digital, 33⅓ rpm, 45 rpm, mono stereo quad				
	Slide : sd. col. b.&w.				
	Videocassette disc ( ) sd., si., col., b.&w., in.				
	Computer cassette : sd., col.; × in.				
	(Computer) laser optical (disc) : sd., col., 5¼in. chip cartridge + user manual				
	Poster : col. b.&w. × cm.				
	Wallchart : col. b.&w.; × cm folded to × cm.				
	Other material designation	Extent	Other physical details	Dimensions	
Series					
Notes	— Spread sheet, with graphic capabilities — System requirements : IBM PC or fully compatible MS-DOS				
Standard number	Serial no: ASA 11 64-26	Terms of availability			
Tracings	1. TRIUS 2. AS EASY AS 3. 005. 369				

Figure 27. Continuation

658.054

> COMPUTERS in business : spread sheets [videorecording]/
> Sunday Times; presented by Andrew Neil and John
> Humphrys.
> — [Liverpool] : Taylor Made Films, 1988.
>
> 1 videocassette (20 min) : sd. col. — (Sunday Times
> business video series) — VHS. — TMF/ST—2

Figure 28. Completed catalogue card for 'Computers in business'

382.9142

> HAYWARD, O.G.
>
> The Common Market [multimedia] / by O.G. Hayward.—
> London: C.I. Audio Visual, 1971.
>
> > 1 sound cassette (40 min.:1⅞ ips, mono.
> > 16 slides: col. — (International studies; IS1).
> >   Historical background to the EEC, organization and
> >   prospects. Teacher's notes.

Figure 29. Completed catalogue card for 'The Common Market'

005.369

> As easy as [computer file]/Trius. — Version 3.01. —
> Programs (8 files). — [USA?]: Trius; Beer, Devon :
> Shareware Marketing, 1989.
> 1 computer disc; 5¼ in. + user manual. Spread sheet, with
> graphic capabilities.
>
> System requirements: IBM PC or fully compatible MS-DOS.
> Serial No: ASA116426

Figure 30. Completed catalogue card for 'As easy as'

STORAGE AND RETRIEVAL

Storing NBM for easy access and retrieval is important. Books have been placed on shelves for hundreds of years, and this system presents reasonable accessibility combined with fairly economic storage. When NBM first appeared on the scene, they seemed to be so radical in format that librarians felt that only new systems could be adopted. Tied in with this was a concern that these materials were more overtly desirable than books and presented considerable problems of security. Certainly some NBM are expensive, but they cannot honestly be considered excessively so in comparison with the current cost of books.

One solution was to lock them in special cupboards to which only the librarians had access. They would then be released for use on the premises by the clients. Another was to relay the information to special booths or carrels from a remote source so that, once again, control was almost entirely in the hands of the librarian and not the user. Those enlightened libraries that felt that some responsibility could be given to the client decided to arrange them on open access in collections according to the format, as it was considered that these did not necessarily mix well. If the catalogue was organized so that books and NBM were integrated, it was possible that a casual search for a subject would reveal the presence of items in a variety of formats. In the absence of such information, however, the client was faced with deliberately searching for the subject within the medium that had been preselected.

Recognition of these drawbacks has encouraged library organizations towards the final logical step, intershelving the different media. Multimedia storage has proved a perfectly satisfactory arrangement for most formats, as the majority of items can be packaged so that they sit like books on shelves or rest in journal boxes. Transforming filmstrips into slides and packaging them in plastic wallets solves the most difficult problem, and as vinyl discs are progressively replaced by CD audio they too can fit among the other items.

Computer programs on discs may be stored in this way too, either in separate packages or in boxes. Many institutions, however, offer network facilities from a hard disc or server. If this system is adopted, it is advisable for economic reasons to have at least 12 machines in such an arrangement. An alternative organization is to provide microcomputers with their own hard discs as individual workstations. In particular, generic programs like wordprocessors, databases and spread sheets are ideally provided from hard discs.

Subject-specific programs may be better drawn individually from shelved packages, from large mainframes or even from optical stores. In making decisions on such arrangements, it is useful to take into account the relative importance of the documentation that accompanies the program. While this may be retrieved from the beginning of the program, experience shows that it is more effective if it is permanently available to the user on paper, especially as it is such an aid to browsing. It can be argued that local availability of such programs is probably more valuable and convenient for the user than a central distribution system.

The growth of optical systems and the appearance of 'juke box' collections of them provides the potential for a promising high density storage arrangement for data and information as well as programs in the future. If initial experiments with fibre optic links on university campuses for the distribution of information to individual workstations prove successful, then they could be seen as the forerunners for large bandwidth distribution systems from libraries to individual premises for the general public.

In the section that follows, the storage issues for the various media will be discussed. First, some consideration of the criteria for selecting a system is necessary. Such criteria need to reflect both the needs of the clients and the managerial problems of the librarian. Underlying them must be the demand for maximum use combined with optimum security, safety and availability. Any decisions that are made will necessarily be compromises, for the totally secure system will preclude free access; but in reaching such decisions the librarian should at least have considered the reasons and have some understanding of the consequences.

Labelling
While consideration will be given to labelling throughout this section, it is useful at this stage to be aware of the main principles. Labels should:

(a) carry information which ties various parts of a package together;
(b) have space for additional local information;
(c) explain any equipment standards required for use;
(d) carry a brief description of content and treatment, particularly with regard to materials that are difficult to browse;
(e) explain any prior knowledge that the user should have or indicate a level of treatment and its objectives, where relevant;

(f) be legible to the level of literacy likely for the potential user;
(g) be fixed firmly so that they do not come off easily.

Browsing

Some NBM are difficult to browse easily. Good labels and transparent packaging as appropriate are a help, and equipment nearby to provide rapid search facilities is an asset. Equipment for videocassettes and the CD formats permits rapid sampling of different parts of the materials. Computer programs sometimes contain sample 'runs' so that the user can see a version of what can be undertaken; but as these become increasingly sophisticated, an increasing length of time is required to explore the possibilities available. Accompanying documentation is particularly valuable to give an indication of the potential usefulness.

Keeping the parts together

Most formats separate readily into a number of parts. These may be merely the material and its box, but the individual pieces may be more numerous than this. Cross-labelling does help to bring the pieces together, but it is also important that external labels should provide all the necessary information about the number and type of elements inside.

Security

Storage should resolve problems of security without imposing prohibitive conditions on use. There are some potentially unpreventable losses because the items, such as microforms and slides, are so small. However, many of the standard library security systems act effectively with NBM (care must be taken to avoid magnetic systems being used with magnetic materials or X-ray systems with film). Some security systems also act effectively with equipment, but in most libraries this is satisfactorily restrained by screwing it firmly to benches and shelves. Finally, a decision has to be made to balance carefully the cost of security against the cost of replacement. Unique and irreplaceable material should generally not be available in any form other than copies.

Packaging

Packaging should facilitate storage. Now that intershelving is the accepted system, a major criterion for selecting packaging is its support for this. In addition, the packaging should be durable, reflecting the degree and manner of use of the material involved. Some packages are so durable that access to the contents can be excessively troublesome, while others open so readily that the librarian is fortunate to find the contents still present even if the package has hardly been moved from its shelf. Finally, the packaging should protect the contents from damage, but in so doing should not damage the user. The principal enemies of NBM are dust, excessive temperature variation and humidity, all of which should be taken into account in a good packaging system.

Difficulties over storage come not from the type of material, but from the different formats in which they are arranged. Below, each of the major formats is discussed separately.

Portfolios of paper materials and photographic prints
The early system adopted was to file the materials in wallets in drawers or in racks. Although the wallets had flaps, an accidental drop could shed the contents. More recently, there has been a trend towards binders — ring, lever arch or even albums. In these the contents are more secure and in some cases better protected, particularly when each item is in its own clear plastic sleeve within the binder. Shelving is also easy. Labelling is important to ensure that each item is cross-referenced to its container, and this should also carry the relevant information about the materials the binder is supposed to hold.

Filmstrips
These are usually supplied in small canisters with separate explanatory notes. In many cases, librarians have sensibly transformed them into slides.

If such a policy is not adopted, various packaging systems are available. A binder-type box can be used; the canister held in a sponge rubber former, the notes in an internal flap. Cardboard can be used instead of sponge rubber, but it deteriorates with use. Hanging transparent wallets, similar to those used for slides, are available with attached bags, in which the canister and notes may be stored. These can be held in filing cabinets, in journal boxes or in binders.

For intershelving purposes, the binder systems are the most suitable. There is also additional space for an audiocassette if that is needed.

Good labelling is needed to ensure good cross-referencing between the notes, the filmstrip and its canister. Each needs to carry the relevant titling and numbers to ensure they are kept together, and this information should be repeated on the external packaging. Scratching the information on the black leader or trailer of the filmstrip is one way of labelling this. Well-prepared notes should provide the user with a browsing facility,

but it is not difficult to extract the filmstrip and hold it up to the light
or over a light box to obtain an impression of the quality of the visual
content.

Slides

All slides should be mounted before storage. Mounts can be divided into
two main types, plastic without or with glass. If the former is adopted,
the film itself is exposed and unprotected, and therefore may be damaged
or fingered or become covered in dust. Adding glass increases the
thickness and cost. If a trace of moisture is present during mounting or
is introduced through humidity changes, the light is distorted as it passes
through and produces a rainbow appearance, the pattern moving under
the influecne of the light's heat. This is called a Newton ring. Some glass
mounts are called anti-Newton and eliminate this distortion.

The common practice is to store master sets mounted in anti-Newton
glass mounts, reference sets in ordinary glass and distribution copies
in glassless mounts. In all cases, however, the slides must be labelled.
Each should have a spot in the bottom left-hand corner, and this is
frequently used to carry the number which indicates its position in a set.
Other labels should give the set title, if there is one, and maybe the
production company. In library collections, it is wise to avoid using a
code number only, although this may be added to the other labels.

Domestic storage is usually a box with individual slots for each slide.
To view or project them, each slide has to be extracted individually and
inserted into a magazine or directly into the projector. For identification,
an indexing system is needed to decide which slide is which. Inserting
new slides into the sequence means reshuffling all the others, a very time-
consuming business. Intershelving is rarely practical with this method.

A more popular and simple system is to store the slides in a plastic
wallet, each in its own slot. The number of slides per wallet varies with
the size of the slot. Note that if a slot is too tight, the more likely it is
that damage to the slide or wallet will occur; whereas if a slot is too
loose, the more likely it is that the slides will fall out. This latter problem
can be discouraged by having a covering flap over the whole wallet.

Browsing can be easily undertaken by holding the wallet up to the light
or resting it on a light box. The wallets may be hung in filing cabinets,
but for intershelving they should be held in binders or placed in journal
boxes. The information on the external labelling should include the
number of slides in the set. To assist in a visual check, some librarians
cut off any slots that are not being used.

Microforms

As microfilm material itself is illegible without magnification, the presence of eye-readable information is essential. This may be attached to the spool, the cassette or the cartridge, to the card of aperture cards, to the top band and any sleeve of a microfiche. The extent of the information should be sufficiently comprehensive for the user to be able to identify important sections rapidly.

Roll microfilm is readily stored on shelves, as the various methods used to hold the film can be easily placed in boxes. To give more substance to the item, it may be sensible to place the reel, cassette or cartridge in a book file or another box.

Microfiche of all types are normally kept in paper sleeves, and as these are approximately 6in. × 4in. in dimension, they can be simply stored in a small drawer. Computer-controlled storage systems are also available for large collections, the program holding sufficient information to help the user identify any individual frame. Microfiche can also be stored in special holders in ring binders, and these are ideal for intershelving.

Films

Films are now rarely kept in general library collections, and so the problem of intershelving does not arise. Stored on their reels in tins or cardboard containers, these are often kept in fibreboard boxes. Films are normally stored in special collections.

As browsing is difficult, labelling and supporting information should be as comprehensive as possible. A short précis is often provided to give users an opportunity to obtain some understanding of the contents. On some projectors, a footage counter is provided, and this may be used to identify particular parts that are of special interest and to which the film may be fast wound.

Films may be seriously damaged by dust, excessive heat and humidity. Maintaining constant suitable environmental conditions is important. Protection from dust can be achieved by ensuring the reels are kept securely boxed when not in use. It should not be necessary to examine the film on its reel in order to find initial information about its content.

Audiocassettes

Magnetic tapes are obviously difficult to browse; there is nothing to see. Comprehensive information is therefore necessary, giving a précis of the content and length of any sections, preferably measured by time. If there are odometers which are reasonably uniform in their readings available on the equipment in the library, it is helpful to include position readings of the major sections of the tapes. In practice, sampling and browsing through the contents of the tape can be undertaken by using the fast forward and rewind controls on a player to certain points and then playing a part of the tape. If such a facility is to be encouraged, suitable equipment should be available close to the various storage areas.

Technical information should be provided, for example mono or stereo, the tape surface (normal, chromium dioxide or metal) and Dolby recording. If the audiocassette holds computer data, then the model, operating system and use instructions are needed.

Cassettes are normally supplied in plastic boxes, usually with an insert providing basic information and any specific instructions or guidelines on use. It is important that these are labelled so that the different parts of the package can be easily brought together.

While cassettes may be intershelved with other materials, it may be helpful to give the package more substance by enclosing it in a bigger box. This method also provides more space for further information. It is always advisable to keep the cassette inside its own plastic box, even when this is placed inside a larger box for shelving purposes.

Magnetic discs

Discs cannot be browsed easily, and depend on accompanying documentation for effective use. As they are relatively fragile and easily damaged by dust and grease, it is essential that they are stored in their paper or plastic sleeves, preferably within another container.

Two arrangements are common. One is to place the discs as a collection inside a small box with a lid, each containing about ten of them. With several programs on each disc, this means that each box could contain eight to a hundred different programs. Although they may be related to each other, this does not encourage ease of access, and unwanted discs get fingered during searches for the one that is required. There will also be difficulties in linking relevant paperwork to each program. The other common technique is to place each disc, with a limited number of programs stored on it, in a plastic folder together with the paperwork describing its use. This is very similar to a slim book in size and can therefore be easily intershelved.

Each disc bears a label; only the lightest pressure must be used on a floppy disc in order to write on its label; otherwise the disc within its cardboard jacket will be damaged. Therefore felt-tip pens are recommended. Minidiscs are much stronger and better protected.

The principal information, in addition to the program names, authors and producers, is that which identifies the computer with which the disc can be used. This means listing the make, model and disc operating system or format; there is no way of identifying this information from the external appearance of the disc. All small discs for computers look identical.

As magnetic discs wear out with use and are relatively easily damaged or corrupted, it is common practice to prepare a copy to be kept safe in reserve. There is no qualitative difference between the original and any copies made from it; all are storing digital information. Thus it does not matter whether the original or a copy is issued for general use. Some publishers sell a copy with the original in the package; some release copyright for this purpose and recommend that a duplicate is prepared. To prevent accidental erasure, it is advisable to write-protect the disc (unless writing is essential in using the program) as that helps to avoid genuine accidents.

Discs are damaged by excessive heat, high humidity and direct sunlight, so they should be stored in a suitable environment. Pressure leads to bending and distortion of the surface and this has to be avoided. Also, because the information is stored on them magnetically, they have to be kept away from strong magnetic fields such as those produced by television sets or even the transformers in the computers.

Videocassettes

The videocassette raises the same difficulties with regard to browsing as all magnetic media. There is nothing to see. Good labelling and the provision of supplementary information is therefore essential. Again, sub-sections of interest should be identified, and the distance from the beginning by time can be indicated. The visual information from fast searching is helpful, but identification through the index system is quicker. Some tapes are recorded with index marks for the different sections, so that the player will stop at each of them. This is unusual with commercial tapes but common with local recordings.

It is advisable to ensure that the lug on the back of the cassette is removed to prevent accidental recording over a programme. For intershelving purposes, the videocassette is supplied in a substantial box and there is no need to duplicate it. However, notes and further information should be kept with it as far as possible. Tapes should be stored upright so that the loops do not have the opportunity to slide over each other.

The main sources of damage are dust, temperature and humidity. Similar precautions should be taken as with other media; it should be ensured that the tapes are kept in their boxes to keep out the dust and are stored in good environmental conditions.

Overhead projector transparencies

Only specialized libraries dealing with education and training are likely to have these materials to store. Because they are normally used only by instructors, it is usual to keep them in any kits to which they refer or to store them as a separate collection rather than to make an attempt to intershelve them.

If transparencies are not framed, they are most suitably kept in folders, wallets or pseudo-record sleeves, separated from each other for ease of use and protection by sulphur-free paper. Framed transparencies may be stored in box files, ring binders or folders in large filing cabinets.

Information about individual transparencies may be written on the upper or most easily scanned edge of the frames, summaries being given on the outside of folders. When wallets are used, information can be written on external labels. Some coding system needs to be developed to bring the various transparencies back together after use.

Vinyl discs

The accepted packaging for these discs is a double sleeve, the inner a protective paper cover (better than plastic because this usually induces static), the outer a strong laminated card which normally carries a comprehensive summary of the relevant information. The individual bands are usually identified, and there is an increasing trend to include the length of each, measured in time. Labels may be fixed to the outer surface of the sleeve for library numbering, and this should be repeated on the label on the centre of the disc. It is also possible to write on the spine of the outer sleeve if the storage method makes this important.

Discs should be stored vertically and fairly rigidly to prevent bending. For convenience in browsing and selection, clients prefer a bin system of storage in which the front of the sleeve faces outwards so that the collection can be flipped through. An alternative storage system is to place the discs on shelves with the spine outwards, but this is more difficult to browse as the information is smaller and less legible. In this system, the shelves should have dividers, 9 to 12in. apart. Discs are heavy, so the shelving needs to be strong.

There are no trends towards intershelving discs, as this could prove damaging to them. If the library wishes to intershelve material available on discs, it is wiser to purchase or rerecord (with permission) on cassettes and then store these.

Optical storage systems
These are supplied in plastic or card boxes, each with a spine that can carry simple information. There is space on the discs for information, a substantial area available on those using only one side for the recorded data. Leaflets carrying further information can be easily inserted into the container. For appropriate stores, the information usually contains descriptions of each section, including the length measured in time. Chapter and selected frame numbers can also be listed where these can be located by the user. Discs that are libraries of pictures can list all these, but that requires a substantial volume to carry all the information.

With systems like WORMS and erasable discs, it is essential that the user maintains an accurate file of the contents as additional information is added or removed.

The boxes can be simply intershelved, or given more substance by being stored inside larger boxes. Special shelf units are available for these formats, but they are not essential in a multimedia library collection.

External labelling
To end this section on storage, it is worth re-emphasizing the importance of external labelling. Frequently the information on materials produced from commercial sources is inadequate and needs to be supplemented by the library staff.

External labelling is important for two reasons. It provides the user with browsing information, and indicates any constraints on operation that may dismiss the item from consideration. Secondly, if the information is sufficiently comprehensive, it saves the user from opening and exploring a package that may prove to be irrelevant, and thus prevents potential damage to the contents. As a minimum, the information on the spine should give the title, author and/or presenter, publisher's insignia and any series or item title and number. Sufficient space should be left for local library labels. On the front and/or rear of the container, further information concerning the level and content of the package is useful, together with the various formats included, particularly where these may lead to incompatibility problems.

The comprehensiveness of this information needs to be increased in the case of extensive multimedia packages or kits, so that it includes references to the relevant users and the most suitable manner to work with it. The packaging and storage of these mixtures have not been described, but there is no reason why they should not be boxed and stored on end on shelves, just like rather fat books.

COPYRIGHT

For librarians the issue of copyright has been a constant source of anxiety. That concern is expressed is important, for the maintenance of the law helps to ensure just reward for authors and producers, and therefore the continual development of new products. In the absence of the upholding of copyright legislation, the potential market disintegrates and there is no economic rationale for continuing to produce material.

Over the years the technology has developed to the degree that copying has become very much easier to undertake. It used to be the case that copies were always inferior to the original, but copies of digital recordings − whether of music, video or computer programs − are always of exactly the same standard as the masters from which they came. Indeed, much of the present equipment provided for the high quality of replay of NBM is designed to provide copying facilities. The intention behind this is to provide the user with production opportunities of a high standard, and with respect to recording from radio and television the option of time shifting, that is recording the broadcast in the user's absence and replaying it later.

Thus good hi-fi systems are provided with facilities for recording radio to audiotape, and vinyl disc and tape to tape as standard options. Videocassette recorders are designed to record broadcast television, and are easily linked to support transfer from one tape to another. Dubbing sound over a videorecording is a standard facility to support the use of video cameras, and these options make it relatively easy to pirate video and films. Computer discs are expected to be copied so that masters are not used as working copies, and the personal development of programs, now that they are so complex, often involves using libraries of procedures that have been developed for that purpose. If the procedure comes from the middle of a published program, it is a mere extension of the same principle. Digitizers have been developed to transfer a photograph or a still video picture into a computer program as a creative act, although the pictures so recorded may themselves be copyright. Facsimile facilities are now incorporated into the computer so that the images received in this way can be manipulated or stored in an electronic − as opposed to a paper − file. Great efforts continue to develop inexpensive equipment that will read the individual letters into the computer as well, so that any text, whether received by facsimile or digitized, can be absorbed into the text that the user is creating.

The opportunities offered by the new technologies are far wider and more integrated than the traditional photocopying systems that first alerted librarians to the anxieties of the copyright law. Taking paper copies of parts of books or print-outs from frames of microforms at least produced copies that were representative of the original, but many of the newer technical developments lead to copies that become manipulated and absorbed into new creations. When this was done by painfully copying pieces of text by hand, the labour was such that many turned a blind eye. In these new developments, extensive pieces can be absorbed with a few strokes on the keyboard.

Vigilance and care is therefore even more important now. Users must be constantly made aware of the importance of respecting other people's rights, not just because it is the law but because it will deprive the rights owner of the opportunity to create further works and material. Stealing other people's rights can be responsible for ensuring that new material is not created, and everyone loses by this. Librarians have a responsibility to encourage users to appreciate this and to respect copyright. Perhaps, if clients recognized that any material they created — provided it had some originality — was automatically their own copyright, they would have more understanding. There is no legal act or registration required to obtain the rights, merely the act of creating the item. Given royal assent in November 1988, the long-awaited Copyright, Designs and Patents Act 1988 was implemented on 1 August 1989. All rights determined before the date of implementation will continue as long as they would under previous legislation, but from that date all copyright is subject to the Act. Most of the rest of this section refers to the implications of the new Act.[18]

The duration of rights on items prepared before the Act will continue as before, but that for materials created following its implementation will generally last for 50 years. The exception is published texts that are copyright for only 25 years. The difficulty with NBM is that there are so many different rights attached to them. For example, a video has the ownership rights of the producer, those in the particular format, the rights of the performers and those relating to the music, and at least the 'moral rights' of the author and producer. If the production was originally broadcast, it is unlikely that the company responsible owned more than the rights to transmit it.

Copying in any form is illegal. A photograph of a painting and a paper print of a microform frame are as much copies as a duplicate in the same material form. If a photograph is digitized into a computer, the rights in it are being broken.

In the privacy of one's own home and for use in purely domestic circumstances, almost anything can take place, and although rights are often being transgressed there is little likelihood of any notice being taken. Naturally any copies made cannot be sold or performed in public. Legally, all the normal copyright regulations apply, although recording from broadcasts for the purposes of time shifting is permissible. There are many attempts by manufacturers to discourage copying, especially with video and computer software, but almost all of these can be overcome by the skilled user. However, they do discourage the amateur in his or her own home from making copies too freely.

Some copying is legal, provided a substantial part is not taken, and this means not just a large chunk but also the central feature of an item – the summary graph or core algorithm in the computer code, for example. Commercial agencies have introduced another protection to try to thwart some of this copying as part of the contract of the right of supply when the item is purchased, and this should be noted. Under the new Act, fair dealing rights for personal use and research continue although this does not apply to sound, film or videorecordings. Copies of extracts from these media are permissible for use in teaching.

Some libraries will be given the right to copy for archival purposes, but this will not apply to all. All libraries will be able to allow the copying of 1% of an item per quarter of a year for personal use, but this must not form part of a repeated set, for example for a class set. Abstracts at the top of journal articles can also be copied, particularly when they form part of a guide to contents. This right may, however, lapse if a licensing scheme is introduced.

Satellite technology introduces new problems as the origination of the signal may not be clear, and the ownership may not be defined. However, until legal cases have been decided, it is better to assume that all the restrictions that bear on normal broadcast transmissions apply to those via satellites. Cable requires a licence for installation, except within one site, and so if a group of libraries wish to be interconnected in this way a licence will be necessary. However, if a university library wishes to interconnect with all the buildings that form its campus, it is likely that this will be permissible without a licence.

Some libraries will be identified by the Secretary of State so that they have extended rights of copying to support their particular users. Until the statutory regulations are issued, it is not clear what these will be or whether they will cover NBM at all. On the other hand, the Act includes the right for owners of certain material to charge the library if their items are borrowed, that is, removed from the premises for use. This is a rental charge under another name, and will have to be paid by the library. The funding for it may come from the library's own funds or from a charge to the client; the Act does not suggest any mechanism, merely that the producer has the right to receive payment from the library. While this rental scheme does not apply to books, it does cover sound, video, film and computer programs.

Another new aspect introduced in the Act is pressure towards the adoption of licensing schemes.[19] Particularly with regard to off-air recordings and photocopying of texts, but also with regard to any other areas in which producers and rights owners feel there would be advantages, the Act encourages the development and adoption of licensing schemes which will permit copying for certain fees. It is for the producers to suggest a scheme that is acceptable to representatives of the users, and in the case of disagreements there will be special tribunals set up to ensure fair play and to arbitrate.

These schemes will cover certain libraries, most likely in the education sector, and not necessarily all of them. It will be up to the producers to decide which they wish to include. There is little doubt that, finances permitting, such arrangements can be a satisfactory way of serving clients efficiently without there being constant anxiety about the copyright regulations that may be bearing on what is being undertaken.

Such is the widespread nature of the effect of the new Act that it is incumbent on librarians to familarize themselves with its conditions, in particular noting the relevant statutory regulations. Special sections of these regulations apply to libraries and need to be studied. The comments in this section have been prepared before they have been fully analysed.

REFERENCES

1 British Library Research & Development Department, *Annual report*, London, British Library, 1989.
2 Cornish, G. P., 'Report: National Committee on Regional Library Cooperation', *Audiovisual librarian*, **15** (2), 1989, 106.
3 Tibber, M., 'The national discography', *Audiovisual librarian*, **15** (1), 1989, 25.
4 Noble, I., 'Public domain software for librarians', *LAITG news* (Library Association Information Technology Group), **19**, 1989, 24—37.
5 Jones, J., 'The appraisal of audiovisual software', *British Universities Film Council newsletter*, (30), February 1977, 12.
6 Foskett, A. C., *The subject approach to information*, 4th ed., London, Bingley; Hamden, Ct, Linnet, 1977, 1.
7 For a detailed discussion of the problems involved in cataloguing a specialist slide collection, see Clark, W. R. and Harrison, K., 'LANSLIDE: the automation of the University of Lancaster Library's slide collection', *Audiovisual librarian*, **14** (4), 1988, 196—200.
8 Harrison, H. P., 'Media resources in the Open University Library', *Audiovisual librarian*, **1** (1), 1973, 13—14.
9 See the following articles concerning NBM and the automated catalogue: Morse, H. and Holland, M., 'Cataloguing av materials on DOBIS/LIBIS', *Audiovisual librarian*, **15** (3), 1989, 134—41; Knowles, C., 'OCLC and me — computerizing the av catalogue', *Audiovisual librarian*, **15** (2), 1989, 80—5.
10 *Anglo-American cataloguing rules*, 2nd rev. ed., Chicago, American Library Association; Ottawa, Canadian Library Association; London, Library Association, 1988, 1.
11 Cutter, C. A., *Rules for a dictionary catalogue*, 4th ed., Government Printing Office, 1904; 1st ed., 1876.
12 Weihs, J. R., *Non-book materials: the organisation of integrated collections*, 3rd ed., Ottawa, Canadian Library Association, 1976, 8.
13 Furlong, N. and Platt, P., *Cataloguing rules for books and other media in primary and secondary schools*, 5th ed., School Library Association, 1976, 8.
14 *International standard bibliographic description: general*, IFLA, 1977, 5.

15 *Anglo-American cataloguing rules*, op. cit., 623.
16 Price, S., 'Up the Umzimvubu', *Observer*, 21 March 1976, 33.
17 Library Association Media Cataloguing Rules Committee, *Non-book materials cataloguing rules*, London, National Council for Educational Technology/Library Association, 1973, 16.
18 The legal situation with regard to copyright is complicated and the Copyright, Designs and Patents Act 1988 still requires clarification in practice. Guidance is available from the Library Association and the Council for Educational Technology.
19 The Copyright Act 1988 authorizes licensing schemes and the Copyright Licensing Agency and the Educational Recording Agency provide licences for print and off-air recordings.

Part 5

MANAGEMENT

INTRODUCTION

If users and materials are to interact successfully within the library, good management techniques are essential. Without them, the user is left to flounder in a mass of disordered material without either advice or guidance. The basic techniques for managing a library are, of course, appropriate for both book and non-book collections. In this part, the discussion is limited to those extra problems introduced by the presence of NBM, and deals with the four topics of the physical environment, satisfying requirements, financial implications and problems of control.

A very thorough guide to the organization and management of NBM in a college setting has been provided by the Council for Educational Technology in their packs *Learning resources in colleges* and *Management of information technology in further education.*[1] Although aimed at the educational market, the questionnaires provided are of value to any library manager considering the place of NBM in the library and its community.

Many of the problems of management are a result of the inadequacies of clients' conceptions and their difficulties in making use of the service provided. To some extent, NBM add to these problems, for many of the formats require the availability and use of specialized equipment. Here is a new dimension to the much discussed topic of 'user education'. The technologies involved in information technology have led to a re-examination of the library as a provider of information. Gateshead Public Library have provided shopping services for pensioners based on Prestel. Libraries in some areas are developing community video workshops. In academic institutions there has been the merger of librarians and computer centres to form information services, as at Aston University.[2] In the USA librarians have been involved in telecasting their own and other productions. Public libraries have cooperated with local community groups in providing viewdata facilities and in loaning out microcomputers. It is not the purpose of the comments in this part to consider the extra problems involved in managing activities such as these. Nevertheless, it is worth noting that libraries have a central role in 'managing' these developments for the local community and ensuring that all members have the right of access to this source of power. To a remarkable extent information is a source of power in Western society; it is of vital importance for the industrial, commercial and cultural success of the United Kingdom.

A great deal of research has taken place into ways and means of educating the library user. NBM are widely employed by library staff to introduce facilities to clients, ranging from the simple chart or map to complex programmes involving videorecordings and Hypercard stacks on microcomputers. In educational institutions, seminars and lectures for students are given on projector transparencies, slides and tapes and in teaching packages. 'Librarians now see their primary role as maximizing the use and effectiveness of their collections, rather than acting as custodians.'[3] There has been tremendous interest in research into information skills and the aim of this has been summarized as 'getting the user to use the library with maximum effect'.

The development of the idea of an information skills curriculum has emphasized the sequences of stages inherent in any finding-out activity. These have been summarized as:

(a) What do I need to do? (formulation and analysis of need)
(b) Where could I go? (identification and appraisal of likely sources)
(c) How do I get the information? (tracing and locating individual resources)
(d) Which resources shall I use? (examining, selecting and rejecting individual resources)
(e) How shall I use the resources? (interrogating resources)
(f) What should I make a record of? (recording and storing information)
(g) Have I got the information I need? (interpretation, analysis, synthesis, evaluation)
(h) How should I present it? (presentation, communication, shape)
(i) What have I achieved? (evaluation).[4]

Here the library and its resources have been placed in an overall pattern of the use of information. The roles of the school teacher and librarian are of great importance in developing such early knowledge. As many schools use NBM as a natural part of their teaching, and children are using much of the appropriate equipment at home, the process is not new or difficult. The development of simple information retrieval computer software has assisted this process by integrated catalogues created by the pupils themselves.

The Travelling Workshops Experiment in library user education was a major testing ground for the study of user education. Its most important aim was 'to demonstrate to teaching staff in higher education how various aspects of information handling may be taught and incorporated in to the students' curriculum'.[5] It also tested the value of teaching packages, centrally produced, concluding that they may be more effective than individual programmes which have been unable to draw upon a wide range of experience. These packages comprised student handbooks, practical work, sound tapes, slides and posters. The conclusion of the report emphasizes that 'it is the context of user education that most influences its relevance. Content and method are of secondary importance; this is borne out by the often striking differences in the success of the [same] TWE materials and approaches, when used in two different situations.'[6] It is the use made of NBM and the style of the presentation which are important.

The problem for NBM use rests far more on the inadequacies of the older clients than on the young. Not only are the former less willing to trust and use the materials (as shown, for example, in the antipathy to microform *vis-à-vis* books) but they are also more fearful and reluctant to handle the equipment. As far as the library staff are concerned, considerable effort will be required to overcome this distaste by means of example and recommendation. The difficulties with equipment can be allayed by the development of simple procedure charts or pamphlets which must be carefully placed with the individual items. A number of libraries, particularly in the educational world, have already developed successful ones.

When NBM are issued to new clients, librarians may also feel it is necessary to enquire whether they have the technical ability and facilities to use and look after them. A common-sense approach to this should be adopted, initial questions perhaps being raised around knowledge of the recording standards, speed, pulsing etc. of the materials. Clients may even benefit from simple advice or discussion on techniques of use and obtaining the greatest value from the materials. User education raises much wider problems than those discussed here. Effective exploitation of all information resources is an area that requires much further research to develop appropriate strategies and techniques. However, NBM add only a few additional issues to those encountered with all materials and these have been mentioned above. Carefully planned procedures and structured learning packages using NBM can also assist in their resolution. While many of these may be provided from a central source, perhaps as core material, additional items from local sources are likely to be necessary to supply answers to the special needs of the clients of a particular institution.

THE PHYSICAL ENVIRONMENT

Incorporating NBM into the library invariably raises questions about physical conditions and layout. Many of these are more the result of staff trepidation than real problems, and in this section the intention is to consider the actual effects of these materials. In general, apart from the points discussed below, NBM do not require special features or considerations. Conditions that are suitable for books are usually satisfactory for NBM.

Coping with hazards

The major hazards to NBM are extremes of temperature and humidity, dust and magnetic fields. If staff and clients can work comfortably in the environment, then the temperature and humidity levels are likely to be satisfactory for materials and equipment. Note should be taken of the likely damage if these conditions vary excessively (see pages 158–161), and a check should be made regularly if there is any doubt. Staff should also take care that conditions do not alter much when the library is closed.

Problems with magnetic fields are unusual. Electric motors and transformers may be present in the library to provide supplies for particular equipment such as air conditioners or cleaners, and they should be kept away from NBM using magnetic tape. Some security devices also include magnetic devices and these should be checked for their effects.

The worst hazard is undoubtedly dust — not only because it coats film and lenses, but also because it tends to be ground into the materials as they are used, causing poor reproduction or even scratches. While a totally dust-free atmosphere is impractical, every effort should be made to ensure cleanliness. When not in use, all NBM and equipment should be kept covered, and a regular system for cleaning the machinery is advisable. Plastic materials need to be wiped with anti-static cloths at fairly frequent intervals, particularly if plastic protection sleeves are used around them.

Electricity supply

Most equipment requires a mains supply of electricity for economic operation. While some can make use of battery power sources, these are very expensive. It may be worthwhile to invest in rechargeable batteries. There is no guide to numbers of power sockets, the simplest rule being that there are never enough.

For safety reasons all sockets should be flush with the surface to which they are fixed and should have individual switches. They should also be internally guarded, access to the live and neutral parts being prevented until the plug removes a guard through insertion of the earth bar. As a further safety measure, they should be easy to reach so that it is possible to insert or remove plugs without having to pull on the wires or having to bend them acutely as they emerge from the plug, both of which can be dangerous.

There are a number of possible systems for locating the sockets. Unless there is a definite policy to make use of fixed furniture, in which case electrical conduits to the sockets on the tables are simply arranged, the problem of flexibility is the most difficult to surmount. Certainly wires trailing around the floors are to be avoided at all costs as they are very dangerous − both for the equipment and the users. Some libraries have chosen floor sockets, sometimes covered by flaps of carpet. While these are usually safe, some types of shoe heels can cause problems. Wires are still present at ground level with all the potential dangers implicit in this. In libraries where there are pillars, sockets can be provided on them and on the walls, benches being moved close to them when equipment needs supplies. Another system is to hang sockets from the ceiling, a safe method (unless users walk into them) but aesthetically not very pleasing.

Although each library will make its own decisions, it is necessary to bear in mind both the safety and the convenience factors. In the latter category, it is sensible to site the sockets at table-top height about 0.75m from the ground, to avoid the need for the user to stoop. Anything which prevents easy access can discourage use and encourage misuse and possible danger.

Lighting

Many NBM deteriorate under direct exposure to sunlight, so this should be avoided, particularly with photographic materials. However, the major problem is the difficulty of seeing pictures on a screen when the surrounding light is bright. To reduce this, many rear projection screens can be easily protected by having hoods around them. In some circumstances, it may be considered necessary to keep the equipment in special areas of reduced light, but generally this is not essential. Provided some care and consideration is given to the direction and level of lighting, the problem is not difficult to surmount. Where equipment uses number display systems similar to those used in pocket calculators, there may be visibility difficulties in bright light. This is particularly apparent where fluorescent tubes are used, and some means of shading such displays may be necessary. Some modern tape recorders use these types of number in the odometer and difficulties may arise with them.

Fluorescent tube lighting may be the cause of interference with electronic equipment; this is particularly obvious on television monitors/ receivers. In prime condition, the lights usually produce no problem, but defective tubes, especially at the end of their life, generate transmitted waves which can cause crackles on sound reception and white lines on television screens.

Now that television sets or monitors are used for continual reading and study, it is necessary to consider the brightness of light on them. Stray reflections should be avoided where possible, and the user should be able to sit about 1m away from a 14in. screen to view and work in comfort. The ambient light needs to be at a similar brightness to that of the screen so as to reduce any potential eyestrain. Careful consideration to avoid excessive use of VDUs is important, and clear criteria should be established. Users should note that most VDUs have a brightness control.

Viewing/listening positions

When NBM first appeared in libraries, there was some anxiety about possible disturbing effects on the book users. The problems of distribution of mains power and security also seemed insurmountable unless the viewing/listening areas were enclosed in some way. As a result, there was a rapid development of carrels, small enclosures either of three sides only or complete, in which the equipment was housed. In some libraries, NBM − or rather those considered to be audiovisual − are kept and used in one special room only. This makes cross-referencing between information in different types of document even more difficult than usual. In others, carrels are blocked together in one part or spread in small patches for particular subject areas. It is apparent that a client wishing to use paper materials will go to the open tables, and to explore NBM to a carrel.

The resulting seclusion meant that the activities of NBM-using clients did not distract other users, and that any noise from the equipment was restricted to a small area. However, they were seen to be doing something special, and NBM became imbued with a special quality which seemed to make their use different from that of other documents. More recent trends of thinking, and indeed the argument of this book, incline towards the attitude that NBM and all other documents are equally valuable information carriers. Any secreting of NBM users into special areas runs against this thinking.

Further support for the development of isolated carrels came from the complexity of some equipment. Tape-slide presentation, for instance, requires a sound tape recorder, a connecting box, an automatic slide projector and a screen. In the early days all these were separate items, which were most conveniently kept joined together in specially made furniture cabinets. The Surrey carrel, developed at the University of Surrey, was a successful development of this type. A number of other institutions produced their own, particularly medical schools. In some libraries, a decision was made that television programmes would be distributed on demand from a central bank of videotape recorders and not put on by the client personally. To view them, carrels — fixed structures wired to the video distribution centre — were essential. In American colleges, the 1960s saw a considerable development of these systems to various levels of sophistication. Known as dial-access-retrieval, the client using them dialled a telephone code for the particular programme required from the selection being transmitted at the time. However, this never proved attractive to British institutions, partly because of its considerable expense, but more importantly because of its inflexibility.

Nevertheless, although the full complexity of dial-access-retrieval was discarded, librarians still felt it necessary to isolate NBM use to carrels. A number of commercial models are available, many demountable and therefore easily movable to different areas. For convenience, most of them also interlock, usually in fours, and where they are fixed a central core carries all the wiring, which is distributed four ways. Some of the most successful have been made to the special designs of Dundee College of Education. A further development in the carrels produced for the Polytechnic of the South West is a sliding top which acts as a shield against interference from overhead lighting, and also locks up the carrel completely when pulled farther out.

Yet the necessity for having carrels at all must be questioned. With improving technology and client skills, the early anxieties over mechanical noise and user incompetence have been reduced. If the philosophy of similar value between books and NBM is to be evident in practice, surely it is better that they should be seen to be used in any part of the library.

Distractions for other library users can prove much less than many expect. Generally, viewing screens are comparatively small in the library as they are used by individuals or pairs at most. (Special group viewing rooms are excluded from this discussion.) A reader who is distracted by people moving around the library is likely also to be distracted by a bright picture in another part of the room, but most people are not distracted in this way. Noise is now rarely a problem. Whether in carrels or not, sound is listened to by users through headphones, and so others are unaware of it. There may also be a problem with microcomputers and their peripherals. A number of microcomputers provide a sound system which can be irritating to users if not channelled through headphones. Similarly, the provision of printers can cause a noise problem. The introduction of laser printers has alleviated this. However, mechanical noise from other equipment is limited to the sound of cooling fans which is unobtrusive when compared with most air conditioning and microcomputers. Apart from the problem of cinefilm projectors, distraction as an argument in favour of carrels is increasingly weak. However, it may be necessary to identify particular areas for siting the connecting equipment to mainframe computer systems like Prestel or major databases overseas. The high telephone connection charges cannot be used without control.

Complex equipment is also not such a difficulty as it was. As has been stated, users are becoming progressively more aware and confident with it through their own experience in school and home. Machines which used to be separate and bulky are now manufactured as one compact model. Microcomputers have integral disc players and modern videocassette equipment, being relatively foolproof, can be entrusted to the client with considerable confidence.

Security will always be a problem, and librarians are right to be anxious about the attractive nature of much NBM equipment to the potential thief. It is worth noting that some of the library security systems developed to prevent the loss of books can be used to similar good effect with NBM equipment. While carrels afford a measure of protection against loss, usually by screwing or chaining the equipment down, similar measures can be taken with equipment placed more openly in the library. Naturally, unscrewing has to be possible to allow for servicing and repair, and the determined thief will find a way of doing this surreptitiously. Nevertheless, the screw is a deterrent against casual loss.

Whether the library decides on a separate room for NBM, on carrels or the open table, display and use will depend on a balance of weighting between the points mentioned above. All three choices offer an acceptable practice for which there are particular advantages for different libraries. A final point is worth noting, however; the equipment for NBM does occupy space, and therefore if the client is to make notes or refer to other materials at the same position, an adequate table-top area has to be provided.

Browsing
If users are to be encouraged to browse through the library's NBM, it should not be necessary for them to take the materials to the main viewing/listening positions. Light boxes for transparent materials and simple sound cassette players for listening to tapes can be fixed alongside stacks easily and inexpensively. With computer software and videotapes, browsing is difficult and must be confined to the printed information supplied with the containers.

Technical area
A library dealing with NBM will normally require access to a technical area. This will have three main functions.

1   *Repair of equipment*   A store of spare parts, including lamps, will be necessary for instant replacement. Depending on the skills of the staff, it may be possible to undertake repairs also. A sufficiency of measuring devices for identifying faults, soldering irons, mechanical jigs etc. may be present. However, increasingly equipment is maintenance free, and it may be cheaper to replace than repair.

2   *Repair of materials*   The sophistication of this will depend on the level and type of stock present in the library, and on a calculation of the relative costs of instant in-house repairs and more time-consuming external agencies. Simple laminating equipment and binding will normally cover damage to paper materials. Damaged still pictures are most economically discarded, but film can be spliced. To identify areas of damage in a film, sophisticated and expensive apparatus is available to check a reel automatically, but unless there is a large stock this may be more cheaply undertaken by hand. Sound tape can also be spliced, but videotape should be rerecorded. Damaged plastic materials are best discarded, and action to be taken on models, specimens etc. will depend on their value and nature. Decisions on the level of repair to be undertaken will dictate the quantity and type of equipment provided.

3   *Production*   The standard of provision of equipment and space for

this will also depend on policy decisions. If duplicate copies are to be issued to clients, then provision of the appropriate machinery is necessary. Original materials may also be made: this may require simply transferring one format to another, for example microfilming periodicals or transferring disc recordings to sound cassettes (it is important to check on copyright restrictions). Another method may be taking off-air recordings from broadcasts, in which case good aerials connecting to the equipment will normally be essential. The library may also have decided on the active creation of new materials to fill apparent gaps in its stock, and the level of provision will depend on the forms in which such NBM are to be made. Any decisions on this will need to be considered in relation to the costs of in-house production compared with the costs of using an external agency.

STAFFING REQUIREMENTS

Do NBM cause special staffing problems? Some would argue that they only demand extra skills from the professional librarians, while others point to the need for extra differently qualified personnel. This debate led to a major consideration by Gerald Collier of staffing structures for the Council of Educational Technology. He attempted to analyse and clarify 'the managerial and professional level tasks involved in providing a teaching and learning support service or unit in a wide variety of educational institutions',[7] recognizing that information provision was embracing the work of librarians, media specialists and computer staff. Integration is the aim but the rigid demarcations drawn up by these groups have prevented this aim being achieved in some institutions.

In this section the issues involved in staffing are discussed, but it must be emphasized that this is only in terms of the impact of NBM. Some of the points will have a more general application, although the development of the concept is based on the results of introducing these materials. If a library is adding to its stock, it may be necessary to increase the staff to deal with it; that is a normal calculation for the management which is not of importance here. NBM may be additional stock in this sense and require that response, but that is a decision based on the quantity of materials, not their nature. Here the discussion is concerned with the impact of stock of a different type and the effect that it has on the skills of the staff employed.

The audiovisual librarian?

When libraries first admitted audiovisual materials such as slides and videorecordings, the initial response was to employ a special librarian to look after them. Few of the professional staff had any experience with such materials. Basic training mostly emphasized books, and the bibliographic tools commonly available and used were slanted in their direction. A similar response was made towards records and music scores when these were introduced into the general library; and in this case, as the field had a subject coherence, this was very logical. But the AV librarian was in a different situation. The subjects were disparate, the materials forming the only link.

AV librarians were also allocated only a limited proportion of the full range of NBM. For example, it was unusual to find them responsible for portfolios or even microforms. The latter were usually carriers of government publications, back runs of newspapers and periodicals, and were assigned to the relevant subject specialists. To the AV librarian was given the responsibility of all the 'awkward' materials, from slides to wallcharts and models.

Such an approach is the anithesis of normal academic library practice. The trend over the years has been towards greater subject specialization, fundamentally for two reasons: firstly, such a system meant that one member of staff at least became deeply familiar with one particular field and hence was able to operate a sensible and carefully thought-out acquisition policy; secondly, such specialization produced more effective advice to clients because of a deeper knowledge of the field and a fuller appreciation of the likely interests. A specialist AV librarian could offer a good knowledge only of the different formats and the relevant equipment; understanding of the content was naturally superficial.

The philosophy underlying this book is that NBM and books are equally valuable as information carriers within the capabilities of their formats. Conversely, the existence of the specialist AV librarian emphasized the opposite, highlighting the difference between the two types of materials rather than the similarity of the information they carried. At the beginning of this evolution in the library's responsibilities, the management solution to inadequate staffing may well have been considered the only logical one. However, now it is surely clear that all subject specialists should be responsible for the NBM in their area, and it is towards the necessary in-service training of such staff and the appropriate basic training of new entrants that the profession must look.

In the modern library, clients will expect to find the NBM in the same area as the other materials on the subject, and to seek advice on all the relevant stock from the same person, not to have to consult one for books and someone else for the rest. To this end, all staff should understand 'the application of librarianship to the new media which should be covered in the initial education of every librarian, whatever his eventual specialization'.

The skills required

To be able to exploit NBM, it is necessary for the librarian to have certain extra skills. Here, only a series of general points are made to demonstrate the range of needs.

1 *Technical skill* It is not necessary for the professional staff to be technical experts, and it is important to avoid 'the ever present danger

... that the machines can be transmuted from simply a means of unlocking informational riches to an end in themselves, with ... interest becoming centred upon how to work the magic boxes and their care in sickness and health'.[8] For some people there is a compulsive delight in exploring the mysteries of electrical equipment and gadgetry, but this fascination is not a requirement for a librarian. It is important that the machines are seen as a means to an end, not as the end itself.

All the same, it is necessary for the staff to be able to use the equipment with confidence, and to be able to assist clients to do so as well. A basic knowledge of how the equipment works, following what is described in this book, is all that is normally needed by way of preparation to achieve the appropriate information-revealing operation. If the equipment does not work, a qualified technician is needed, not a librarian. However, it is probable that most professional staff will also be required to undertake basic maintenance, as outlined in Part 3. The growth of the domestic market for NBM equipment — for example videorecorders — has meant that manufacturers have had to make the equipment more idiot proof; they have also supplied better instruction manuals. Another important factor is that the younger generation of librarians has itself grown up with the technology and has often attended equipment training courses at library schools.

Some librarians who work with NBM would also argue that there is much to be gained from the development of an empathy with these materials, similar to that which many people have with books. The truth behind this is difficult to ascertain — it is almost impossible to measure — but it probably evolves from enjoyment of the way the information is transmitted and an appreciation of the techniques of production. While this is not a technical skill, its possession leads to a more constructive approach to the care of the materials and to more sensible advice on their exploitation. While a knowledge of computer programming skills may be of assistance to the librarian involved with computer software, it is not a prerequisite. The provision of software with adequate documentation is crucial in assisting the user, rather than the ability to explain how the software was written.

2 *Bibliographic skills* While the bibliographic tools are less well organized than for books, there are still a considerable number that can be used. The approach is not quite so straightforward as the use of Whitaker's *British books in print*, but their exploitation is not difficult and should be a skill acquired by all librarians.

3 *Advising clients* The exploitation of stock will always involve

advising clients, helping them to locate appropriate items and to make use of them. Certain technical variations in the organization and storage of NBM, and sometimes even limitations on their use, will mean that guidance may often be more necessary than is the case with books.

Advice on selection and use will be related to an analysis of the client's needs and situation. Because some NBM require equipment, advice will be needed to ensure that the client has the appropriate items and understands the problems of compatibility. However, more important is advice on the appropriateness of selections for the particular circumstances; the only relevant question to answer is whether the materials are designed for individual or group use.

Educational circumstances are, however, different. While some NBM have been created for independent study by students, many will be found in educational libraries for class use by teachers. Compared with books, NBM can be used in teaching in a wide variety of ways, and the librarian who is exploiting his or her stock fully should be giving relevant advice. This demands considerable understanding of teaching methods, which is not normally part of the background of the librarian. Although some would suggest that such knowledge is unnecessary because the professional teacher should know what to do with particular classes, considerable uncertainty arises when he or she is faced with a varied stock offering a number of different opportunities. Advice, supported by a realistic understanding, is then very useful, particularly if further information on successful use by other people can also be given. The importance of such skills is gradually being recognized. Some librarians are now seeking additional teaching qualifications, although the full teacher training course is probably excessively detailed. Unfortunately other relevant courses are difficult to find. A number of academic institutions have recognized this shortage of suitable courses and have provided in-house courses. For example, Teesside Polytechnic runs a certificate for teaching in higher education for its new teaching staff and enabled information librarians to attend the course. One result of this was a learning pack designed to improve the librarian's teaching skills and providing guidance and rationale for the creation and use of NBM such as OHPs and tape-slide programmes. Other courses which would be beneficial to librarians would be those leading to diplomas in curriculum development and educational technology.

The argument here tends towards the need for librarians in educational institutions to have considerable knowledge of teaching and also of the methods of student learning. Not all the activities of professional staff require such understanding. For example, cataloguing and basic bibliographic control can be undertaken without it, and this may lead to the development of different types of staff — those who advise clients requiring this type of educational skill, and those dealing with the mechanics of organization and control.

Such knowledge of learning may also have other benefits. Firstly, assistance to students in finding appropriate study pathways can be given from a background of deeper understanding, and an exploitation of a wider variety of approaches to the subject might well be made possible, using the full range of NBM. Secondly, many NBM are published with very little information on how they are to be used for effective teaching/learning. To improve this, the librarian may feel it is helpful to provide basic guidance sheets. These should include headings such as the learning objectives and the equipment and other materials required; briefing on how to set up and organize the setting; and even perhaps a debriefing which lists possible ways of following up the work to develop its potential further. In order to prepare such sheets as these, a librarian requires more knowledge than comes from present training in librarianship.

The concepts outlined here are still controversial, but they are mentioned because they evolve from the presence of NBM in the library of an educational institution. The level of efficient exploitation is one decided upon, to a considerable extent, by the general management policy. Because NBM offer such a variety of approaches to learning, it is difficult to conceive of useful advice being given without such a background of knowledge.

4 *Advising colleagues* While NBM are still accepted by a number of professional staff, librarians committed to their use may employ their skills in demonstrating and explaining their value. This requires an ability to advise and assist without causing irritation, which can be very useful and encouraging in an embryonic organization.

5 *Being aware of developments* No librarian in the present technological age can feel that all methods of storing and exploiting information have now been fully developed. New techniques will continue to emerge; new means and materials will evolve. It is therefore important that the modern librarian has an open mind, and will watch for new approaches and evaluate their benefits for his or her institution. The profession has had an unfortunate reputation for stasis and unwillingness to recognize trends and manipulate them to its advantage. However, although the first generation of NBM has caused a rethinking and a

somewhat reluctant acceptance, it is clear that the next generation is being received more willingly. The eagerness of librarians to pilot viewdata systems and the formation by the Library Association of an information technology group are indications that the profession has learnt the lesson of earlier debates concerning NBM. Its further establishment of an electronic network, LA NET, in 1989 gives this view even greater credence.

Technical assistance
A library with equipment for NBM will need professional technical assistance to undertake regular servicing and cope with the inevitable serious repairs. Whether full-time posts are created or not will depend on the amount and types of equipment involved. The technicians should be fully qualified, whether by experience or through academic courses. It is probably wiser to look for electronic rather than mechanical expertise, as the latter can be readily acquired by a person with the former skills. Most serious mechanical breakdowns have to be returned to the factory or to accredited servicing agencies because they require special tooling which it is uneconomic for the library to acquire for the few occasions when it is likely to be needed.

Other technical experts, such as a photographer, will depend on the policy adopted towards duplication of NBM for clients and in-house production. A team of skilled technicians can be costly, and the library will need to decide whether it can employ them, or whether hiring from an outside agency may not be more appropriate.

Summary
As was made clear at the beginning of this section, the discussion has been limited to the additional staffing needs caused by the incorporation of NBM. There can be no conclusion as to the number or level of staff required.

The viewpoint here, as in the whole of this book, has centred on the general library. However, some librarians are already employed in subject resource centres, the stock limited to one small topic area. Just as they will be using subject indexing systems appropriate to their collections, so they will also be responding to the particular needs of their special situation by using technical skills further to those mentioned above. Some will even be undertaking simple production work.

The comments in this section have concentrated on the general basic needs of the librarian, not those introduced by special circumstances.

Given a good training in the skills outlined above, the professional librarian should be able to adapt and modify his or her approach to meet the needs of specialist clients in these more limited surroundings with ease.

FINANCIAL IMPLICATIONS

When the constraints preventing the development of the effective use of NBM within the library were discussed, the problem of the book fund was mentioned (see page 46). This has always been the centre of librarians' budgeting requirements and it has appeared in the past to be sacrosanct. Continuing the theme of this book that it is the information carriers and their exploitation that should be considered sacrosanct, it must be realized now that there is little justification for separate estimates for books and NBM in libraries. This becomes clear particularly with the development of online bibliographic services or CD-ROM where the same information is provided as in the printed services. Indeed one decision may be to dispense with the expensive capital costs of providing a shelf copy of, say, *Chemical abstracts* and to offer instead a user-financed service to the online provision. If the library is to react to its clients' needs, it must not be hampered by separate funds. It will need to consider the view, expressed by Hallworth, 'that the book fund becomes a materials fund, which allows experts of various kinds within the system to apply a corporate approach for the good of the total service; separate funds for each different form of stock is an anachronism'.[9]

The financial implications of housing NBM within the library should not be considered a result of an extra, rather tiresome, even gimmicky, addition to services; but rather as a recognition of what the library should be doing — supplying a complete information service.

While extra staff may be needed, these are not necessary to cope specifically with the NBM but rather to deal with the increased volume of stock. In many cases, additional NBM can be dealt with satisfactorily by the present staff, although some cost of retraining them may be involved. It may be necessary to establish a technical department to service equipment, but it may prove less expensive to rely on outside contracts.

Perhaps the major financial implication is the cost of equipment. The initial purchase price should be keenly studied; discounts are available and bulk purchasing can also result in significant savings.

Maintenance of equipment has been discussed in Part 3, and some people have suggested that 10% of the initial cost should be allowed annually for this. It is wise to budget for the complete replacement of a piece of equipment after five years. There may be increased insurance costs, especially where clients have free access to electrical equipment, and also extra premiums for theft. The running cost of equipment is small, although extra estimates will have to be made for spare projector bulbs and other replaceable items. If it is decided to use carrels or special storage systems for the equipment, this will be extra to the initial purchase price. There is also the use of services which depend upon telephone links, for example telesoftware or viewdata. This will involve telephone charges, costs for accessing the service and often a fee for using particular pages. The library may decide to earmark a certain sum of money for this service and withdraw the provision when this money is spent rather than give open-ended commitment.

Finally, there is the ever-present problem of equipment development and the obsolescence of old models. In presenting the final requirements, the librarian must make allowances for this, for it reflects the need to be aware of and responsive to advances in technology, equipment, and materials. The multimedia library manager needs to ask, for example, what advances have been made in microcomputers? These advances in technology become budget concerns because they mean that technology has solved a problem or met a need or created new fiscal requirements that must be reflected in it.

The librarian may also be faced with a novel situation, the decision whether to purchase or hire. This relates especially to interactive videodiscs and videorecordings, which may be hired through a number of commercial libraries. Therefore an amount must be earmarked for hiring material. If material is previewed before purchase it may also be necessary to hire, although the cost of this can often be subsequently deducted from the cost of purchase.

The majority of NBM are not more expensive than books and therefore any increase in the materials fund should not be excessive. However, one area of extra cost may be that of repackaging and processing. The servicing of NBM may require extra staff, particularly if standardized packaging is not used. In particular, kits, slides and computer discs can be expensive in staff time. If a policy of integrated shelving is adopted, then repackaging in book-like containers will have to be considered. Many publishers are now providing their materials in suitable packages. The microcomputer publishers are following a similar pattern. There is a bonus in that labelling and pocketing of such rebound documents is more analogous to that of books and new library stationery need not be bought. Indeed, a library supplier will often label and pocket free of charge using the library's own stationery. The full range of library processing — class lettering, issue cards, accession number, ownership stamp — will be more easily fixed to standardized packaging than to the original published format. The cost of repackaging should also be compared with the extra cost in separate shelving if a non-standard approach is adopted. Consider, for example, the additional expense of purchasing sound cassette stands, plastic wallets and filing cabinets for slides.

The cost of security must also be taken into account. Certain formats — such as sound cassettes — and equipment are susceptible to theft and need to be protected. However, this should fit into the security system already in use in the library. For a library without a system it may be necessary to consider installing one as a result of a decison to purchase NBM.

The selection of stock may be more expensive in staff time because of the nature of some formats and the cost of equipment for previewing. Similarly, the cataloguing process may be slower and there may indeed be a major cost factor to consider if the book cataloguing is by MARC tape as the majority of NBM is not included in these services. Thus a larger staff may be required to cope with a smaller quantity of material.

A final element in the financial implications is the difficult one of charging for the service. A number of public libraries are charging clients for borrowing videorecordings, sound cassettes and pictures. This is a tempting approach to get a new service started. The political philosophy involved here is outside the scope of this book, but the central tenet must surely be to provide the same service for all materials. Thus the logical step would be to charge for books. It can even be argued that the success of charging for NBM has recently caused some pressure from financial committees to impose such charges. Indeed, the financial implications of NBM may be very much wider than those of the cost of material, equipment, processing and staffing! The Green Paper established a core service for public libraries and the debate on income generation is a very real issue, particularly in the light of the new Copyright Act.

PHYSICAL CONTROL

The question of the centralization of the service must be discussed. There seems little doubt that centralized processing is the most efficient. Particularly within educational institutions, it has been argued that NBM should be located in the areas where learning takes place, perhaps as a result of their traditional use as teaching aids. However, this takes no account of the use of NBM by other departments, their value in individual study situations and the need for access outside teaching times. If the materials are in the library, access can be controlled for the benefit of all. Within the public library it may be necessary to process centrally but the individual branches can then be left safely to establish their own stock. Expense has caused one or two branches of some public libraries to be established as 'the sound cassette library' or 'the picture library'. This can result in resentment from some clients who cannot visit these branches. Where possible, there should be equity of service.

The physical processing of the documents should be done centrally or by an outside supplier. As with all materials processing, there will be four objectives: to identify the library's ownership; to process for issue; to locate where the document will be stored; and to protect from damage and theft. Individual formats can result in time-consuming procedures; for example marking the ownership of a slide set could involve labelling the slide wallet, stamping the notes and, finally, labelling the container for the notes. Decisions also have to be made on the balance between time-consuming processing and security. A set of 36 slides could have an accession number on each of them or just on the container, a choice between absolute security or the minimum necessary. The librarian involved in the processing procedure must have knowledge of the storage facilities and the possible damage and deterioration the NBM will face from continued use. For example, computer floppy discs should not have their security tags removed. Linked to this is the lack of browsability of some of the forms and the need to provide full information labels on the actual item. While the physical processing method is a highly logical exercise and includes the use of work flows, the librarian still needs to use his or her initiative and imagination to cope with the variety of NBM.

Shelving may be in specialized cabinets or integrated with the book stock. In either case, shelving staff should be trained to be careful and accurate in the placement of NBM: for example videorecordings should be securely fastened in their containers; film cans should be carefully handled to prevent damage and staff should not carry an excessive weight; sound cassettes should be stored away from the magnetic sealing system; and illustrations will need to be accurately replaced in sequence.

There must be a policy decision as to whether material shall be on loan or for reference only. This is a decision that cannot usually be made for all NBM or even for one particular form. Rather it depends on the needs of the clients. There may be pressure to restrict access to specific groups; for example, only lecturers or the representatives of a particular organization. This should be resisted as a general policy, for all clients should have access to all services. The degree of access will depend on individual circumstances. Some material may be for reference only. Microcomputer software is often available only within the library because of a licensing agreement. A video collection with a large demand for its stock may restrict loan to a short period, perhaps 48 hours, or be limited to individuals representing groups and therefore have no provision for one-person viewing. However, bearing these points in mind, 'circulation is a primary task of the multimedia library. Its goal is to maximize the availability of all materials to the patron and to actually implement [sic] the use of such materials.'[10]

The method of loan issuing adopted must be able to handle all materials, whether a book, a computer disc or a model of a dinosaur. There are numerous systems available and these should be assessed on how simply and accurately all material can be issued. However, problems may arise in deciding how far to check NBM prior to issue. If there are 16 slides in a set and only 15 are returned, the client may claim that one was missing on issue. There is a similar problem with damage to sound discs and film. The best method is to check on return and make an accurate record, then to use damage labels for sound discs (on which scratches may be marked). For slide sets a supply of 2in. × 2in. cards with 'slide number — missing' printed on them is needed to place in vacant pockets. Videocassettes and microcomputer software are time consuming to check and the librarian must often rely on a complaint from a subsequent client. A decision on when documents should be withdrawn from stock should be left to the judgement of the librarian. The slide set could be withdrawn from circulation until a replacement slide has been obtained, but individual slides are sometimes difficult to acquire. Portfolios and kits with their profusion of items are a difficult problem. The easiest solution is to provide a contents list together with a note asking users to inform the library of any missing items when they return the kit.

Security is a problem in most libraries and the introduction of NBM, and in particular the equipment, has made the library a temptation for thieves. Equipment such as sound cassette recorders is easily resold. Both equipment and documents can be protected by sensors. All systems should be checked with the manufacturers for their use with magnetic tape as these may be affected by the electrical field incorporated in some devices. Loss may also be prevented by siting equipment close to the issue point or any other easily observable area.

The librarian concerned with managing his or her library to the highest standards often relies on outside evidence to help finalize decisions and to offer evidence to controlling bodies. The British librarian must rely upon the more general statements concerning library provision; for example, the recommendations contained in *College libraries: guidelines for professional service and resource provision*, third edition (Library Association, 1982).

The American Library Association has published *Information power: guidelines for school library media programs* (ALA, 1988). The British school librarian equivalent is *Library resource provision in schools*, new edition (Library Association, 1977), which includes recommendations for school library resource centres and for the School Library Service.

CONCLUSION

The addition of NBM to the library stock does not cause major problems for management. In this part, the areas where significant problems may arise have been looked at, and the logical conclusion should be that a rational analysis of the problems leads to only minor modifications of existing arrangements. Perhaps the most important, and unmentioned, role of management is to encourage in the library staff a commitment to the concept of NBM as valuable information carriers and thence an eagerness to purchase and exploit them. Traditional book-oriented librarians will treat NBM sceptically, perhaps to the extent of creating unsurmountable difficulties; but staff with a wider outlook and efficient training will work hard to overcome any difficulties that may arise. Providing clients with the opportunity to use a variety of materials will encourage more interest from them, and probably also increase their number. In this way, the library may find itself playing a central role in the development of the life of the community it serves.

REFERENCES

1 Donovan, K. G., *Learning resources in colleges: their organisation and management*, London, Council for Educational Technology, 1981. The same author has produced *Management of information technology in further education*, London, Council for Educational Technology, 1986.
2 See articles on this topic in *British journal of academic librarianship*, **3** (3), 1988.
3 Clark, D., *The travelling workshops experiment*, London, British Library, 1981, 1.
4 Marland, M., *Information skills in the secondary curriculum*, London, Methuen Educational, 1981, 50.
5 Clark, D., op. cit., 2.
6 Clark, D., op. cit., 175.
7 Collier, G., *Teaching and learning support services: 1. Higher education 2. Further education 3. Secondary comprehensive, middle and primary schools*, London, Council for Educational Technology, 1981.
8 Butchart, I. C., Shaw, W. B. and Watson, W. M., 'Course guide 1: the application of the librarianship of the new media which should be covered in the initial education of every librarian, whatever his eventual specialization', in *Media awareness for librarians: course guidelines*, London, Council for Educational Technology, 1977, 11–18.
9 Hallworth, F., 'Publicity and promotion', in Lock, R. N., *Manual of library economy*, London, Bingley; Hamden, Ct, Linnet, 1977, 375.
10 Hicks, op. cit., p.183.

Part 6

BIBLIOGRAPHY AND INDEX

BIBLIOGRAPHY

The items listed below are mainly works published since the second edition.

Akeroyd, J. *et al.*, *Using compact disc read only memory as a public access catalogue*, London, British Library Research & Development Department, 1988.

Aumente, J., *New electronic pathways: videotex, teletext and online databases*, Newbury Park, Sage, 1987.

Bayard-White, C. and Hoffos, S., *Interactive video: introduction and handbook*, 4th ed., London, National Interactive Video Centre, 1988.

Birnhack, J., *Audiovisual resources in a hospital medical library: their organization and management*, London, Mansell, 1987.

Blease, D., *Evaluating educational software*, London, Croom Helm, 1986.

Brand, S., *The media lab: inventing the future at MIT*, New York, Viking, 1987.

Carter, C. and Monaco, J., *Learning information technology skills*, British Library Research & Development Department, 1987.

Casciero, A. J. and Roney, R. G., *Audiovisual technology primer*, Littleton, Libraries Unlimited, 1988.

Chesterman, J. and Lipman, A., *The electronic pirates: diy crime of the century*, London, Routledge, 1988.

Clarke, A., *British Library's compact disc experiment*, London, British Library Research and Development Department, 1986.

Copyright, Designs and Patents Act, 1988, London, HMSO, 1988.

Cornish, G. P., *Archival collections of non-book materials: a listing and brief description of major collections*, London, British Library, 1986.

Cowley, J. and Hammond, D. N., *Educating information users in universities, polytechnics and colleges*, London, British Library Research & Development Department, 1987.

Cullen, P. and Kirby, J., *Design and production of media presentations for libraries, Aldershot, Gower, 1986.*

Curtis, H. (ed.), *Public access microcomputers in academic libraries: the Mann Library model at Cornell University,* Chicago, American Library Association, 1987.

Desmaris, N., *The librarian's CD rom handbook*, London, Meckler, 1989.

Doll, C. A., *Evaluating educational software*, Chicago, American Library Association, 1987.

Donovan, K. G., *Learning resources in colleges: their organisation and management*, London, Council for Educational Technology, 1981. This has been complemented for information technology by the following:

Donovan, K., *Management of information technology in further education*, London, Council for Educational Technology, 1986.

Duke, J., *Interactive video: implications for education and training*, (CET working paper no. 22). London, Council for Educational Technology, 1983.

Ellison, J. W., *Media librarianship*, New York, Neal-Schuman, 1985.

Ellison, J. W. and Coty, P. A., *Non-book media: collection management and user services*, Chicago, American Library Association, 1987.

FIAF, *Preservation and restoration of moving images and sound*, London, FIAF, 1986.

Fleischer, E. and Goodman, H., *Cataloguing audiovisual materials: a manual based on the Anglo-American cataloguing rules II*, New York, Neal-Schuman, 1985.

Forester, T. (ed.), *The microelectronics revolution*, Oxford, Basil Blackwell, 1980.

Fothergill, R., *Implications of new technology for the school curriculum*, London, Kogan Page, 1988.

Frost, C., *Media access and organisation: cataloguing and reference sources guide for nonbook material*, Littleton, Libraries Unlimited, 1988.

Gilman, J. A., *Information technology and the school library resource centre* (CET occasional paper no. 11). London, Council for Educational Technology, 1983.

Hanford, A., *Panorama of audiovisual archives*, London, BBC Data, 1986.

Harrison, H. P., *Picture librarianship*, London, Library Association, 1981.

Harrison, H. P., 'Audiovisual materials, in Walford, A. J.', *Reviews and reviewing: a guide*, London, Mansell 1986, 214–26.

Harrison, H. P., *The archival appraisal of sound recordings and related materials: a RAMP study with guidelines*, London, Unesco, 1987.

Heery, M. J., *Audiovisual materials in academic libraries: report*,

London, Library Association Audiovisual Group, 1984.

Hendley, T., *CD rom and optical publishing systems*, Hatfield, CIMTECH, 1987.

Hunter, E., *An introduction to AACR2: a programmed guide to the second edition of Anglo American Cataloguing rules 1988 revision*, London, Bingley, 1989.

International Visual Communications Association, *Commissioning a programme: the professional approach*, London, IVCA, 1988.

Intner, S. and Smiraglia, R., *Policy and practice in bibliographic control of nonbook media*, Chicago, American Library Association, 1987.

Isailovic, J., *Video disc systems: theory and applications*, London, Prentice Hall, 1987.

Jones, M. C., *Non-book teaching materials in the health sciences: a guide to their organization*, London, Gower, 1987.

Kaslow, B., *Video to on-line: reference services and the new technology*, Birmingham, Haworth Press, 1985.

Lambert, S. and Ropiequet, S., *CD rom: the new papyrus: the current and future state of the art*, Redmond, Microsoft, 1986.

Laurillard, D., *Interactive media: working methods and practical applications*, Chichester, Ellis Horwood, 1987.

Library Association Audiovisual Group, *Bibliographic control of audiovisual material*, London, LAAVG, 1986.

Liebscher, P., *Audiovisual librarianship: a select bibliography, 1965–1983*, London, *Audiovisual Librarian*, 1984.

McPherson, A. and Timms, H., *The audio-visual handbook: a complete guide to the world of audio-visual techniques*, London, Pelham, 1988.

McQueen, J. and Boss, R. W., *Videodisc and optical digital disk technologies and their implications in libraries*, Chicago, American Library Association, 1987.

Malley, I., *A survey of information skills teaching in colleges of further and higher education*, London, British Library Research & Development Department, 1988.

Malley, I., *Educating information users in colleges of further and higher education*, London, British Library Research & Development Department, 1988.

Marland, M., *Information skills in the secondary curriculum*, London, Methuen Educational, 1981 (Schools Council curriculum bulletin no. 9).

Marsterson, W., *Information technology and the role of the librarian*, London, Croom Helm, 1986.

Maybury, R., *Beginners' guide to satellite tv*, Harmondsworth, Penguin, 1987.

Megarry, J., *Compact discs and computers: converging technologies*, London, Kogan Page, 1989.

Miller, P., *Production and bibliographic control of non-book materials in the United Kingdom*, London, Polytechnic of North London, 1985.

More than just toys, London, National Toy Libraries Association, 1986 (video).

Noble, P., *Resource-based learning in post compulsory education*, London, Kogan Page, New York, Nichols, 1980.

Olson, N. B., *Cataloguing microcomputer software*, Littleton, Libraries Unlimited, 1988.

Olson, N. B., *A manual of AACR2 examples for microcomputer software*, 2nd ed., Lake Crystal, Soldier Creek, 1986.

Pack, P. and Pack, P. M., *Colleges, learning and libraries: the future*, London, Bingley, 1988.

Papert, S., *Mindstorms: children, computers and powerful ideas*, Brighton, Harvester Press, 1980.

Parr, M. and Stasiak, J., *The actual boot: the photographic post card boom 1900–1920*, Northallerton, A. H. Jolly, 1986.

Pinion, C. F., *Legal deposit of non-book materials*, London, British Library, 1986.

Pinion, C. F., *Video learning services in public libraries*, London, Library Association Audiovisual Group, 1984.

Reed, M. H., *The copyright primer for libraries and educators*, Chicago, American Library Association, 1987.

Robl, E. H., *Organizing your photographs*, New York, Watson-Guptill, 1986.

Saffady, W., *Optical storage technology, 1989: a state of the art review*, London, Meckler, 1989.

Saffady, W., *Video based information systems: a guide to educational, business, library and home use*, Chicago, American Library Association, 1985.

Silverman, E., *Satellite and education: a report on the current situation*, London, Council for Educational Technology, 1987.

Smith, V., *Public libraries and adult independent learners*, London, Council for Educational Technology, 1987.

Stonier, T., *The wealth of information*, London, Thames Methuen, 1983.

Teague, S. J., *Microform, video and electronic media librarianship*, London, Bowker-Saur, 1985.

Templeton, R., *Computer software: issues affecting the provision of bibliographic control*, London, British Library, 1986.

Tydeman, J. and Kelm, E. J., *New media in Europe: satellite, cable, video cassette recorders and videotex*, London, McGraw, 1986.

User's guide to VDUs, London, Team Video, 1988 (video).

Vieth, R. H., *Visual information systems: the power of graphics and video*, London, Gower, 1988.

Wall, R., *AV materials and electronic copyright*, London, Library Association, 1988.

Weihs, J. R., *Accessible storage of nonbook materials*, Phoenix, Oryx, 1984.

Weihs, J. R., *Non-book materials: the organisation of integrated collections*, 3rd ed., Ottawa, Canadian Library Association, 1988.

White, B. H., *Collection management for school library media centres*, Birmingham, Haworth Press, 1986.

Williamson, R., *Knowledge warehouse*, London, British Library Research & Development Department, 1987.

Wood, L., *British films 1927–1939*, London, British Film Institute Library Services, 1986.

Woolls, E. B. and Loertscher, D. V., *The microcomputer facility and the school library media specialist*, Chicago, American Library Association, 1986.

Yates-Mercer, P. A., *Private viewdata in the UK*, London, Gower, 1985.

INDEX